EMINENTLY VICTORIAN

EMINENTLY VICTORIAN

PEOPLE AND OPINIONS
edited by John F. C. Harrison

ARTISTS OF THE AGE
by Basil Taylor

PERCEPTIONS IN POETRY
by Isobel Armstrong

British Broadcasting Corporation

Originating from a series of
programmes prepared in consultation
with the BBC Further Education
Advisory Council

First published 1974

Published by the British
Broadcasting Corporation
35 Marylebone High Street,
London W1M 4AA
Printed by Jolly & Barber Ltd.,
Rugby, Warwickshire

ISBN 0 563 10890 8

CONTENTS

LISTS OF PLATES

plate numbers indicated in bold type

3 PERCEPTIONS IN POETRY

FOREWORD

The studies that are published in these pages were originally commissioned by BBC Radio's Further Education department as a three-part series of programmes first broadcast on Radio 3 (Study) from January to May 1974. The underlying aim of the series was to suggest how scholars use the evidence of contemporary sources to derive greater insight into, and understanding of, the past. The emphasis in each part of the series was on a different type of source material: letters, memoirs, speeches and diaries; paintings and drawings; and poetry. No social historian in fact, of course, limits himself to a particular type of evidence – there may be as much social comment in a painting or a poem as in a speech or letter – so the sub-divisions introduced may seem somewhat arbitrary. But the fuller interpretation of each type of evidence benefits from the special expertise of different scholars, be they art critics, students of literature or of politics in the widest sense. Within these pages, their distinctive skills as well as their common interests are reflected, as they were in the broadcasts; but the printed record also allows the divisions to be crossed, for example by the inclusion of illustrations to accompany those studies based principally on verbal sources.

In translating the substance of these broadcasts from one medium to another, care has been taken to reflect in print, as far as possible, the texture of the programmes. In the first part, *People and Opinions,* for example, the quotations set in smaller type with indented margins represent matter that, on the air, was conveyed by other voices than the expositor's own. But anyone who meticulously compares the text with the original source will discover phrases and sentences omitted within some of the quotations. These omissions, made in the interests of broadcasting, could not effectively be indicated on air and are similarly ignored in print. Contrariwise, in the third part, *Perceptions in Poetry,* while the smaller type setting again signals other voices in the programmes, some poems are here published in slightly longer extract than was practicable on air. For *Artists of the Age* a different convention is introduced. At the time of the broadcasts, many listeners had availed themselves of a smaller publication which reproduced many of the paintings referred to in the programmes, so that they were able to study the pictures when listening to the speaker. In the middle section of this book these same pictures are represented, with captions and notes, expanded from the earlier publication; while the text in smaller type is matter selected from the full script of the broadcasts.

It was my own particular pleasure to undertake studio production of the programmes on *People and Opinions* (those on *Artists of the Age* and *Perceptions in Poetry* being produced, respectively, by my colleagues Dennis Simmons and David Epps) and I must here record my appreciation of the special contribution made by John Harrison. Professor Harrison could, no doubt, have matched with his own set of biographical essays the individual studies of Victorian art and poetry developed by Basil Taylor and Isobel Armstrong. But in treating sources considerably more varied and indeed more voluminous than either paintings or poems, it seemed appropriate that the task should be shared with other scholars in the same discipline under his editorship. That two of them share his surname is entirely coincidental! And that he himself has contributed more than one study was entirely at my instigation.

Michael Stephens

1

PEOPLE AND OPINIONS

edited by John F. C. Harrison

THE MENTALITY OF THE AGE

The period of early and mid-Victorian England, from c.1830 to c.1880, was an immensely exciting and disturbing time in which to live. It was a period of great social change and consciousness of change, to which the accident of Victoria's long reign has given an illusory impression of uniformity and continuity. The first twenty years, ending with the Great Exhibition of 1851, was a turbulent, confusing era, variously labelled the Age of Reform, the Age of the Chartists, or the Hungry Forties. It was followed by a quarter of a century of calm, stability and prosperity – dubbed by historians the Victorian Heyday or the Age of Equipoise. There is need for a healthy scepticism regarding some of the commonly-attributed opinions of the Victorians. When we hear that the Victorians believed this or always did that, it is prudent to remember that the world of 1830 was a very different place from that of 1880; that a man's active life spans more than the historian's neat division into decades and quarter centuries; and that even in a given year our great grandparents were as much divided over the important issues confronting them as we are today.

In the pages that follow nine figures have been selected for study. And the immediate question that springs to mind is: why these people and not nine others? Any selection of this nature is bound to be personal and rather arbitrary, and I would not claim any special merit for this particular gallery of Victorians. But the selection is not without its rationale. First, the nine were all people who made a very definite impact on their contemporaries in their respective spheres of influence; they were people whose careers were noted by others and whose opinions were listened to. Second, they are people who have attracted the attention of scholars working in the field of Victorian social history in recent years. The contributors to this series have each made a special study of the character presented because they felt that he or she was in some way particularly relevant to an aspect of Victorian society worthy of investigation. These studies therefore present both a picture of the past and a guide to historical thinking about it.

How far these nine people were 'typical' Victorians is very hard to say. Clearly they are all representative of certain recognisable positions found in the middle years of the nineteenth century. But the total picture of Victorian England conveyed should be considered as impressionistic rather than representative. None of the nine ranks among the Top People of Victorian England: nor did they qualify for inclusion in Lytton Strachey's list of Eminent Victorians. But neither were they obscure people, about whom nothing is known beyond the dates of their birth and death. They belonged (either by origin or assimilation) to what a previous age had called the middling sort of people, and which the Victorians themselves preferred to label as the middle and respectable classes. In this sense they were the most eminently Victorian of all classes in Victorian England.

From the nine studies some of the great themes of early and mid-Victorian society emerge. Implicit in the thinking of all these people is the assumption of progress – the great regulator of early Victorian thought. Yet belief in the onward and upward march of mankind and the triumph over all material obstacles did not blind the Victorians to the great imperfections in their society. Their faith in progress led not to complacency or withdrawal, but to intense activity in order to change things for the better. Robert Owen devoted his self-made fortune and the best years of his long life to proclaiming the need to build a new moral world. Josephine Butler set aside the comforts of home and family to crusade for poor and 'fallen' women. Thomas Cook's successful business as a travel agent was combined with his devotion to temperance reform. The world (and particularly England), thought the Victorians, was progressing at a prodigious rate, but that very progress served only to point to new possibilities and new expectations. We, who have come to expect the ever-accelerating rate of social change even though we have difficulty in adjusting to it, can hardly appreciate the novelty of this situation. In the lifetime of any of our nine characters society changed more than it had done for many generations previously. A favourite image was to see the world careering forward like an express train – and it is perhaps symbolic that in the lives of three of our figures (Hudson, Smiles and Cook) the railway was crucial.

This sense of being caught up in the vortex of social change was commonly expressed, either implicitly or more directly. An individual's particular orientation towards it helps to define his position and role in mid-Victorian England. This is equally true for a Tory like Hudson and a Radical like Cobden. The converse of this concern with change was an awareness of the need for some degree of stability if society was not to fall apart. 'The first duty of society is the preservation of society,' wrote Walter Bagehot, whose political liberalism was based on a robustly empirical, commonsense attitude to change. None of our nine figures wanted the stability of an aristocratic hierarchy: indeed most of them strongly repudiated the aristocracy as effete and obsolescent. But they were conscious that the new industrial civilisation lacked many of the social virtues which had acted as a bond in the England of the parsons and squires. The problem as these Victorians saw it was essentially this: given the undesirability and impracticality of trying to put the clock back, how could the whole process of change be contained and directed in ways which they approved? Each of them made his own answer; but all the answers are within a certain context. Noticeably their ideas and values do not stray beyond the bounds of what we can recognise as the mentality of the age.

The tone of that mentality was unmistakably religious. In the nineteenth century men framed their thinking about all kinds of subjects in religious terms, to an extent far beyond our present practice. From devout and committed Christians like Josephine Butler, to self-proclaimed infidels like Robert Owen, the language and habits of thought of Protestant Christianity were everywhere employed. Salvation, conversion, and the puritan virtues of hard work, sobriety and self-help, were widely accepted. Private doubts there were in abundance. But beyond and above all credal differences, doctrinal disputes, and even loss of faith, there remained, as a kind of moral cement, the great evangelical belief in duty and service beyond the mere satisfaction of self. Perhaps Thomas Carlyle, the prophet of the early Victorians, was right when he commented with his usual perspicacity that the age was 'destitute of faith and yet terrified at scepticism'. This and other themes can be heard from the voices that follow.

John F. C. Harrison

For further general reading see also books listed after each chapter

BEST, G. F. A. *Mid-Victorian Britain, 1851-1875* Weidenfeld and Nicolson, cased and paperback 1971; Panther, 1973.

BRIGGS, A. *The age of improvement* Longman, 1959

BURN, W. L. *The age of equipoise* George Allen & Unwin, 1964; paperback 1968.

HARRISON, J. F. C. *The early Victorians, 1832-51* Weidenfeld and Nicolson, cased and paperback 1971; Panther, 1973.

HOUGHTON, W. E. *The Victorian frame of mind, 1830-1870* Yale U.P., cased and paperback 1957.

KITSON CLARK, G. *The making of Victorian England* Methuen, 1962; paperback 1966.

PERKIN, H. *The origins of modern English society, 1780-1880* Routledge and Kegan Paul, 1969; n.e. paperback 1972.

WEBB, R. K. *Modern England: from the eighteenth century to the present* George Allen and Unwin, cased and paperback 1969.

WOODWARD, L. *The age of reform, 1815-1870* O.U.P., 2nd edn. 1962.

YOUNG, G. M. *Victorian England: portrait of an age* O.U.P., 1936; 2nd edn. 1960.

YOUNG, G. M. ed. *Early Victorian England, 1830-1865* O.U.P., 2 vols. 1934.

ROBERT OWEN

On 26 June, 1830, Robert Owen was presented at court to the young Queen Victoria, by the Prime Minister, Lord Melbourne. There was an immediate outcry in the press. The *Manchester Courier* editorialised:

> Anything in the shape of comment on this disgraceful circumstance would be superfluous indeed. We may safely leave it to be dealt with by people of all parties. The Premier of England, the chaperon of a notorious infidel in the court of a young Queen! What, past *all* shame, my lord?

And the *Liverpool Mail* said:

> Christians of England! Will you tamely submit to this outrage upon your baptismal faith? Is it not enough that roués and debauchees in disguise infest the neighbourhood of the palace? Is it not enough that the sacred feelings of virtuous and honourable ladies are outraged in what should be the very sanctum of purity? Are not these and a thousand other outrages upon decency, morals, and religion enough, but we must also submit to see the Prime Minister of England present at the court of the youthful Queen of England an avowed infidel and a public apologist of despisers of the marriage vow?

1 Robert Owen (1771–1858)

Yet the object of this vituperation was a benign old gentleman, getting on for seventy years of age, and the father of a happy family, now grown up. He had been a friend of the Queen's father, the late Duke of Kent, and had in fact lent him money. Twenty years earlier Owen had been the greatest cotton spinner in the kingdom, and had made a fortune out of his mills at New Lanark in Scotland. Why then was he so bitterly attacked? What was it about him that gave so much offence? What did they mean when they called him a notorious infidel?

To answer these questions we have to go back a little in time. We do not usually think of Owen as a Victorian, for he was born in 1771. But he lived until 1858 – when the Queen had already reigned for over twenty years. And this brings out a point which is worth remembering at the beginning of these studies of the Victorians — that many of them had grown up before the Queen came to the throne, and that their ideas and attitudes and assumptions were closer to those of the Regency, or even earlier, than to anything which came after. It is for this reason that I have chosen to talk about Robert Owen, rather than about someone who was conveniently born about 1820 and died in 1901. Owen's ideas were formulated during the Regency and earlier. But their full impact was not felt until the 1830s and 1840s. By 1839 Owenism, as it was called, was widely known; hence the reaction when Owen was presented at court.

One of the difficulties with talking about Owen is that he was such a many-sided person. You can talk about him as a business man (one of the great success stories of the Industrial Revolution), as an educator, as a pioneer of the cooperative movement, as the father of English socialism, as a factory reformer, as a trade unionist — even as a prophet. He was all these things — and more. So I shall have to select only some aspects of his life and work, leaving many important parts unmentioned. I shall limit myself to talking about Owen as a social reformer, as a critic of early Victorian society.

We sometimes think of the Victorians as being tremendously smug, self-satisfied, and hypocritical. Some of them were. But others were immensely self-critical, and fully aware of the shortcomings of themselves and their society. Owen's starting point was the well-known premise of the philosopher, Jeremy Bentham: 'The object of all human exertions is happiness. The happiness of the greatest number is the only legitimate object of society'. Which in Owen's words became:

> The end of government is to make the governed and the governors happy. That government then is best which in practice produces the greatest happiness to the greatest number, including those who govern and those who obey.
>
> Robert Owen *A New View of Society* 1817

Yet when he looked around, Owen concluded that happy individuals are rare. And he argued that since men are governed by reason, this failure to produce universal happiness must be due to some error of judgement.

> From the earliest ages it has been the practice of the world to act on the supposition that each individual man forms his own character, and that therefore he is accountable for all his sentiments and habits, and consequently merits reward for some and punishment for others. Every system which has been established among men has been founded on these erroneous principles. This error cannot much longer exist; for every day will make it more and more evident that the character of man is, without a single exception, always

formed for him; that it may be, and is chiefly, created by his predecessors; that they give him, or may give him, his ideas and habits, which are the powers that govern and direct his conduct. Man, therefore, never did, nor is it possible he ever can, form his own character.

A New View of Society

This was not a particularly original idea – it had been around at least since the time of the philosopher, John Locke, in the late seventeenth century – though Owen was always convinced that his ideas had never been thought of by anyone else before. He also claimed to have discovered the science of society; and he had important things to say about ideology and social change. Here is part of an address he gave to his workers at New Lanark in 1816:

What think you, my friends, is the reason why you believe and act as you do? I will tell you. It is solely and merely because you were born, and have lived, in this period of the world – in Europe – in the island of Great Britain – and more especially in this northern part of it.

Had they been born elsewhere or in other times, he added, they would have been quite different. And he concluded from this that class antagonism was irrational and irrelevant, since each class was the victim of its own ideology. The lesson for the working classes was plain:

You must be made to know yourselves, by which means alone you can discover what other men are. You will then distinctly perceive that no rational ground for anger exists, even against those who by the errors of the present system have been made your greatest oppressors. They are no more to be blamed than you are; nor you than they.

Owen *Address to the Working Classes* 1819

For Owen, social change always could, and should, be peaceful. He went out of his way, time and time again, to emphasise that the changes he proposed could be brought about without violence or upset of any kind.

Society did not destroy the old gravel roads before it commenced and completed the railways which were to supersede them. And when the railways were made ready to receive travellers, even then the gravel roads were allowed to remain for the use of timid persons. In like manner, without destroying or injuring the old system of society, the new will be made ready to receive willing passengers from the old. And thus will conflict be prevented.

Owen *Life, by Himself* 1857-8

Owen wanted to change society because he thought it was on the wrong track. All these great developments in technology and science which we call the Industrial Revolution, seemed to him to be producing nothing but misery and upset for most of the British people. His eldest son, Robert Dale Owen, was closer to his father than anyone else, and he describes Owen's great preoccupation:

> The problem loomed upon him. We may imagine his reflections. Why, as the world advances in knowledge and power do the prospects and comforts of the mass of mankind darken and decline? How happens it that centuries of improvement have left the British labourer twofold more the slave of toil than they found him? Why must mechanical inventions – themselves a rich blessing as surely as they are inevitable – stand in array *against* the labourer, instead of toiling by his side? Momentous questions these! My father pondered them day and night. If he had tersely stated the gist of his reflections they might have assumed some such form as this: Will any man, who stands on his reputation for sanity, affirm that the *necessary* result of over-production is famine? that because labour produces more than even luxury can waste, labour shall not have bread to eat? If we can imagine a point at which all the necessaries and comforts of life shall be produced without human labour, are we to suppose that the human labourer is then to be dismissed, to be told that he is now a useless incumbrance which they cannot afford to hire?
>
> Robert Dale Owen *Threading My Way* 1874

> In the time of our ancestors fifteen millions of men could produce enough to supply the wants of fifteen millions and no more. But now a population of twenty-five millions can with the same expenditure of energy supply the wants of six hundred millions. And yet the bulk of the people pass their lives in poverty. There is poverty and misery everywhere instead of wealth and happiness, because of the irrational basis of all existing institutions.
>
> Owen *Book of the New Moral World* 1836-44

Today, unfortunately, the paradox of poverty in the midst of plenty no longer shocks us – though if we project the problem on to a world scale it is still with us. But for Owen it made all the talk of progress and improvement and the 'blessings of civilization' sound quite hollow. He insisted on asking basic questions about the quality of life for the majority of ordinary people. And he refused to accept the orthodox answers of the time. This, I think, was remarkable in two ways. In the first place we have to remember that Owen himself had benefited enormously from the developments he criticised. He had started as a poor boy from Newtown in Wales, and had risen to become a wealthy manufacturer, solely by his own efforts. Yet he was in no way reconciled to the system, nor under any illusions about its implications. Second, it is remarkable that his critique came so early. It was only during Owen's lifetime that an industrial capitalist civilization had developed – indeed he was one of the leading figures in its development. Yet right from the start its limitations and injustices were clearly perceived, and continued to become more and more apparent as the century wore on.

> My father's conclusions were:
> First, that the enormously increased productive powers which man in modern times has acquired, involve, and in a measure necessitate, great changes in the social and industrial structure of society. Second, that the world has reached a point in progress at which cooperative industry should replace competitive labour. Third, that society, discarding large cities and solitary homes, should resolve itself into associations, each of fifteen hundred or two thousand persons, who should own land and houses in common, and labour for the benefit of the community. In this way, he believed, labour-saving power would directly aid, not tend to oppress, the workman.
> *Threading My Way*

Owen's 'New View of Society' as he called it, was pretty widely ridiculed, and his socialistic schemes were condemned as utopian by those who thought they knew better. But this hardly accounts for the outburst of indignation which greeted his presentation by Lord Melbourne at court. The appropriate response to his socialism was disbelief or mockery, not anger. No, it was not Owen's socialism that aroused such fierce opposition. If that was all that was involved, Owen could have been written off as just another dreamer, a rich philanthropist playing reformer; harmless enough, if a bit tiresome. But Owen did not stop there. He went on to attack religion, private property, and the family, which was a very different matter. For these were the basic institutions of Victorian society; and to question them was to make people feel very uncomfortable indeed. The fury with which Owen was condemned tells us something important about Victorian England. It shows what aspects of society the Victorians regarded as important, where their fears and hopes lay. Owen had evidently touched a sensitive social nerve. At this point he appears as a true radical, one who goes to the roots of things.

> I am not of your religion, nor of any religion yet taught in the world. To me they all appear united with much – yes, with very much – error. My friends, I am content that you should call me an infidel.
> Owen *Address at the City of London Tavern* 1817

But he went on to make things worse by attacking the institution of the family, and even (horror of horrors) the ideal of Christian marriage. At first glance it is rather puzzling to see why Owen attacked religion. Most of his contemporaries agreed with Robert Southey that this was Owen's biggest mistake. The Victorian age was one of the most religious there has ever been. To go out of your way to attack the churches (not just the Church of England, but all of them) was asking for trouble. Yet that is precisely what Owen did.

He spoke of religion as a kind of insanity, and as the cause of most of the evil in the world.

> I believe that the only worship that ought to be offered is correct practice, that is, to speak the truth always in all simplicity, and to act at all times in perfect accordance with it.
> *The Social Bible*

2 'Owen was condemned by bishops and nonconformist ministers alike'. Cartoon from *The Penny Satirist,* 1840

No wonder Owen was condemned by bishops and nonconformist ministers alike. He was the arch-infidel.

The fragmentation and disharmony which Owen deplored in competitive society he attributed largely to the institution of the private family. He regarded the family as a fundamentally divisive force, much more so than class. So he attacked the family and refused to regard class divisions as primary. Protected from the world at large by strong walls of legal and religious custom, the family seemed to him an autonomous and alien element in society. It isolated men from each other. It bred loneliness and self-centredness. Worse still, it was an organ of tyranny, by which the wife was subjected to (in fact made the property of) her husband, condemned to a life of petty domestic drudgery and endless child-bearing.

The truly radical nature of Owen's critique of the family was well appreciated by his contemporaries. Marx and Engels praised him for advocating the abolition of the family as much as they condemned him for neglecting the class struggle. We usually think of the Victorians as being essentially a home-loving people – 'Home,

home sweet home', and all that. And it is perfectly true that the cult of home was very widely advocated. But there was also an undercurrent of persistent criticism of the family and its role – and also, of course, a vast underworld of crime and prostitution which flagrantly denied domestic virtue. In many Victorian novels the inadequacy of the family is brought out. The theme is familiar: husband is out all day at business; wife remains at home; the couple lead separate lives, and after a time become strangers to each other; only when the man goes bankrupt and loses all does he at last discover his home. The Owenite community was an attempt to remedy this failure of the family.

Owen was also convinced that the existing system of marriage was undesirable. He protested against marriages by family arrangement, and he also advocated birth control. In Owen's view the basis of marriage could only be the affection of the two spouses. A marriage without love was prostitution. Celibacy he regarded as unnatural and likely to lead to disease of body and mind. The indissolubility of marriage was a prime cause of personal unhappiness and social evil.

> Marriages should be solely formed to promote the happiness of the sexes; and if this end be not obtained, the object of the union is defeated.
> Owen *Lectures on the Marriages of the Priesthood* 1840

And so he advocated a system of carefully controlled divorce. Unfortunately, Owen's fundamentally sensible views on marriage were obscured by his desire to blame the clergy. Christian marriage, he felt, reinforced the isolation, privateness and secrecy of the family in relation to society; and within the family it strengthened prudery and false shame, and prevented a happy, frank, sexual relationship between the partners. As one of his early followers, George Jacob Holyoake, put it:

> Mr Owen regarded affection as essential to chastity. But his deprecation of priestly marriage set many against marriage itself. This was owing to the newness of his doctrine in those days, which led to misconception on the part of some, and was wilfully perverted by others. He claimed for the poor facilities of divorce equal to those accorded to the rich.
> G. J. Holyoake, *Sixty Years of an Agitator's Life* 1902

Owen's denunciation of marriage and the family was part of his attack on private property. He believed that society suffered because of its over-emphasis on the individualising, as opposed to the socialising, aspects of life. He wanted to do away with private institutions, especially the institution of private property, and put social institutions in their place. That is why his followers were called socialists – the first to bear that name.

To Owen the new industrial order was not a true society because it lacked the necessary characteristics of wholeness, unity, and stability. Instead it offered only fragmentation, loneliness, and strife. Karl Marx described much the same phenomena as alienation. The worker becomes a mere commodity, and his work is meaningless to him, being only a means to other ends. He becomes, in fact, alienated from the product of his labour, and, in time, alienated from himself and his fellow-men. He is denied that community with others which is essential for each individual to cultivate his gifts to the full. This was what Owen had in mind when he described society as artificial and atomized. He saw his task as the restoration of harmony to the world. Harmony was to be the keynote of Owen's new moral world, in sharp contrast with the discord of existing society, the old immoral world. Owen was not able to define the problem of community in psychological terms, but he saw clearly enough that the implications of industrialism could not be confined to physical changes. He took account of the uniqueness of industrial society and tried to explain what industrialism was doing to the lives of ordinary people by reference to the concept of community.

But what about his practical solution to these problems? – for Owen always prided himself on being an essentially practical man, a man experienced in the ways of business, and so on. You have probably already guessed by this time that his answer was community life. Abandon private homes, and live together in a community. Pool all your resources, and carry on agriculture and industry on a cooperative basis. Build the community (or village of cooperation, as he called it) rather like an Oxford college, with private apartments on one side of the court, and dining rooms, schools,

3 Robert Owen's plan for a Cooperative. Cartoon of 1830

A MUTUAL LABOUR COMITTEE sitting for the admission of members.

The poor may do without the rich, combine to suply each other with the necessarys of life, live in perfect equality & have leasure to improve their minds. (own

4 A view of New Lanark (from a contemporary engraving)

Building far left: Top part a School for the Children – the under part a Public Kitchen

Building second left: A School for the Formation of Character

Other buildings: Cotton Factories

The figures represented in the foreground are the Village Band.

children's dormitories, laundries and libraries on the other sides.

> Mr Owen of Lanark, has, it seems, a scheme which is nothing short of a species of monkery. This gentleman is for establishing innumerable communities of paupers! Each is to be resident in an inclosure, somewhat resembling a barrack establishment. I do not clearly understand whether the sisterhoods and brotherhoods are to form distinct communities, like nuns and friars, or whether they are to mix promiscuously.
>
> *Political Register* August 1817

William Cobbett, the great radical journalist, might have a great time sneering at 'Mr Owen's parallelograms of paupers'. But other people – and not paupers – decided that there was something in what Owen said. And they were prepared to try and make a go of community life. In America at least sixteen communities, either avowedly Owenite or influenced by Owenite ideas, were founded. In Britain there were seven Owenite communities, and another three experiments in which Owenites participated. The last, and largest of the English ones was called Queenwood, at East Tytherley, in Hampshire. It was begun in 1839, two years after Queen Victoria came to the throne. But like the other Owenite communities, Queenwood folded up after about five years. The reasons for its failure are numerous. But probably Holyoake put his finger on the main cause when he wrote later:

> The cessation of Queenwood was primarily caused by insufficient capital to last while the new order of life consolidated itself, and the conditions of industrial profit were found. No social community in Great Britain had a long enough time allowed to give it a reasonable chance of succeeding.
>
> G. J. Holyoake *History of Cooperation* 1908

Oddly enough, Owen was never disheartened by the apparent failure of his plans. He merely said that they had never been properly tried out. To the last he believed in communitarianism.

In his old age he was attracted to spiritualism, which had suddenly in the early 1850s become all the rage in America. Significantly, his new convictions were not opposed to his previous teaching, but supplemented and confirmed it. The spirits conveniently assured him that his ideas were correct, that he was on the right track.

Was this just the natural credulity of an old man? Most historians have thought so, and have tried to slide over this last episode of Owen's life, as being in some way derogatory to his reputation. Why bring it up, except to discredit the memory of a great reformer? My answer is twofold.

First, the significance of spiritualism does not depend on the fraudulence or otherwise of table rapping. There was much more to the movement than that. Owen was by no means the only reformer to turn to spiritualism in the fifties. And not only to spiritualism. For spiritualism can be seen as but the latest in a series of movements and causes which attracted progressively-minded men in early Victorian times. Mesmerism, phrenology, vegetarianism, hydropathy – all claimed their devotees. And socialists were often found among them. Men were searching for a solution to their problems which arose from living in a period of peculiarly intense social and economic change. There is a sort of affinity between these seemingly very different 'isms'. The vision of a new heaven will perhaps be most gladly received by those whose eyes have already been opened to the vision of a new earth; or, to put it another way, they will have little difficulty in seeing the one in terms of the other.

Which brings us to the second point – which is that Owen's interest in spiritualism was not primarily an interest in a revelation of a future life. He only used it as a medium by which to proclaim his life-long message of the socialist millennium. His followers referred to him as the Social Father – for they had perceived the truth about him: that he was a prophet, as well as a critic, of the Victorian age.

John F. C. Harrison

OWEN, Robert *A new view of society, and Report to the County of Lanark* ed. by V. A. C. Gatrell. Penguin Books, n.e. 1970.

BUTT, J. ed. *Robert Owen: Prince of cotton spinners* David and Charles, 1971.

HARRISON, J. F. C. *Robert Owen and the Owenites in Britain and America* Routledge and Kegan Paul, 1969.

PODMORE, F. *Robert Owen: a biography* George Allen and Unwin, 1923; Clifton, N. J.: Kelley, new impression of 1906 edition, 1969.

POLLARD, S. and SALT, J. eds. *Robert Owen: Prophet of the poor* Macmillan, 1971.

RICHARD COBDEN

5 Richard Cobden (1804–65)

Cobden's career provides an insight into one element in the complex story of Victorian radicalism. 'Radicalism' is something of a vague term, but as a working definition we may think of Victorian radicals as those politicians who wanted to see progressive changes introduced more quickly than either of the major governing parties would allow. This does not mean that there was otherwise any particular unity about Victorian radicalism – there were radicals for and against the new Poor Law of 1834, there were radicals on both sides of the disputes about factory reform, and radicals differed widely amongst themselves as to the proper course to be adopted in both domestic and foreign policies. Cobden was a leading figure in one of the strands which went to make up this complex fabric.

He was born in 1804, the son of an unsuccessful farmer, but by the age of thirty he had contrived to build up a prosperous business in the expanding textile industry and thereby to secure the financial resources necessary to pursue a political career. By then, too, he had already formed the political opinions which were to actuate him throughout his career. He believed that the social evils which afflicted his day were largely the fault of economic mismanagement; that the periodic depressions, with their consequent unemployment and suffering, were largely the consequence of foolish government intervention in matters economic. He argued that if trade were allowed the maximum degree of freedom from tariffs and other hampering restrictions, then commerce would flow in natural and healthy channels, each country and each region would specialise in the production of the articles which it could best provide, and a free interchange would be far and away the best promoter of prosperity for all concerned.

He was one of the many members of the industrial interest who resented the continuing aristocratic predominance in British society. To his way of thinking, the landed aristocracy, for entirely selfish reasons, imposed limitations on trade and restricted the free development of national energies and so were a major barrier in the way of the changes he desired. Such concepts could win considerable support from a new industrial Britain then emerging, and some at least of those who stood spellbound at the prodigious

25

achievements of British industry resented the continuing ascendancy of the old landed interest in national life. Sometimes this kind of feeling could receive remarkably romantic expression.

Trade has now a chivalry of its own, a chivalry whose stars are radiant with the more benignant lustre of justice, happiness and religion, and whose titles will outlive the barbarous nomenclature of Charlemagne. Trade can be scorned no longer; it has burst forth with the splendour of heaven-made genius, and compelled the reluctant homage of all ranks. Industry now stands side by side with hereditary opulence; the owner of ten thousand spindles confronts the lord of ten thousand acres; the one grasping the steam-engine, the other the plough; each surrounded by an equal number of dependants, and bearing an equal share in the burdens and dangers of the state. Now the time has arrived when the shadow of an injustice between such rivals could no longer be endured. Trade shall no longer pay a tribute to the soil.

Rev. Henry Dunckley *The Charter of the Nations* 1854

6 Membership certificate of the National Anti-Corn Law League

The tribute to the soil which Cobden and his friends most resented in the later 1830s was the Corn Laws, which imposed duties

WORKING MEN!

You pay a Tax of Tenpence
Upon every Stone of Flour you and your wives and little ones consume.

If there was not an Infamous CORN LAW you and your Families might buy THREE LOAVES for the same money that you now pay for Two.

Upon every Shilling you spend for Bread, Meat, Bacon, Eggs, Vegetables, &c., you pay 4d. Tax for Monopoly.

DOWN, DOWN
WITH THE
Infamous Bread Tax!

7 A handbill distributed during the Anti-Corn Law campaign

on the import of foreign food in order to protect the British landed interest. This was seen by the free trade radicals as a tax levied by the landlords on the remainder of society, and a major attack on the Corn Laws was launched by the Anti-Corn Law League – ably led by Cobden – in the early 1840s. Its backbone support came from industrialists for whom the availability of cheaper foreign food for workers would mean reduced production costs. At the same time, primary producers overseas, enabled to sell their food here, would earn the resources with which to buy British manufactures in return. This attitude is simple and clear enough, but Cobden's own aims went a great deal further. He wanted free trade, certainly, but unlike many of his followers in Anti-Corn Law League days, free trade was for him only the first step towards the realisation of wider and nobler visions. He believed that if nations all over the world were to adopt a policy of free exchange of goods – which he believed to be in their own economic interests anyway – then this free interchange would bring about not only a state of ever-expanding prosperity, but also a state of such intimate economic interdependence that war would become impossible and armaments necessarily wither away. Throughout his career, this over-riding hope for a world of peace and co-operation remained the end objective for which he worked.

> How impossible it is to ensure the peace of the world, and guarantee us against all the burdens which our present warlike attitude entails upon us by any means excepting a free commercial intercourse between all nations.
> Cobden to Bright, October 1846

A crucial factor in considering Cobden's career is to understand that, while he could find a good deal of support within the expanding industrial interests where the immediate advantage of the industrial interest could be anticipated – as in the repeal of the Corn Laws – his wider visions of peace and international co-operation were not acceptable to very many of those who would follow him against the Corn Laws. I shall come back to this point, but first let us look at some of the qualities which Cobden brought to his political work as a radical leader. He possessed undeniable personal charm – no negligible asset in a politician, and he deployed in addition considerable powers as speaker and organiser. One of his supporters at the height of the Anti-Corn Law League of the 1840s has left this impression of him at work.

> I had been waiting all the evening to receive this credential letter from Mr Cobden, who was in his bedroom, with a large fire, receiving people on business, of which he had a vast deal on his hands. He wrote this letter while I was in the room with him; and it struck me as an example of his great aptitude for business that though he had been occupied for several hours by a succession of visitors who sought his counsel or direction on the business of the League, quite apart from the business on which I came to him, he immediately proceeded to write the letter with such precision and accuracy that he did not need to alter a word or even a letter, as I can see from the original letter now lying before me.
> A. Bissett *Notes on the Anti-Corn Law Struggle* 1884

But although Cobden undeniably held high principles, he was – shall we say – possessed of a useful flexibility in the methods he was prepared to use to forward them. Cobden's attitude to electoral malpractices illustrates his flexibility as a politician. In public he invariably denounced the scandalous practices of aristocratic borough-mongers; but in private his own record for electoral skulduggery was pretty impressive. He took a leading part in the Anti-Corn Law League's first electoral adventure in a by-election at Walsall early in 1841, when, as one of the agents working for him on that occasion recalled.

> Staid and sober Quakers presided over convivial meetings and sung flash songs. Others bottled voters or carried them off drunk to places many miles off and by darkening windows persuaded them to sleep until the poll was over. I remember at an out-district where free and independent electors were kept amused and in liquor, one fellow was particularly noisy singing 'Rule Britannia'. At last a very staid Quaker exclaimed 'I can stand this no longer!' and left the room. All of a sudden the noise ceased and the Quaker reappeared saying 'I've settled him' – Egad, he had put snuff in his grog.
> I saw two men come up after a third (to vote). One was asked his name and on giving it a man exclaimed, 'Why, that

man is in America!' When the other gave his, another cried, 'I buried that man on the third of last month!' They however voted and the third man said with a wink, 'Come away to your graves again'.

J. B. Smith *Corn Law Papers*

Only a few months after Cobden helped to arrange these activities, he was denouncing the Conservative-dominated House of Commons elected in 1841 as the 'Bribery Parliament'. At grass roots level early Victorian politics were often very rough. Many radicals who in public denounced any form of political intimidation were in practice prepared to use such methods when they could. In the early 1840s, for example, when the Anti-Corn Law League was being attacked by Chartists because they felt that political reform was more important than free trade, Cobden was quite prepared to negotiate an unholy alliance between his own strong arm men and the Manchester Irish to bring the Chartists down. Edward Watkin was Cobden's right hand man in these activities, and he reported to his chief the descent of these vigorous allies on a meeting held by the Manchester Chartists to welcome their leader, Feargus O'Connor, in March 1842.

> The result was a tremendous fight – all the furniture was smashed to atoms; forms – desks – chairs – gas pipes – were used as weapons and the result is something like as follows. 'The lion' – the king of Chartism – Feargus O'Connor – knocked down three times – has, he says, seven wounds – six he can tell the position of – the seventh was inflicted as he was running away – which he did after fighting about two minutes.
>
> Christopher Doyle very much hurt – Bailey confined to his bed – Murray ditto – four others (Chartists) seriously hurt – Reverend Schofield – black eye – loose teeth – contusions behind (got in following Feargus) – four of the (Irish) 'lambs' badly hurt – two with their sculls fractured – they however are used to it and will soon be well.

All of this is as much a part of Cobden the politician as the lofty motives he expressed in lucid and dignified speeches in Parliament or on the platform; he was neither the first nor the last politician to stoop to distinctly dubious methods in pursuit of noble ends.

But with all his high personal qualities, and with all the shifts and expedients to which he was willing to resort, Cobden was never in a position to exercise effective power in Victorian Britain. His aims had certain tactical advantages; the landed aristocracy could be made to fit the useful political category of an enemy to hate and work against. Unfortunately, such feelings were neither so strong nor so general as to make any very effective dent in the dominance of the landed interest during Cobden's lifetime. Even within the industrial interests themselves, hostility to the landed aristocracy was by no means general. Not all merchants and manufacturers shared Cobden's anti-aristocratic views. In 1840, for example, Manchester itself – Cottonopolis – selected a landed gentleman as one of the town's two MPS – much to Cobden's fury.

> As for the conduct of our men here in selecting Gibson, a young untried man and a Suffolk squire to become member for Manchester, I am quite disgusted at it. What wonder that we are scorned by the landed aristocracy, when we take such pains to show our contempt for ourselves? We save our enemies the trouble of trampling on ourselves, by very industriously kicking our own backsides.
> Cobden to Place, October 1840

In 1846 the repeal of the Corn Laws seemed to demonstrate the success of industry as against the land. One of the measures that accompanied the repeal was a great national fund collected for Cobden's benefit. But he cannot have liked the spirit in which one of the organisers, himself an industrialist and a supporter of the Anti-Corn Law League, approached this task.

> Nor have I any notion of its being desirable that the public man whom his country shall have qualified to sit down on his own broad acres, should remain subject to the contingencies of an active trade, of watching, either personally, or by deputy, the processes by which 6d a piece is to be gained, or 2s 6d to be lost, in the production of beggarly printed calicoes.
> Thomas Hunter to Cobden, March 1846

The predominance of the landed aristocracy in British society was very deeply rooted and difficult to overthrow. If Cobden sometimes cherished hopes that the days of this dominance were numbered, his more sensible associates tried to ensure that he appreciated reality rather than took comfort in wishful thinking. Joseph Parkes, an able lawyer who served as an electoral specialist for the Whigs and Radicals, had no doubts about the realities of the situation, which he often conveyed to Cobden in his letters.

> You are not so ill-informed of the Class-interests of this country, of the power of the Aristocracy, of the State of Parties, as to dream of the practicability or *possibility* of a *Radical* or '*Free Trade*' Cabinet and administration. You know, or ought to know, that the *men* for such a Ministry do not exist – that our Representative System would maintain none such if the Ministers could be found, and that our existing political and social system could not realise your vision.
> January 1844

These basic truths lie at the root of Cobden's failure to obtain effective influence. He had great abilities, but the changes in national policies which he wished to see could only be implemented by parliaments and by governments. He was unhappy with both Whigs and Tories, but only those great political groupings were able to control the machinery of the state.

In 1846, for a short time, it was possible to believe otherwise. After the League which Cobden had led with conspicuous ability for eight years had built up an organisation of impressive size, the Corn Laws were in fact repealed. But the hard fact was, that the repeal was effected by the Prime Minister, Sir Robert Peel, and that without the Whig and Peelite votes mustered in favour, the League's objective would have remained unrealised. Nevertheless, Cobden could hope then that with this first major step taken, in the ensuing years he would be able to persuade his fellow-countrymen to follow him in the path, not only of free trade, but also of peace and non-intervention in the internal affairs of other States. There were encouraging signs to be seen. At the 1847 General Election, for example, Cobden received one of the greatest electoral compliments of the nineteenth century, being elected MP for the West Riding of Yorkshire, without his knowledge and while he was absent abroad. To represent in the House of Commons this vast concentration of wealth and influence was esteemed a high honour, usually afforded only to the Riding's most distinguished citizens. But for Cobden, it was an empty honour, for unless the personal prestige and popularity which he had gained during the Anti-Corn Law crusade could be maintained, his hold on that parliamentary seat must be precarious indeed.

Unfortunately for Cobden, the next ten years saw his popularity wane markedly, as his fellow-countrymen who had supported him against the Corn Laws made it unmistakably plain that their support did not extend to his wider visions of peace and international co-operation. Cobden wanted few armaments and a studious refusal on Britains' part to claim any right to determine the affairs of other States; but many of his fellow radicals, in the 1850s, fired with sympathy for Kossuth, for Mazzini or for Garibaldi, talked of adventures abroad to free Hungary, to free Poland and to free Italy which went far beyond anything which Lord Palmerston himself would ever seriously contemplate. As one of his old friends and supporters wrote to him in 1853:

> I will become a convert to your peace principles after one more general war for freedom. This must come within ten years. I had hoped that a war between Russia and Turkey would give Hungary and Italy a chance to be free.
>   J. R. Thompson to Cobden, August 1853

As the eighteen fifties wore on, the essential isolation and impotence of Cobden and his diminishing band of associates became increasingly plain. The Crimean War outraged all his pacific and internationalist beliefs, and he and his friend John Bright made no secret of their outright opposition to a war which in fact gained a

8 Cobden, the giant-monopoly killer, and his Anti-Corn Law League boots.
Cartoon from *The Penny Satirist,* 1845

great deal of popularity at all levels of British society. The way of a peace party in time of war can be a very hard one. If Cobden's private correspondence of these years had been made public he would have become even more unpopular.

> Speaking in the interests of our children, I doubt whether it be desirable that our arms should have a great triumph in the Crimea – for it would only foster the war spirit – and make us more eager for further intervention. Nothing I fear short of the loss of an army by disease will break up this confederacy and turn the public mind against both government and public instructors.
> Cobden to Bright, May 1855

The decline in Cobden's popularity was sufficiently obvious during the Crimean War, but the unmistakable demonstration of this decline did not come until 1857. Ironically enough, it was then sparked off by a notable parliamentary triumph on his part. In China our local agents had embroiled us in a major quarrel with the Chinese authorities at Canton on the flimsiest possible basis. Palmerston's government, while privately aware of the weakness of the British case, determined to back their local agents at the risk of major war. Cobden's motion of censure on the government's China policy was supported by many of the ablest in the Commons.

> I am obliged to the House for having heard me. In all sincerity I wish this Motion to be taken without reference to its consequences, and with the sole desire to do justice to the merits of the case. I think it hard that any Hon. Gentleman should be debarred from giving his honest vote on a question of this importance. I will admit that Parliamentary government must be carried on by parties. If parties were more advanced and came up to my standard, I might join them; but as it is I am isolated, and am content to be a pioneer. But there are great occasions upon which all parties ought to give an honest and conscientious vote. We all of us have moments when we look back upon such a vote as this with more satisfaction than any vote given in the mere scramble of parties.

The motion of censure was carried by a transient combination of radicals and Conservatives, but the reaction of one moderate liberal MP, confided to his diary, was significant.

> I at first had some inclination to vote with Cobden, before I heard his speech. But Cobden's speech, Bulwer's, and indeed all the speakers on that side of the question, made it more and more impossible for me to have anything to do with Cobden. They were so un-English, so ingeniously unfair against ourselves and in defence of the Chinese.
> D. W. Hewett (ed.) *Diaries of Chichester Fortesque*

Palmerston knew his fellow-countrymen and declined to resign after his defeat. Instead, Parliament was dissolved, and the dissolution at once exposed the hollowness of Cobden's position. There seemed to be no constituency which he could contest with any great hope of success, so great was his unpopularity. He finally stood for the industrial borough of Huddersfield, where he was beaten by a local business man of markedly inferior talents but plain Palmerstonian leanings.

Cobden's recipe which coupled free trade with peace and non-intervention abroad was rejected by the Victorian electorate. They could accept free trade, with its intelligible immediate advantages, but into his wider aspirations the majority of them would not go. Cobden himself fully appreciated the significance of this rejection.

> I will never again be a party to the old movement, carried on in such a way as to allow everybody to join in the 'Hallelujahs' for *peace*, and nine-tenths of them to run off and cheer any minister who will offer to make war with any people on earth I have a similar feeling arising out of the late war, respecting 'Financial Reform'. It is a delusion to propose economy in the public expenditure so long as the people of this country as represented by almost every leading politician and newspaper lay it down as their duty that they must regulate the affairs of the whole world, and protect Europe in particular against the encroachments of Russia or any other ambitious power. So long as such a policy is seriously professed by the country, I cannot honestly tell it that there should be a moderate peace establishment. On the contrary, a nation which undertakes to sway the destinies of Europe by bullying one half and protecting the other must make up its mind to bear the expense of such an attitude. The little that I shall have to say will be to link together cause and effect in this unpalatable way. But there is no party as yet in the country that I can see to support one in those views. The Radicals have turned more warlike than the Tories – what have *they* to promise the country in the way of practical benefits as a result of Parliamentary Reform? Not 'peace, retrenchment and reform', which were Lord Grey's watchwords, but the very opposite. No, depend upon it, the Radicals have cut their throats before Sebastopol. The aristocracy have gained immensely since the people took to soldiering.
>
> Cobden to George Wilson, September 1856

The catastrophe of the General Election of 1857 was not the end of Cobden's career. He returned to Parliament in 1859 as Member for Rochdale, and regained a position of some prestige as a respected liberal politician. In 1860 he succeeded in negotiating a limited measure of international free trade in an Anglo-French commercial treaty which was, however, to be very short lived. Cobden did not live to see the effective birth of the Gladstonian Liberal Party, to which he might have made a major contribution. He died in April 1865 at the age of sixty.

Let us leave Cobden with an account of an incident which illustrates the eminently amiable aspects of his personality. When Palmerston formed his second government in 1859, he wished to incorporate in it as wide a range of liberal opinion as possible, and in his cabinet-making he reserved the post of President of the Board of Trade for Cobden, who was then absent in America. When Cobden returned home, he immediately called on Palmerston and there ensued a fascinating confrontation between these two men who had been political enemies for decades. Cobden had repeatedly assailed Palmerston's bellicose foreign policies in bitter terms, yet when the two men met together in this way the atmosphere was cordial, and it is clear that in personal terms they could not help liking each other. Palmerston strongly urged Cobden to accept cabinet office, and argued with a good deal of truth that it was only from inside the governing circle that he could hope to exercise any effective influence on the nation's policies. But Cobden persisted in his refusal to take office on the grounds of the long and public opposition which had subsisted between the two of them. He described his parting with his old arch-enemy in a letter written soon afterwards.

> I rose to depart, expressing the hope that our personal and political relations might be in future the same as if in his government. As I left the room he said – 'Lady Palmerston receives tomorrow evening at ten?' – to which I instantly replied 'I shall be happy to be allowed to present myself to her'. 'I shall be very glad if you will' was his answer, and so we parted.
>
> The next evening I was at Cambridge House for the first time, and found myself among a crowd of fashionables and politicians, and was the lion or rather the *monster* of the party.

John Morley *The Life of Richard Cobden* 1893

For Cobden, arrival among the fashionables and politicians of office-holding status came much too late. His health was deteriorating already, and he was never to have the experience of deploying his undoubted talents in the complex responsibilities of government office. While he remains one of the most interesting and prominent radical politicians of Victorian Britain his positive achievements were relatively few. And few because the great decisions of that age were made not by radical leaders operating outside the governing system, but essentially by the men of the governing parties who actually held the reins of power in that society.

Norman McCord

MCCORD, N. *The Anti-Corn Law League, 1838-46* George Allen and Unwin, 2nd rev. edn. paperback 1968.
READ, D. *Cobden and Bright* Edward Arnold, 1967.

GEORGE HUDSON

George Hudson was the wonder of his age. Born poor – or so he said – he reached dizzy heights of power and wealth proving, to the satisfaction of his contemporaries, that advancement in English society was open to men of merit and probity. Then, after a decade and a half when he was sought after and fawned over by dukes and earls, he fell, was exposed as a swindler of monumental proportions and publicly humiliated by the very people he had once helped; who had lost their money; yet who deserved – many of them anyway – no more sympathy than they got from Thomas Carlyle, one of the few to express sorrow over the fall of the erstwhile 'Railway King'.

> King Hudson flung utterly prostrate, detected 'cooking accounts'; everybody kicking him through the mire. To me and to quiet onlookers he has not changed at all. He is merely detected to me what we always understood he was. The rage of fellow-gamblers, now when he has merely lost the game for them, and ceased to swindle with impunity, seems to us a very baseless thing. One sordid, hungry *canaille* are they all. Why should this, the chief terrier among them, be set upon by all the dog fraternity? One feels a real human pity for the ugly Hudson.
>
> J. A. Froude *Thomas Carlyle: A History of his Life in London 1884*

Hudson was born in 1800 in the East Riding village of Howsham. According to his biographer, R. S. Lambert, he was from 'a prosperous yeoman farming family in straitened circumstances'. In fact there is no evidence to support that contention whatsoever. He was the fifth son of John Hudson, who, it is said, left a fortune of £10,000. Lambert seems to have been taken in by Hudson's own statements and fooled by the fact that young George was sent to York, at the age of fifteen to be apprenticed to a firm of drapers and silk mercers. Hardly a pursuit worthy of the son of a wealthy yeoman farming family, Lambert seems to have reasoned, therefore the family *must* have been poor. In actual fact there is a much more human and commonplace explanation for Hudson leaving How-

9 George Hudson (1800–71)

sham. The parish poor book for the period April 1815 to April 1816 records that he had disgraced himself.

Received of George Hudson for Bastardy—12s 6d.

Sent to York on account of a youthful indiscretion, Hudson worked in the firm of Nicholson and Bell, married one of Nicholson's daughters and eventually became a partner. After his downfall he looked back nostalgically on those years, and inflated the profitability of his business.

> The happiest part of my life was when I stood behind the counter and used the yard measure in my own shop. I had one of the snuggest businesses in York, and turned over my thirty thousand a year, five-and-twenty per cent of it being profit.
> *Daily News* December 1871

Hudson became relatively well-off – a respectable tradesman. But the profits from the shop, whatever he said, were certainly *not* enough to launch him on his career of politician, banker, businessman and railwayman. Where did he get the money that enabled him to start this? How did he achieve the 'take-off' in his career? In 1827 an event occurred which entirely changed the current of Hudson's life. A wealthy great-uncle of his, Matthew Bottrill, died at the age of seventy and left practically the whole of his fortune, worth – some said – about £30,000, to his great-nephew. Bottrill made his will on his deathbed; and 'scandal was not slow to play with the fact that Hudson had been assiduous in his attendance on the old man during his last hours'. But the will was uncontested, and at a stroke Hudson became one of the richest men in York. The concluding clause is of great significance.

> I give and devise all the residue and remainder of my freehold and copyhold messuages lands tenements hereditaments and real Estate whatsoever and wheresoever not hereinbefore specifically disposed of and also all my Personal Estate and Effects whatsoever not hereinbefore specifically bequeathed unto the said George Hudson his heirs executors administrators and assigns respectively according to the nature of the same Estates respectively Subject nevertheless to and charged and chargeable with the payment of my just debts funeral and Testamentary expenses and the pecuniary legacies hereinbefore bequeathed.

Lambert mentions, then dismisses, the idea that Hudson exerted pressure on old Bottrill. But had he seen the will, he would have been forced to admit that it lends weight to the rumours of 1827. The will *was* changed on the old man's deathbed, and George *was* the main beneficiary. Given the lands that Bottrill left – which did not have to be mentioned in the probate – Hudson could have benefited by even more than £30,000. And the significance for the historian is this. If we *do* have him behaving crookedly in 1827 – long before his railway career – then we have him behaving *in character* at the height of his power, during the railway mania; behaving then in exactly the same way that he had behaved as a young man. His standards then were the same as they were when Matthew was dying.

With his new found wealth Hudson entered enthusiastically into the political life of York. He became treasurer of the York Tory party, the briber-in-chief who had to appear as a reluctant witness before a parliamentary select committee which investigated activities at the city's elections of the early 1830s. There he was shown to be an able organiser and an effective briber on behalf of John Henry Lowther. Thomas Foster, a voter, told a witness that he had received a gift of two sovereigns for his vote.

> The postman brought a letter to my house. I opened it, and found two yellow boys in it; I called to my old woman, and said, here are two yellow boys; give me two shillings for them to drink Mr Lowther's health; she did, and I drank his health.

Hudson, as a Tory, was shut out of politics in Whig dominated York, but in 1835 municipal government was reformed and thrown open to annual elections. This gave Hudson, now the acknowledged party leader, another role to play. He organised, bribed and bullied, and within two years of that reform he had toppled the Whigs from power. He became Lord Mayor of 'the second city in the country' and his party remained in control for a decade and a half. The *Yorkshire Gazette* commented:

> the Whig-Radical party may bid adieu to that power which they so long wielded in the old close corporation, and which, by mere luck, they held for a short space under the new order of things.
>
> November 1837

But before this happened Hudson had taken part in his first railway venture. He was wealthy and anxious to stop being a draper and become a gentleman. He became a banker, and dabbled in other ventures. In late 1833 he was one of a group of York businessmen who met at Tomlinson's Hotel and decided to promote a railway line into York that would eventually link up with a Stephenson line at Altofts. Capital (gained more honestly than Hudson's) was abundant and seeking outlets; lines elsewhere had proved that railways were reliable, were practical and were profitable; a political calm had descended on the country; and investors were prepared to plunge wildly into railway speculation, regarding every venture 'as a stereotype of the best'. Latter day admirers of Hudson have presented him as a visionary bent on making York a great rail centre, and as the moving spirit behind the Tomlinson's meeting. He was neither. He was just one among many of the city's business community who were anxious to invest and obtain cheap coal so that their city could become industrialised – another Bradford or another Leeds. 'Cheap coal was what they wanted, and a railway was the only way of getting it'. Cheap coal, not some grandiose scheme to attract other lines to York was their objective. George Stephenson declared that the committee's aims were 'extremely moderate', and 'most honourable and praiseworthy'.

Hudson was now launched. First he was treasurer of the York and North Midland and one of the largest shareholders. Soon he became chairman of the company. But why did his colleagues, established businessmen and political opponents like James Meek, allow him to become their leader? The answer seems to be a simple one. Hudson, with fewer commitments than Meek and the others, and with that drive to become respectable, was simply willing to spend more time on company business than they either would or could. After all *they* were *already* recognised leaders of local society. The building of the line went on rapidly and during Hudson's second mayoralty on the 29th May 1839 it was opened. York at last was connected with the industrial areas of the West Riding. (And a line was being built from Darlington to connect it with the North East). The *Yorkshire Gazette* reported the day's events:

> A cloudless sky of an azure more deep than is often seen above our misty atmosphere and a sign of intense brightness and warmth might have belonged to a southern clime, but that a gentle breeze from the North East of refreshing coolness, preserved the temperature at such a point as to prevent the lassitude and enervation which are felt under a too sultry day.

The day began and ended with feasting. And at seven minutes past one:

> the huge snake-like body was seen making way with an imperceptibly accelerating speed, and, stealing away under the broad arch of the Holdgate Lane bridge, was soon lost to the sight of the crowds who thronged the station, the adjacent bar-walls, and the ramparts, while the gay travellers experienced the exciting sensation of the gradually increasing swiftness, till they were borne along with the speed of a race-horse past the admiring spectators, that still for many a mile thronged both sides of the line.
>
> *Yorkshire Gazette* June 1839

In the next few years Hudson became the most sought after railway magnate in Britain. Company after company invited him to take them over, amalgamations followed, new lines were built. Eventually he controlled practically the whole of the railway system of the north eastern part of the country. John Francis, a contemporary, described his empire in 1844.

His influence extended seventy-six miles over the York and North Midland; fifty-one miles over the Hull and Selby and Leeds and Selby; over the North Midland, Midland Counties, and another, one hundred and seventy-eight miles; over the Newcastle and Darlington, and the Great North of England, one hundred and eleven miles; while over the Sheffield and Rotherham, the York and Scarborough, the North British, Whitby and Pickering, it affected nearly six hundred more, making a total of 1,016 miles, all of which were successful in developing traffic, and equally successful in paying good dividends.

J. Francis *A History of the English Railway* 1851

KING HUDSON'S LEVEE.

10 'Hudson became the most sought after railway magnate in Britain.' Cartoon from *Punch*, 1845

Why was Hudson so sought after? The answer lies in the profitability of the York and North Midland. In February 1840 a dividend of 21 shillings per share was declared; a year later it had gone up to 35; in 1843 it was 50 shillings. It is true that, at first, a few people – like Amos Coates and Joseph Rowntree – questioned the chairman about the way the accounts were kept and asked for outside accountants, but they were shouted down. At the half yearly meeting of January 1841 Hudson turned on Coates who had suggested the company should have auditors like 'insurance offices and banks'.

The manner in which the accounts [are] kept, and the fact that the books of the company [are] open to the searching investigation of every shareholder, [is] a guarantee that there [can] be no opportunity of jobbing, if the proprietary [will] only look after their own interests. This [is] the first time [I have] ever heard such a suggestion in a meeting of railway proprietors, as that a clause should be introduced into an act of parliament for the appointment of auditors. The accounts [are] always audited by the directors, and every book [is] open for inspection by the proprietary.

Yorkshire Gazette

But those dividends were paid recklessly, out of capital, a fact that should have been obvious to shareholders. Hudson's methods may have *looked* dubious but the profits were rolling in. Why rock the boat, they seem to have reasoned. Thomas Backhouse, a Quaker businessman, confided in his diary that *he* was unhappy, and his daughter Mary wrote that he felt 'deeply troubled and most earnestly prayed for preservation from the evils which surrounded him'. But he never spoke out in public about his suspicions. The *English Gentleman* carried an article on the man Backhouse dared not attack when he was at the height of his powers.

In manner he is singularly abrupt – we may say, indeed, insolent. Naturally impatient of control, and accustomed to unlimited command, he occasionally *says*, and *does*, things, which would subject other and more responsible men to severity of rebuke. But no one thinks of questioning the Railway Monarch.

Hudson went from strength to strength, taking over more and more lines, and promising, when he did so, immediate increases in profits. He eventually became an MP for Sunderland, standing as the confirmed Tory protectionist taking on, and beating, the powerful Anti-Corn Law League. Richard Cobden wrote of his overwhelming influence.

A more formidable opponent he could not have [had] than this railway King – He [went] into the constituency with an *intangible* bribe for every class – The Capitalists would hope for premiums – The smaller fry would look for situations for their sons in the vast railway undertakings over which he rules absolutely, & the rope, iron, coal, & timber merchants all bid for his patronage – His *undetectable* powers of corruption are greater than the prime minister's. I would rather face any man than Hudson in a contest for Sunderland.

Hudson's version of the contest was different. He fought, he said,

an enemy exceedingly crafty, and not very scrupulous whose object has not been the truth but to deceive the people – men who have no regard for private character, nor as to the means by which they might carry out the object they had in view.

To the Sunderland electors he confided why he had stood for election.

> it is BECAUSE I have made a fortune and am independent that I come here to ask for your suffrages to send me to Parliament – *that there I may crown all.*
>
> *Yorkshireman* August 1845

Again Hudson was playing the poor boy made good, but parliament was not an unmixed blessing for him. There he spoke on matters other than railways and he sometimes made a fool of himself; giving papers like the radical *Yorkshireman* – at last – an opportunity to attack him. They exposed his gaffes, made fun of his diction and they hinted that he was fond of the bottle. They warned him of what to expect.

> Out of Parliament he [is] a great man, wielding immense influence. In Parliament he will be nobody and destitute of all influence. He will discover this himself by and bye. It is quite a different thing to address a meeting of railway speculators panting for ten per cent, and the congregated intellect, learning, and gentlemanly accomplishments such as the British Parliament contains. Men find their level in the House of Commons, and Mr HUDSON will find his. Perhaps, too, it may do him good.
>
> August 1845

Hudson cut a sorry figure in Parliament – though he had some admirers, like the Earl of Lonsdale, a wealthy relative of John Henry Lowther.

> He is in his bluff exterior the most remarkable man I have ever known. He is a most influential political character and [has] a most effective, common-sense sort of way of treating questions in the House of Commons that enables him to carry and defeat great measures, and turns the scale of many elections.
>
> L. J. Jennings (ed.) *The Croker Papers* 1884

Shortly after Hudson's return to Parliament his party split and the Railway King started on the slippery slope downwards. Lowther, York's Tory MP, followed Peel, and Hudson, a protectionist, forced a nominee of his own on the city. He forced the York City council to oppose a direct London to York railway link that was a threat to his own lines, and he ordered it to build a bridge to serve his railway stations, without any guarantee of railway contributions to its cost. This revitalised the liberal opposition to him and for the first time for many years he was attacked in his own city. He rode out the storm, but he did it by bullying, threatening and bribing – using the mailed fist when the situation demanded the velvet glove. But then, hints that all was not well in the railway world came to be heard. The *Yorkshireman* carried an editorial early in 1847, while Hudson was in trouble with his party in York.

> We beg to direct attention to a special report of an extraordinary railway meeting held in Manchester, on Wednesday last. It is worth perusal from the startling facts it discloses in railway management. Among other strange circumstances which came out at the meeting, was, that Mr George Hudson had had allotted to him, at his own request, 1,000 shares; that he had signed the deed for that amount; but that he had never paid a farthing of deposit – *another* gentleman performing that obligation, and he retaining the shares. Ha! ye small fry of railway stags rejoice, and clap your hands with joy. The Railway King is at your head. Yes, in verity, he is the 'royal railway stag!' – 'To what base uses must we come at last, Horatio?' But more of this anon.
>
> February 1847

These were but murmurings of the storm to come. 1847 was a bad year, 1848 was even worse. Hudson's world crashed around him. One by one his companies took alarm and set up committees to investigate his activities, and one by one those committees told men what they should have known all along; that the profits were bogus, and the dividends paid out of capital; and they showed that the Railway King had been guilty of graft on a grand scale. He was never really tried in a court of law – he was protected by parliamentary privilege – but he *did* appear as a witness in a libel trial at York where he was forced to admit to monumental frauds or indiscretions – it depended on one's point of view. Some like William Etty, the painter and York's second favourite son, believed in him until the end.

> I feel I should be safe were I to risk my existence on the honour and honesty of George Hudson. If ever I set eyes on a man – and I have had some experience – whose manly port, physiognomy, and whole bearing, characterised *an honest man,* a man superior to all meanness, it is George Hudson! a man I am proud to call my friend!
>
> *York Herald* April 1849

Etty died before the trial of Richardson versus Wodson took place. Richardson was one of Hudson's closest followers – a York Tory councillor and solicitor to the York and North Midland Railway Company. Wodson was the publisher of the *Yorkshireman* who had printed details of how – with Hudson's connivance – the manager of the Railway Kings's York Union Bank had speculated with bank funds and 'overdrawn', as the *Yorkshireman* had it, 'to the tune of some £20,000 or thereabouts'. Had Etty lived, even he could not have ignored the remarks of defence counsel, Serjeant Charles Wilkins, a Tory like Hudson, who catalogued his swindles and called him:

AN INTERVIEW

Between an

OLD ENGLISH GENTLEMAN,

and

The Ex Railway King,

respecting the

RAILWAY SCRIPT

Held by the former, at the Persuasion of the latter,

AT ONE TIME, 2 WARM BOSOM FRIENDS.

See the change! Can it be wondered at, when we read the following Verdict given by a British Jury, in the Trial for Libel, of *Richardson* v. *Wodson*, publisher of the " Yorkshireman" Newspaper.

1. That the Article complained of was not libellous.
2. That there had been "ARTIFICE, MISMANAGEMENT & DEFALCATIONS in *every* Joint Stock Company, over which the Plaintiff and Mr. GEORGE HUDSON had had control."
3. That although there was no evidence that the Plaintiff had been personally corrupted, yet he had received a certain number of Shares (*to wit*, 100) from Mr. Hudson.

UNDER VERY SUSPICIOUS CIRCUMSTANCES.

Vide Pamphlet of Trial, published by C. Mitchell,
Red Lion Court, London.

[Printed at the Free-press-Office, York.]

11 '. . . . he was forced to admit to monumental frauds or indiscretions.' A contemporary lampoon

43

the greatest enemy of mankind in his day. One who has brought about more misery, and produced more ruin, than any man of his age. A stain upon the nation in which he lives – a stain upon the land – a blot on the commercial honour of the nation.

The Recent Trial for Libel, 'Richardson v. Wodson'

Hudson lived another twenty years after his disgrace, most of the time abroad. His will shows that he was, at one stage, speculating in the building of railways on the continent. In disgrace he behaved with far more dignity than he ever did while in power. While his erstwhile lackeys turned on him, as Carlyle said, like a hungry crowd of animals, Hudson kept quiet. He never implicated anyone in his crimes and he deserves credit for that, though the historian must regret that his version of the events of the railway mania was never given. *Punch* (1849) plagiarised Cowper with a poem which was prophetic.

> The Royal GEORGE is gone,
>   His iron rule is o'er –
> And he and his Directors
>   Shall break the lines no more!

Hudson took most of the credit for the railway boom and most of the blame, and that seems to be a reasonable verdict. He, by his lies about the York and North Midland, more than anyone taught people to believe that railways were tremendously profitable. Having taught them that, the boom got underway, and the railways were built. Britain gained a tremendous advantage over her neighbours. But was this only a short term gain? Surely it was. What would have happened if Hudson – or someone like him – had not existed? What would have happened if the real profitability of railways had been known? (Before Hudson stepped in The Great North of England, for example, paid only some $3\frac{1}{2}$ per cent.) Certainly there would not have been that mania to invest. Would the state have had to step in? Would a smaller more rational railway network have been the result? It is useless to speculate. Hudson did exist and he did, more than anyone, cause the mania of the late 30s and 40s.

A. J. Peacock

12 'Off the Rail'. Hudson's bankruptcy depicted in *Punch*, 1849

EVANS, D. M. *The commercial crisis, 1847-1848* David and Charles, n.e. of 1848 edition, 1970.

LAMBERT, R. S. *The railway king, 1800-1871 : a study of George Hudson and the business morals of his time* George Allen and Unwin, 1934, reprinted 1964.

PEACOCK, A. J. and JOY, D. A. W. *George Hudson of York* Dalesman, paperback 1971.

TOMLINSON, W. W. *North Eastern Railway : its rise and development* Longman, 1915.

WILLIAM HOWITT

13 William Howitt (1792–1879)

The practice of social morality in Victorian times meant keeping a balance between tradition and progress. Everybody who tried to change society felt this dilemma. William Howitt was no exception. In fact, he had ideological difficulties which an earlier campaigner, William Cobbett, never faced. Cobbett's was a single-minded devotion to the English peasantry and traditional life. He had no desire to think about progress, or social improvement that moved away from traditional norms. After Cobbett's death in 1835 Howitt was looked upon as his successor – 'the foremost partisan of the traditional life of rural England'. Although this radical Quaker did not make the sort of impact on the public mind that Cobbett made, he was by no means without influence.

Like other Victorians, and whether he liked it or not, Howitt was caught up in this struggle between the old and the new. By his time the Industrial Revolution was being fought out at the level of individual, family and community. Even though Howitt had to turn his face both ways, toward town and country, he had learned the internal truths of rural life while growing up on his father's farm in Derbyshire. Continually in books such as *The Rural Life of England* and *The Year Book of the Country* his mind went back to earlier years.

> How rapidly is the fashion of the ancient life of rural England disappearing! Everyone who lived in the country in his youth and looks back at that period now, feels how much is lost. Modern ambition, modern wealth, modern social proprieties, are all hewing at the poetical and the picturesque, the simple and the cordial in rural life, and what are they substituting in their stead?
>
> William Howitt *The Rural Life of England* 1844

Like so many others before him Howitt found pleasure in recalling the tightly-knit peasant community which had become so enmeshed in his memory. He felt as Clare, Crabbe, Goldsmith – and Cobbett himself – had felt, that it was withering away. Town and village labourers were becoming restive in the 1840s. Chartism

45

14 Howitt's birthplace in the village of Heanor, Derbyshire

was a way out for some – but not always for those living in rural areas. Howitt put the peasant first in his scale of values. It was his opinion that beauty and ability could be found outside country mansions, that is in poor homes where the 'arbitrary power' of the State seldom entered. There was one type of interference which appeared philanthropic on the surface but drew no distinction between misfortune and crime.

> Our New Poor Laws have aimed a deadly blow at this blessed security, and, till the sound feeling of the nation shall have again disarmed them of this fearful authority, every poor man's family is liable, on the occurrence of some chance stroke of destitution, to have to their misfortune, bitter enough in itself, added the tenfold aggravation of being torn asunder, and immured in the separate wards of a POVERTY PRISON.
> *The Rural Life of England*

In other words there was little difference between a labouring family and a pauper's family. Howitt emphasised this truth. Sometimes perhaps he allowed himself to become a bit nostalgic. He could sound wordy and ineffective. But he was not. His concern was genuine and he tried to report what he saw. He was as conscious of the existence of the 'two nations' as was Benjamin Disraeli. He did his best work when writing of rural life and it is sometimes difficult to see much difference between his novels and his descriptive works. His fiction was of an 'improving' kind. This can be seen in a novel, or tract, entitled *The Hall and the Hamlet*. He portrays two groups here in his writing – those who are privileged to manage, instruct and give orders, and those who are obliged to obey.

> The Hall may, and must, do much to elevate the Hamlet, and the Hamlet, in a more elevated and prosperous condition, can add much to the interest of living at the Hall. Every lover of his country must be anxious to see rural life so well and healthily balanced that the old English character may wholly survive in the new English progress of society.
> Howitt *The Hall and the Hamlet* Vol. 1, 1848

46

The people who had to be directed were never invented figures. They were the mole-catchers, shepherds, stone-breakers, ploughmen that he remembered from his farm and village. So his reports are free from the easy distortions of urban ignorance. The English peasant was reckoned to be a simple monotonous animal. Most people were content to call him a clown or a country hob. But the prejudices of the English squires were not mysterious to Howitt, and what he opposed was the traditional hierarchy. He saw the evil of class division at its root and wanted labour to have its due. This was a plea by a simple man who had seen how the poor were kept in their place. He respected the human being whose very identity was being denied.

> All that has been wanted in him has been cultivated – good sturdy limbs to plough and sow and reap and mow, and feed bullocks, and even in these operations, his sinews have been half-superseded by machinery. There never was any need of his mind, and therefore it has never been minded.
>
> Howitt *The Year Book of the Country* 1850

Howitt minded. So did other people. Some were busy writing books and novels like Charles Kingsley or letters to *The Times* like the Dorset peer and parson, Sidney Godolphin Osborne. Howitt was different from both these men. He did not have their ability to pay attention to specific problems but was ready to look at too many too briefly. His social concern was really a type of patronage. As a Quaker, though, he asked very inconvenient questions. He was never a revolutionary, but he was an innovator, and innovators can be an inconvenience in any locality. Whether he lived in town or country his mind was occupied with 'good causes'. As an educator of the 'lower orders' he wondered whether teachings and preachings would ever draw people together. Could Christianity put some sort of bridge of sympathy between landlord and tenant, between what he called grade and grade? He was always an optimist and had as much faith in education as did Robert Owen. He argued that the great voice of the time was that reforms must go on, and education should be extended to every human creature. As a Victorian living near an explosive crater of change he could not afford to look back too often. In this he was the reverse of his older contemporary, Sir Walter Scott. William Hazlitt remarked of Scott:

> He is a prophesier of things past. The old world is to him a crowded map; the new one a dull, hateful blank. His mind receives and treasures up everything brought to it by tradition or custom – it does not project itself beyond this into the world unknown, but mechanically sinks back as from the edge of a precipice.
>
> William Hazlitt *The Spirit of the Age* Vol IV in *The Works of William Hazlitt*

15 Ebenezer Elliott, The Corn
Law rhymer

Howitt was the opposite of this. Although the past was so alive
to him, he was also looking for what was new or challenging. He was
consciously a representative of the age of transition from the placi-
dity of rural life to the bustle of town and factory. He resembled his
friend from Sheffield, the worker-poet, Ebenezer Elliott. Elliott's
poem *The Village Patriarch* could have been written by Howitt.
Or at any rate it expresses his feelings as he contemplated the rapid
growth of industrial society. As Elliott wrote of the bewildered
countryman he spoke for many migrants and exiles.

> New streets invade the country and he strays
> Lost in strange paths, still seeking and in vain
> For ancient landmarks, or the lonely lane
> Where once he played at Crusoe, when a boy.
> Fire vomits darkness, where the lime trees grew.
>
> E. Elliott *The Splendid Village, Corn-Law Rhymes and other Poems*

As a writer, Howitt was for improvements; for anything that
would give poor folk a chance to live as human beings rather than to
exist as serfs. He applauded the coming of steamboats, and the
cheap fares on railways which enabled seven thousand people to
visit the home of the Duke of Devonshire at Chatsworth in one day.

> The spirit of improvement has been met by a fitting spirit in
> high quarters. Our excellent Queen has thrown open
> Windsor – the most royal of all royal palaces in the world – to
> the free and unpaid entry of all her loving subjects. The
> royal example has been emulated by the nobility who have
> thrown open their parks, their gardens, their picture galleries
> to the feet and eyes of those who have long fought, worked
> and suffered for the maintenance of the stately glory of those
> things.
>
> *The Year Book of the Country*

Sometimes Howitt appreciated the condition of England. At
others he was much more critical. He thought the two main rivals
in the field of educational advance – Joseph Lancaster and the Rev.
Andrew Bell – had gone much too far in their enthusiasm. Such
popular methods as they favoured added up to what he called a
steam and railroad system of education, with the schoolmaster
acting like a drill-serjeant marching poor children by regiments
toward the mysteries of ABC. They took them no further and Howitt
believed they had simply taught them to see further into mischief.

The whole shape of society in fact changed as Howitt grew older.
Minds and habits were affected by machinery, transport and the
breakdown of local ties and associations in parish administration.
It has to be remembered that Howitt's writing life spanned more
than fifty years. And of course in talking about him and his opinions,
his wife, Mary, can't be ignored. The Howitts were both professional writers and as mutually involved in their work as were Sidney

16 William and Mary Howitt.
A contemporary drawing

and Beatrice Webb. The Corn-Law Rhymer, Ebenezer Elliott, said they were as inseparable as 'the heads of William and Mary on the face of an old coin'. So in any close-up of Howitt, his wife hovers like a shadow. She may have been an inferior thinker; she was sentimental and occasionally insincere; but she was also a strong character who had a lot to say about her husband. I daresay she acted as a brake on his political activities; and certainly there is evidence to show that whatever you call *him*, she certainly was no true radical. In 1822 they came to live in Nottingham. They stayed there until 1836. In 1824 they witnessed the mourning for Lord Byron in Nottingham when the hearse came into the town and they joined others in filing past the coffin twelve at a time. Mary spoke of what happened when this man who had influenced her husband was being taken to the family vault.

> Nottingham, which connects everything with politics, could not help making even the passing respect to our poet's memory a political question. He was a Whig, he hated priests, was the author of *Don Juan* and *Cain*. So the Tory party, which is the same as saying the gentry, would not notice even his coffin. The parsons had their feud, and therefore not a bell tolled when he came or went. He was a lover of liberty which the Radical Corporation here thought made him their brother; therefore all the rabble from every lane and alley, and garret and cellar came forth to curse and swear and shout and push in his honour. The rude crowd of country clowns and Nottingham Goths paid no regard to the occasion, and no respect or decency was to be seen.
>
> Margaret Howitt (ed.) *Mary Howitt, an Autobiography* 1889

Obviously, the degree of Mary's radicalism must always be suspect. She clearly was not sympathetic to the 'rabble', the 'common people'. That poses questions about William too. I am not at all sure whether, but for her constant caution, in the public sense, William Howitt would not have made a more definite mark in the

17 A view of Nottingham when the Howitts were resident in the city

political life of Nottingham. A man who had such strong opinions on so many subjects might have been expected to make a more permanent mark on his era. He did probe fairly deeply into rural life and he cannot be dismissed entirely as a light-minded reporter. In 1833 he caused some excitement in Nottingham when he published *A History of Priestcraft*. It was bought by members of Mechanics' Institutes and caused a lot of controversy. The Radical tailor, Francis Place, an agnostic, criticised it. But religious people in the town took it very seriously.

The first public meeting in the kingdom to consider the abolition of a Church Establishment was held in Nottingham in 1834. A deputation to Earl Grey was decided on, and Howitt was a leading member. The blunt straightforwardness, racy English, and ready tact in his interview with the Premier tell with quite dramatic effect in the dull pages of the Annual Register.

The report in the Annual Register made it clear that Lord Grey presumed Howitt and a colleague were following similar lines to those of other dissenters.

> William Howitt replied that on reading the Memorial his Lordship would be better able to decide that than they were; for he believed the Nottingham Dissenters had not been looking here and there to see what other Dissenters were doing, but had considered what was their duty, and had proceeded honestly to do it. Mr Howitt agreed that it was the duty of a Christian country to protect Christianity but that it was only to be done by making it free; to establish one sect in preference to another, was to establish a party, not a religion.
>
> January 1834

With the passing of the Municipal Corporations Act in 1835 Howitt found himself elected an alderman. He was described as an eloquent speaker, and working men in Nottingham were sure they had found a champion. Unfortunately for the people who had followed him, he appeared to lack any political ambition. As an observer he scrutinised society and then complained that the radicals he had associated with were more politicians than people of taste. Charles Kingsley, a Christian Socialist, was concerned with this sort of question and had an answer for hesitant folk like Howitt.

> I am trying to do good but what is the use of talking to hungry paupers about heaven? It is very easy to turn our eyes away from ugly sights, and so consider ourselves refined. The refined man to me is he who cannot rest in peace with a coal mine or a factory, or a Dorsetshire peasant's house near him, in the state in which they are.
> *The Life and Works of Charles Kingsley* 1901

Even if Howitt, by comparison, seems not to care, he was an associate of Kingsley's teacher, the theologian F. D. Maurice and of the non-violent Chartist, William Lovett. And he never really sought the burdens of public office. They were thrust on him. So finally a decision about his career had to be made. His business as a druggist did not prosper but he was making headway with his writing. His daughter, Anna Mary Watts, wrote extensively about her father, and she says:

> His work in Nottingham drew to its end. Literature had become his profession, and his literary engagements attracted him to London. The disappointment was great amongst the working men of Nottingham when it became known that the champion of their 'rights' was about to depart. 'We thought', said they, 'that at last we had found the man for whom we have waited *so* long, and now he has deserted us.'
> *The Pioneers of the Spiritual Reformation* 1883

Howitt did not desert the workers of Nottingham. The coal miners he could never forget. They stood as symbols of the new age of technology, of steam, coal and machinery. He had watched the long trains of coal waggons moving without horses or attendants so that they seemed to be driven by what he called 'unseen demons'.

> Only when you went up to them did you realise that these trains were drawn by great ropes worked by a stationary engine out of sight, often at a great distance. Amid all these uncouth sounds and sights the voice of the cuckoo and corncrake came at intervals to assure me that I was still on the actual earth and in the heart of spring and not conjured into some land of insane wheels and machinery possessed by riotous spirits.
> *The Year Book of the Country*

Sometimes Howitt gives the impression that within himself he had to *be* a countryman in his mind and imagination in order to *be* at all.

It does seem a serious lack in the writings of a man with Howitt's interests and knowledge that he did not look a little more closely at the problems connected with pauperism and the Poor Law. We know that he disliked and distrusted the new system which came into being in 1834 but he says far too little about low wages and bad conditions. Even so, he kept some ordinary middle-class people in touch with ideas that were concerned with human betterment. In 1856 an annual publication called *Men of the Time* mentions a book of his which reflects his concern at the inequality in the distribution of wealth.

> In 1846, Mr Howitt who was a practical Administrative Reformer from an early period in his career, published a volume entitled *The Aristocracy of England* in the course of which he brought into one view an immense body of facts to show that five-sixths of the good things which are given away in this country are bestowed upon the aristocracy: pensions, appointments, clerical, naval and military promotions without end.

Another way in which Howitt tried to influence public opinion was by editing two journals – *The People's Journal* and *Howitt's Journal of Literature and Popular Progress*. These were brave efforts to capture the heads and hearts of manual workers. The first could have succeeded because Howitt was simply a partner. There were disagreements. Then the second venture was begun. Both these journals failed. They were meant to help workers to be prudent, careful and independent. Mary Howitt made it clear that there was no desire to set the poor against the rich. They wanted workers to be satisfied to be workers and to regard all labour as a privilege, not a penalty.

One side of William Howitt's nature pushed him toward this world which was imperfect and the other side forced him to think of a more perfect condition. He lived abroad, in Italy and Germany, a good deal, yet his love for the English countryside never for one moment diminished. Possibly the clue to his career rested with his boyhood which he said was like a paradise of opening existence.

> Up to the age of ten this life was all my own, and I revelled in it. Those early days and habits modelled the whole of my existence, and exerted an indomitable influence on my fortunes. With that charming country all around me, I was an Adam in Eden before the Fall.
>
> *Mary Howitt, an Autobiography*

No doubt Howitt had vision and industry and was never afraid to write down his thoughts even if they should injure his career. An optimist by inheritance he believed implicitly that all things worked together for good, that the world was filled with plenty for all but that somehow – even in the Victorian haven of wealth and respectability for the upper and middle classes – the lesson of dividing earthly blessings had not been learned.

It is in our social arrangements that the mischief commences and the misery lies. The frenzy of gain grows desperate, and the whole machinery of society becomes not a machine of blessings, but of mangling and destruction. The country is full of everything that can contribute to human comfort, but the millions cannot come at it. We starve, with warehouses and shops loaded with provisions; we have everything and can get nothing. Care sits and gnaws voraciously at every heart; he is the only thing that feeds.

The Year Book of the Country

Sober William Howitt we could say. Sometimes, though, he could write with wit and merriment. Behind the occasional levity was the gravity of conscience. In his stand on behalf of spiritualism and the supernatural he invited (and certainly received) the scorn of old friends like Charles Dickens and Robert Browning. Dickens, he said, had played with spiritualism as a cat with a mouse. But Howitt was never diverted from the Christianity he had followed from his youth. In one of his last writings, dealing with the history of the supernatural, his answer to his critics was uncompromising.

If you could crush the supernatural in the Bible, there remains yet a little task for you – you must crush it in the whole universe, and to do that you must crush the universe with it, for it exists everywhere, and its roots are in the foundation of all things.

Howitt *The History of the Supernatural* 1863

Perhaps I can end with an item that has no historical relevance at all. Even if their beliefs are out of date and much of their work is hidden away, it is pleasant to think that the surname of William and his wife will be remembered as long as there are readers of James Joyce's *Finnegans Wake*.

And still nowanights and by nights of yore do all bold floras of the field to their shyfaun lovers say only: Cull me ere I wilt to thee! and, but a little later: Pluck me whilst I blush! Well may they wilt, marry and profusely blush, be troth! For that saying is as old as the howitts.

James Joyce *Finnegans Wake* 1939

E. W. Martin

LEE, A. *Laurels and rosemary: the life of William and Mary Howitt* O.U.P., 1955.

BROWN, C. *Lives of Nottinghamshire worthies and of celebrated and remarkable men of the county* . . . London: H. Sotheran; Nottingham: C. Wheatley, 1882.

HOWITT, M. *An Autobiography* edited by her daughter, Margaret Howitt. London: W. Isbister, 2 vols. 1889.

WATTS, A. M. H. *The pioneers of the spiritual reformation* London: The Psychological Press Association, 1883.

SAMUEL SMILES

Every age has its popular prototypes who epitomize the dominant social values of the time. For Victorian Britain Samuel Smiles provided the social heroes. They were not kings and noblemen and great warriors, but the men who had laid the foundations of the industrial greatness of England – mostly self-made men, who had risen from poverty and obscurity to wealth and influence in society. Smiles admired such men, and became the best-known propagandist for the type of social character they represented. He enunciated, in popular form, the social philosophy of the newly-dominant middle classes. He made their views and attitudes, the things they wanted and believed in, intelligible and attractive.

But Smiles' background had not been such as to provide much in the way of breadth or elegance. Quite the contrary: for he was born and raised in the little Scottish town of Haddington, in East Lothian, the son of a shopkeeper. John Knox had also been a native of Haddington, and still cast his shadow across the lives of people like Smiles' parents. One good result of this was a concern for education, and young Smiles was able to have a full-time schooling to the age of fourteen at the local Burgh and Classical schools. But the debit side of Knox's legacy was seen on Sundays. Smiles recalled that:

> Sunday, the 'day of rest', was to us the most exhausting and unpleasant of the week. Our preacher was a combative man. He preached the narrowest Calvinism, and there was far more fear than love in his sermons. We had no sort of recreation on Sundays. Walking, except to the kirk, was forbidden. Books were interdicted, excepting the Bible, the Catechism, and the Secession Magazine, or perhaps some book of Evangelical sermons. I have no doubt it was all intended for our good; but I never in my youth had any agreeable recollection of Sundays.
>
> Samuel Smiles *Autobiography* 1905

Small wonder, then, that when his mother asked him one day if he would like to be a minister, he replied:

18 Samuel Smiles (1812–1904)

Oh, no! I'll no be a minister.

Autobiography

Whereupon the good lady asked if he would not like to be a doctor.

> The question was rather startling at first. There were many prejudices about doctors in my younger days. Our servants used to tell trembling children about the 'black doctors' that were ready to clap a plaster over our mouths, and carry us away no one knew whither. Then, a regular watch and ward was held over the parish burying ground, to prevent the 'doctors' rifling the graves, for the purposes of the dissecting-rooms at Edinburgh.
>
> *Autobiography*

Nevertheless, in October 1826, Smiles was apprenticed to a local doctor for five years and, moving with his master to Leith, was able to attend medical classes at Edinburgh University. He qualified in 1832 and returned to Haddington to practise. He managed to pick up a few patients, mostly among the poorer people, but he was anything but successful. He went abroad to Leyden and acquired the degree of MD at the University there, thinking this might impress future patients. But finding no job on his return to England, he developed a reluctance to pursue the practice of medicine and, at the end of 1838, accepted the editorship of a radical newspaper, the *Leeds Times*.

He had already tried his hand at writing and had decided that this was where his real bent lay. So for four years he plunged into local politics and absorbed himself in the day-to-day life of the smoky city which was the centre of Yorkshire industrialism. But he soon found the pace of life too fast. And, recently married, there were the prospects of a young family to support. Besides quieter pastures, he needed a more lucrative profession than provincial journalism. Returning once more to medicine, he continued what he called 'my literary pursuits' in his spare time, and with no enthusiasm for doctoring he longed for some occupation that would support him comfortably and yet allow him the leisure necessary for writing and studying. In 1845 he found such an opening – as assistant secretary to the new Leeds and Thirsk Railway. For the next twenty years he served as secretary (or, as we should now say, chief executive officer) to successive railway companies. He looked forward to the evenings: for then his official work was done, and he could devote himself to the things he most enjoyed.

> Some people wondered how I contrived not only to perform the secretarial work of a large company, but to write books requiring a good deal of labour and research. I remember once giving this explanation. It all arises from the frugal use of time; and by the thought that once passed it can never be recalled. I never carried any subject of anxiety, or undone

work, home with me. When the day's work was over I went home with a mind comparatively free, and then I was able to sit down in my study with the satisfaction of duty done, ready to take a part in filling up some unoccupied niche in the literature of my country.

Autobiography

'The frugal use of time'. That was one of the bulwarks of Smilesian philosophy. And he certainly made good use of his time in Leeds between 1838 and 1854. He was active in radical politics; he associated himself with popular education, public libraries, mechanics' institutes, cooperatives and friendly societies. He wrote articles, gave lectures, and got to know both the labouring men and the manufacturers. I am sure that the Leeds period is crucial to an understanding of Smiles and his philosophy. After his Scottish puritan upbringing it is the most important element in his intellectual and emotional make-up. It was in Leeds that he got to know the world of industry and began to appreciate the achievements of Victorian technology. It was in Leeds also that he originated his famous doctrine of self-help, in a course of lectures given, in 1844, to a mutual improvement class.

19 A contemporary impression of a working men's evening class

My object in writing out *Self-Help*, and delivering it first in the form of lectures, and afterwards re-writing and publishing it in the form of a book, was principally to illustrate and enforce the power of George Stephenson's great word – PERSEVERANCE. I had been greatly attracted when a boy by Mr Craik's *Pursuit of Knowledge under Difficulties*. I had read it often, and knew its many striking passages almost by heart. It occurred to me that a similar treatise dealing not so much with literary achievements and the acquisition of knowledge, as with the ordinary business and pursuits of common life, illustrated by examples of conduct and character drawn from reading, observation and experience, might be equally useful to the rising generation. It seemed to me that the most important results in daily life are to be obtained, not through the exercise of extraordinary powers, such as genius and intellect, but through the energetic use of simple means and ordinary qualities, with which nearly all individuals have been more or less endowed. Such was my object, and I think that, on the whole, I hit my mark.

Autobiography

He did indeed hit his mark. *Self-Help* went like a bomb. To his surprise (and also, one suspects, to the surprise of John Murray, his publisher), it sold 20,000 copies in the first year, 15,000 in the second, and steadily thereafter. By the time of Smiles' death in 1904 over a quarter of a million copies had been sold, and it had been translated into most European and Asiatic languages. Later in life Smiles loved to tell anecdotes about the reception of *Self-Help* in different parts of the world.

The late Dr Max Schlesinger told me that, while in Egypt some years ago, he had visited one of the Khedive's palaces, then being fitted up by an Italian architect. On looking at the inscriptions and mottoes written on the walls, and on the magnificent furniture of the house, Dr Schlesinger asked what they were. The Italian informed him that they were texts from the Koran. 'But they are not all from the Koran,' he added; 'indeed they are principally from Smeelis'. 'From whom?' 'Oh! you are an Englishman: you ought to know Smeelis! They are from his *Self-Help* : they are much better than the texts from the Koran!'

Autobiography

The Japanese edition of *Self-Help*, for which there was no equivalent in that language, was entitled *European Decision of Character Book*, and in a letter to Smiles the Japanese translator and publisher, Professor Nakamura, wrote:

'Will you allow me to thank you with a sincere mind for your literary work, which has had a good result in our little island of Japan. I am glad to see the results, for almost all the high class of our fellow-countrymen know what *Self-Help* is.'

*

The translated book was a remarkable document. It had become expanded into a book of about 2,000 pages, and read from the end backwards. The characters reminded one of an entymological collection. They stood apart, like insects in a case at the British Museum; but, on closer scrutiny, they seemed to represent, not the lower creatures, but familiar objects such as houses, windows, fireplaces, and various domestic utensils, involved in fantastic flourishes capable of no European explanation. On looking at the book and its characters, it does not afford matter for surprise that the Japanese should be contemplating the abandonment of their own language, and a resort to straight-forward, condensed, and sensible English!

Autobiography

'Sensible English' indeed! Although, later in life, Smiles travelled quite extensively in Europe, he remained, like most members of the Victorian middle class, unashamedly convinced of the immense superiority of the British race over all others.

Self-Help is, in essence, simply a series of potted biographies drawn from all national cultures and periods of history, interspersed with moral reflections and proverbial wisdom. It was a mixture the Victorians liked – though Smiles had his critics, particularly among the socialists later in the century, who were annoyed by such observations as:

Success grows out of struggles to overcome difficulties. If there were no difficulties, there would be no success. If there were nothing to struggle or compete for, there would be nothing achieved. It is well, therefore, that men should be under the necessity of exerting themselves. In this necessity for exertion, we find the chief source of human advancement – the advancement of individuals as of nations. It has led to most of the mechanical inventions of the age. It has stimulated the shipbuilder, the merchant, the manufacturer, the machinist, the tradesman, the skilled workman. In all departments of productive industry, it has been the moving power. It has developed the resources of the soil, and the character and qualities of the men who dwell upon it. It seems to be absolutely necessary for the purposes of stimulating the growth and culture of every individual. It is deeply rooted in man, leading him ever to seek after, and endeavour to realize, something better and higher than he has yet attained.

Smiles *Thrift* 1875

Smiles was well aware that something less high-falutin' was needed if his gospel was to appeal to ordinary men. He had to demonstrate that individualism could offer real benefits to working men, providing they followed a few simple rules of conduct. The first of such rules was to work regularly and steadily. The second was to practise thrift, or saving.

It is the savings of the world that have made the civilisation of the world. Savings are the result of labour; and it is only when labourers begin to save, that the results of civilisation accumulate. We have said that thrift began with civilisation: we might almost have said that thrift produced civilisation. Thrift produces capital; and capital is the conserved result of labour. The capitalist is merely a man who does not spend all that is earned by work.

But thrift is not a natural instinct. It is an acquired principle of conduct. It involves self-denial – the denial of present enjoyment for future good – the subordination of animal appetite to reason, forethought, and prudence. It works for today, but also provides for tomorrow. It invests the capital it has saved, and makes provision for the future.

Thrift

Here was the Smilesian answer to the charge that the new capitalist system reduced the worker to the level of a wage-slave. The working man who did not have anything except his weekly wages *was* a slave, said Smiles. He was at the mercy of others, he could not control his own destiny, he was not truly a free man at all. Thrift offered an escape from this position. It enabled a man to support himself, to stand on his own feet, to be genuinely independent, to be a truly free man.

Of course, working men could see that in one sense this was simply a middle-class device to get them to support themselves during times of unemployment and sickness, instead of receiving some form of public relief. But it also harmonised, to some extent, with an older artisan tradition of what was called 'an independence', the highly valued freedom of the skilled man who was his own master. And the existence of this artisan ideal made it easier, I think, for Smiles' precepts to become acceptable to some portions at least, of the working classes.

But Smiles pitched his claims for self-help much higher than this. He made it the basis of an improvement in the standard of living of the whole of the working classes.

There is no reason why the condition of the average workman in this country should not be a useful, honourable, respectable, and happy one. The whole body of the working classes might (with a few exceptions) be as frugal, well-informed, and well-conditioned as many individuals of the same class have already made themselves. The healthy spirit of self-help created amongst working people would more than any other measure serve to raise them as a class, and this, not by pulling down others, but by levelling them up to a higher and still advancing standard of religion, intelligence, and virtue.

Smiles *Self-Help* 1859

At its best, as the lawyer, A. V. Dicey put it, self-help was the

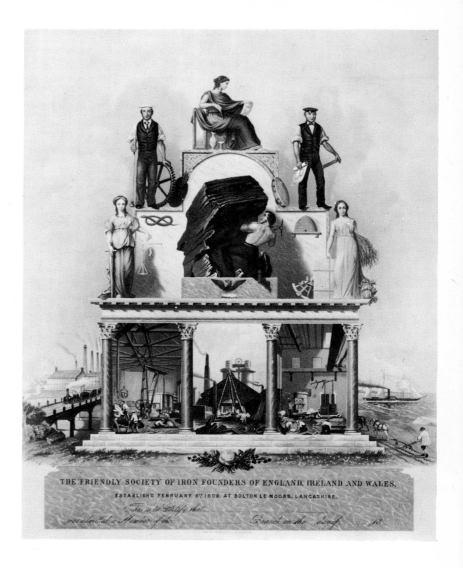

20 Membership certificate of the
Iron Founders Friendly Society

positive side of laissez-faire. And for a minority of working-men,
mainly artisans, it undoubtedly had an appeal. The members of the
Birmingham Flint Glass Makers' Friendly Society, for example,
were advised by their leaders:

> If you do not wish to stand as you are and suffer more op-
> pressions, we say to you get knowledge, and in getting know-
> ledge you get power. Let us earnestly advise you to edu-
> cate; get intelligence, instead of alcohol – it is sweeter and
> more lasting.
>
> *Flint Glass Makers' Magazine* 1850

Smiles liked to quote Gibbon's remark that every person has two
educations, one which he receives from others, and one which he
gives to himself.

Often the best education of a man is that which he gives himself, while engaged in the active pursuits of practical life. Putting ideas into one's head will do the head no good, no more than putting things into a bag, unless it react upon them, make them its own, and turn them to account. That which is put into us by others is always far less ours than that which we acquire by our own diligent and persevering effort. Knowledge conquered by labour becomes a possession – a property entirely our own. A greater vividness and permanency of impression is secured; and facts thus acquired become registered in the mind in a way that mere imparted information can never produce. This kind of self-culture also calls forth power and cultivates strength and it is beginning to be pretty generally understood that self-culture is one of the best possible investments of time and labour.

Self-Help

Self-culture was thus an important aspect of self-help. But Smiles went on to face the inescapable fact that for the majority it would not lead to fame or riches, but would have simply to be its own reward.

Many are apt to feel despondency, and to become discouraged in the work of self-culture, because they do not 'get on' in the world as fast as they think they deserve to do. Having planted their acorn, they expect to see it grow into an oak at once. They have perhaps looked upon knowledge in the light of a marketable commodity, and are consequently mortified because it does not sell as they expected it would do. But to regard self-culture either as a means of getting past others in the world, or of intellectual dissipation and amusement, rather than as a power to elevate the character and expand the spiritual nature, is to place it on a very low level.

Self-Help

I said at the beginning that Smiles, through his writings, popularized a certain type of social character that the Victorians admired. The Victorian age was full of self-made men, men who had risen from rags to riches, men who had 'got on', who had been successful. And there was a considerable curiosity as to how they had done this. A whole literature of success was produced, with titles like *Men who have risen; Small Beginnings, or the way to get on*; or *The Elements of Success – a book for young men*. The self-made man was an almost mystical figure. And his success was attributed by Smiles and others to certain personal qualities. Initiative, energy, frugality, abstinence, punctuality, early rising – above all, thrift and self-help – these accounted for the success of the middle-class heroes.

But it was when he came to define success that Smiles got into difficulties. The problem was this. Suppose (as could well be the case) that a man followed all the Smilesian precepts – hard work, thrift, self-help – and yet failed to achieve wealth or honour or any worldly reward whatsoever, could his life be counted a success? And if so, on what grounds?

Having seen clearly the limitations of the crude appeal to self-education as a means of 'getting on', Smiles fell back on the argument that the object of self-improvement must be to 'elevate the condition of labour, by allying it to noble thoughts'. He knew that the demands of serious study after a twelve or fourteen hour working day were too much for the vast majority of working men. Their scanty leisure was insufficient for self-culture, just as their scanty wages were insufficient for regular saving. But if self-help was, in fact, simply advice to lift themselves by their own bootstraps, what did it have to do with success?

I suppose that at the root of this difficulty is an ambivalence about social and moral values. And Smiles tried to gloss over this by resort to the idea of the gentleman. Most of his self-made men – the inventors, industrialists and engineers about whom he wrote – were not accepted as gentlemen in the social sense; some of them, indeed, were barely successful either in economic or social terms. But, he insisted, if they had 'character' they were nevertheless gentlemen – gentlemen in the true sense.

> Riches and rank have no neccessary connection with genuine gentlemanly qualities. The poor man may be a true gentleman – in spirit and in daily life. He may be honest, truthful, upright, polite, temperate, courageous, self-respecting and self-helping – that is, be a true gentleman. The poor man with a rich spirit, he who has lost all, but retains his courage, cheerfulness, hope, virtue and self-respect, is still rich.
> *Self-Help*

Did Smiles really believe this? Or is it offered as a consolation to those who, despite their best efforts, do not manage to make it? It is hard to be sure. But I am inclined to think that he was being sincere. Like many of the Victorians, beneath his surface optimism he occasionally betrays a mood of doubt and uncertainty. On reaching middle age, he observes:

> The wise person gradually learns not to expect too much from life. While he strives for success by worthy methods, he will be prepared for failures. He will keep his mind open to enjoyment, but submit patiently to suffering.
> Smiles *Character* 1871

Why, then, we may ask, should we strive to improve ourselves by self-help? Why bother at all, if the end may be only failure and suffering? To which Smiles can only reply that we must do our duty.

> We have each to do our duty in that sphere of life in which we have been placed. Duty alone is true; there is no true action

but in its accomplishment. Duty is the end and aim of the highest life; the truest pleasure of all is derived from the consciousness of its fulfilment.

Character

So the gospel of Samuel Smiles ends up with duty – the great evangelical concept that underpinned the structure of Victorian society. And that is rather surprising, because it is a long way from the usual image of Smiles as the banal apologist for bourgeois success. Of course, his doctrines did provide a justification for the ethics of the business man, they did present the values of individualism and competitive society in an attractive light, they did extol the middle classes and hold them up as models for emulation. But Smiles resented the charge that he glorified worldly success, or that he was a spokesman solely for the middle classes. The fact is that he was, to some extent, overtaken by events. We often forget that an average person's life extends across more than one generation or decade; that the period of our youth is likely to have been a very different sort of age from that of our mature years. The social and intellectual climate of England in the 1840s – from which Smiles drew his crucial experiences and in which he formulated his views – was very different from the 1860s and 1870s when his books became popular. The Hungry Forties was a very grim time indeed, when many people genuinely feared revolution. The 1860s was a time of economic prosperity and social optimism. Self-help in the 1840s appeared to be a means by which the working classes might secure some means of personal and social advance. It did not necessarily have to take an individualist form: it could be collectivist – as with friendly societies, mutual improvement clubs, cooperatives or trade unions. These were all institutions of self-help, and Smiles was sympathetic to many of these ideas during those formative years in Leeds. But subsequently the doctrine of self-help underwent a transformation. Individual self-help was stressed more and more, and other forms were largely ignored. What had been originally a device to enable the working classes to grasp some of those cultural and material benefits which were denied them in the new industrial society, became the middle-class reply to workers' demands for better social conditions. Smiles was caught in this transformation of the social scene, without ever quite understanding what had happened. Willy-nilly, he found himself the spokesman for the middle classes. Bourgeois Victorian England was a religious age in many different ways. It took to its heart the gospel of self-help and its prophet, Samuel Smiles.

John F. C. Harrison

BRIGGS, A. *Victorian people* Odhams, 1954; Penguin Books, 1970. University of Chicago Press, cased and paperback 1971.

HARRISON, J. F. C. *Learning and living, 1790-1960* Routledge and Kegan Paul, 1961.

SMILES, S. *Self-help* J. Murray, 1859; centenary edn 1958; Sphere, 1970.

WALTER BAGEHOT

21 Walter Bagehot (1826–77)

When historians of nineteenth-century England are searching for some memorable, penetrating remark by a Victorian writer which sums up the character of his contemporaries for us, there is one author whose name recurs again and again, and that is Walter Bagehot. It is true that the best known accounts of social conditions come from Dickens, or perhaps from Carlyle or Disraeli. Bagehot was a banker and journalist who knew the political world of Westminster and the financial world of the City, and knew also the countryside of southern England, but he had no experience of the new industrial England of the North. It is true also that if we were looking for *the* Victorian philosopher, a man who gave a rigorous logical form to some of the key ideas of Victorian liberalism, we should go, in all probability, to John Stuart Mill. Bagehot is a more middle-of-the-road kind of figure, a liberal in politics, but also a man with a strong vein of conservatism; not a nostalgic, Romantic kind of conservatism like Disraeli's, but one which appreciated and enjoyed the world as it was. He was not a philosopher, or a would-be political leader, or an angry prophet; he was an incomparable observer and interpreter, if not of the whole range of Victorian life in his time, at least of very important and interesting sections of it: of politics and public life generally, and above all, perhaps, of the mentality and opinions of that immensely influential section of Victorian society, the solid, respectable middle classes.

This may sound like a recipe for dullness, but Bagehot was anything but dull. His writing is shrewd and sympathetic, but it is also lively and even satirical in a genial way. He was a journalist, but not one of the dogmatic, partisan, thundering kind. He wrote not for the newspapers but for the sober, thoughtful monthly and quarterly reviews. He wrote on literary and biographical subjects, on political and economic affairs, and eventually he found the perfect niche for himself as editor of the *Economist*. This was through his father-in-law, James Wilson, its first proprietor and editor. And the paper is still distinguished by the kind of informative journalism Bagehot did so much to create.

The chief reason his writings are of such continuing interest is that although he wrote to influence his contemporaries he did not denounce or flatter them. Instead he approached them almost as a modern historian might do, to understand them – and of course he had the advantage of living among them. They fascinated and amused him. And though he obviously enjoyed the feeling of superiority his cleverness gave him – which can sometimes be irritating – basically he liked them; and he understood them because fundamentally he was not unlike them. Bagehot was not taken in by cant or appearances, but there was nothing of a rebel about him. The historian G. M. Young called him not 'the greatest of the Victorians' but 'the greatest Victorian', and by that he meant the Victorian whose greatness was most typical of the mentality of his age. Young was looking, he said, 'for a man who was in and of his age, and who could have been of no other; a man with sympathy to share, and genius to judge, its sentiments and movements', and a man whose ideas 'could transmit, and can still impart, the most precious element in Victorian civilisation, its robust and masculine sanity.' All this he found in Bagehot.

G. M. Young's is only one example of a long line of tributes, from Bagehot's own time to ours – tributes from which there have been remarkably few dissenters. The features Young picked out, sympathy and judgement, companionability and sanity, have been the qualities which have drawn readers of all kinds to Bagehot, but he has particular appeal to men who like to mingle the world of affairs with the world of thought and reflection. They feel, I think, that Bagehot understood the problems of practical action in the world, that he would never be guilty of pushing a theory too far and reaching absurd conclusions, or of mistaking the world as it is for the world as it ought to be. On the other hand they enjoy his clear-sightedness and penetration, his refusal to be taken in by the outward forms of things. So it is perhaps not an accident that the standard modern biography of Bagehot has been written by a leading authority on foreign affairs, Alistair Buchan, or that a front-bench MP, Norman St John Stevas, is editing his collected works. Bagehot himself made one attempt to enter the House of Commons and failed, but his opinion was so valued that Gladstone called him 'a kind of supplementary Chancellor of the Exchequer'. But perhaps his greatest admirer among statesmen was a President of the United States, Woodrow Wilson:

> You receive stimulation from him, and a certain feeling of elation. There is a fresh air stirring in all his utterances that is unspeakably refreshing. You open your mind to the fine influence, and feel younger for having been in such an atmosphere. It is an atmosphere clarified and bracing almost beyond example elsewhere.
> Quoted N. St John Stevas *Walter Bagehot*

Woodrow Wilson was writing many years after Bagehot's death, and his words indicate something very important about the quality of Bagehot's writing. In all his works, even on such austere subjects as financial credit or the working of the Constitution, or in apparently ephemeral studies of minor poets or politicians, the reader always feels he is confronted by a man, a living personality with its own distinctive flavour and a powerful vitality.

I will try in a moment to illustrate that point, but first we need to see what influences shaped the personality we sense so strongly in Bagehot's writings. What kind of background helped to make him what he was? Bagehot was born in 1826, in the small town of Langport in Somerset. Since he died, aged only fifty-one, in 1877, he was not merely a Victorian but essentially a mid-Victorian, sharing in and giving expression to the optimism and stability of the eighteen fifties and sixties. His family were prosperous west country bankers, and one thing Bagehot never had to worry about personally was money – though as a banker himself and an economic journalist he spent much of his time thinking about it professionally. Bagehot was a man who made a virtue of feeling comfortable with the world and with his fellows, and it was no doubt easier for him to cultivate a genial self-assurance than it would have been if he had been a poorer man.

But there was one great tragedy which overshadowed his otherwise happy, secure and comfortable family life: his mother was subject to recurring fits of insanity. Bagehot was a devoted son, and the burden of sustaining his mother fell chiefly on him. Inevitably, too, he must have wondered whether he had inherited any tendency to insanity himself. The famous easy-going worldliness and geniality of his writing was almost certainly not achieved without a struggle. It would be too harsh to call it contrived, but it was a kind of achievement nevertheless, and this may help us to forgive him if he sometimes sounds just a bit too pleased with himself. Like other Victorians who knew or feared insanity at first hand, like Thackeray or T. H. Huxley, he may have clung all the more tenaciously to a tone of shrewd and tolerant sanity and humour because of an intimate knowledge of the darker side of the mind. He once wrote:

> Behind every man's external life, which he leads in company, there is another which he leads alone, and which he carries with him apart. We see but one aspect of our neighbour, as we see but one side of the moon; in either case there is also a dark half which is unknown to us. We all come down to dinner, but each of us has a room to himself.
> Bagehot *Collected Works*

It was partly his mother's instability which led Bagehot, after a brilliant undergraduate career at University College, London, to turn his back on the capital and return to the quiet world of the country bank at Langport. Although his life there had its compensations – he liked an out-of-door life – he had energies to spare, until his father-in-law's death in 1860 precipitated him into the editorship of the *Economist*. But even before that he had found a field for his talents in those extensive political, biographical and literary essays for which the great nineteenth-century reviews provided a ready market. In one of Bagehot's early essays, on the poet William Cowper, he came perhaps the nearest he was ever to come to expressing a sense of rebellion against his fate and against the kind of civilisation he embodied and so often eloquently defended:

> Everything is so comfortable; the tea-urn hisses so plainly, the toast is so warm, the breakfast so neat, the food so edible, that one turns away, in excitable moments, a little angrily from anything so quiet, tame and sober. Have we not always hated this life? What can be worse than regular meals, clock-moving servants, a slow parson, a heavy assortment of near relations, a placid house flowing with milk and sugar – all that the fates can stuff together of substantial comfort, and fed and fatted monotony.
>
> *Collected Works*

Victorian writing is full of celebrations of cosy domesticity. It is odd to find G. M. Young's 'greatest Victorian' rebelling against it. But it is untypical of Bagehot too. As a writer on politics he never forgot the importance of the humdrum. The world, he felt, was kept going by practical men, men who wanted, above all, comfort and security and to go about their everyday business undisturbed. There was a lesson in this for politicians, and the English, stolid and practical as they were, understood it better than anyone:

> The English people have never forgotten what some nations have scarcely ever remembered – that politics are a kind of business – that they bear the characteristics and obey the laws inevitably incident to that kind of human action. Steady labour and dull material – wrinkles on the forehead and figures on the tongue – these are the English admiration. We may prize more splendid qualities on uncommon occasions, but these are for dailywear.
>
> N. St John Stevas *Walter Bagehot*

Bagehot saw this saving dullness as a particularly English characteristic and was fond of ironically complimenting his countrymen on possessing it. The essentially practical nature of politics was something he stressed in his very earliest political writings, the essays he wrote on the *coup d'état* by which Louis Napoleon, later Napoleon III, overthrew the second French Republic in 1851. Bagehot happened to be in Paris at the time and sent his reflections on the event in a series of letters to an English journal. Louis Napoleon had been justified in violating the constitution, he argued, because there was something more fundamental than constitutions, which the continued existence of the Republic would have threatened, namely the everyday security and prosperity of ordinary men.

The first duty of society is the preservation of society. By the sound work of old-fashioned generations – by the singular painstaking of the slumberers in churchyards – by dull care – by stupid industry, a certain social fabric somehow exists; people contrive to go out to their work, and to find work to employ them until the evening, body and soul are kept together, and this is what mankind have to show for their six thousand years of toil and trouble. To keep up this system we must sacrifice everything. Parliaments, liberty, leading articles, essays, eloquence – all are good, but they are secondary; at all hazards and if we can, mankind must be kept alive.

Collected Works

Bagehot went on to apply this argument from fundamental necessity to the recent state of France.

I do not say that but for the late *coup d'état*, French civilisation would certainly soon have come to a final end. Some people might have continued to take their meals. But I do assert that, according to the common belief of the common people, their common comforts were in considerable danger. The debasing torture of acute apprehension was eating into the crude pleasure of stupid lives. Six weeks ago society was

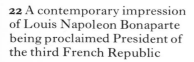

22 A contemporary impression of Louis Napoleon Bonaparte being proclaimed President of the third French Republic

living from hand to mouth; now she feels sure of her next meal. And this, in a dozen words, is the real case – the political excuse for Prince Louis Napoleon.

Collected Works

The argument itself is familiar enough, of course, but the tone is unmistakeably Bagehot's. He was only a young man of twenty-six when he wrote it, and he subsequently came to modify his views on Napoleon III's régime quite considerably. But the manner is already characteristic of him, above all the mixture of condescension and passion when he talks about 'sound work', 'dull care', 'common comforts'. 'The debasing torture of acute apprehension was eating into the crude pleasure of stupid lives' – there is a lot of the essential Walter Bagehot in that sentence.

Many of his English readers must have had their liberal and constitutionalist principles rudely shocked by Bagehot's defence of despotic rule, even when it was presented as an extreme remedy for an extreme situation. Of course, Bagehot shared these liberal and constitutional preferences, but he went on to explain why it was, in his view, that Britain, unlike France, could enjoy the blessings of a free constitution, and many readers, instead of being reassured, must have found themselves even more startled and affronted. Bagehot was a liberal and a constitutionalist, but he aimed at being one without illusions.

I fear you will laugh when I tell you what I conceive to be about the most essential mental quality for a free people, whose liberty is to be progressive, permanent and on a large scale; it is much *stupidity*. I need not say that, in real sound stupidity, the English are unrivalled.

Collected Works

But then, Bagehot went on:

In fact, what we opprobriously call stupidity, though not an enlivening quality in common society, is Nature's favourite resource for preserving steadiness of conduct and consistency of opinion. It enforces concentration; people who learn slowly learn only what they must. The best security for people's doing their duty is, that they should not know anything else to do; the best security for fixedness of opinion is, that people should be incapable of comprehending what is said on the other side.

Collected Works

The trouble with the French as a political nation, Bagehot thought, was their inability to be stupid: 'nations, just as individuals', he said 'may be too clever to be practical and not dull enough to be free'.

Those letters from France were a young man's work, and they show a young man's delight in shocking his elders, but they con-

23 An impression of the City of London at the time of the Great Exhibition in 1851

tain, in a slightly crude form, many of the ideas which were to interest Bagehot all his life. He wrote a number of books; one, called *Lombard Street,* was a study of the City of London as a financial centre. Another, called *Physics and Politics*, was an attempt to understand progress in human history in terms of group psychology, and to show how civilisation depended on a kind of balance between conformity and originality – just the kind of mixture which was represented by his own conservative liberalism, in fact. But by far his best known book is *The English Constitution*, which he published in 1867. It is not only the classic description of the working of the constitution between the 1832 and 1867 Reform Acts; what is more remarkable is that despite the important changes which have taken place, particularly in the development and organisation of political parties, it still remains, probably, the best and certainly the most readable introduction to the working of the constitution that we possess. The reason is that what Bagehot provided, unlike previous writing on the constitution, was no mere formal description of constitutional law and procedures, nor was it just a celebration of the excellence of the constitution handed down to us by our ancestors. Bagehot tried, for the first time, to describe how the constitution actually worked, to distinguish the form from the reality, and in doing so he showed all the startling love of paradox which was evident in those early letters on the *coup d'état* in France. Bagehot's paradoxes have become commonplace now, but they were anything but that at the time.

To start with, Bagehot began not with the monarchy but with the Cabinet. He did so because the first of the traditional myths which he wanted to dispel was the idea that there is in the constitution a so-called separation of powers, a sharp distinction between the executive which governs and the legislature which makes laws. This, Bagehot saw, was simply not so.

> The efficient secret of the English Constitution may be described as the close union, the nearly complete fusion, of the executive and legislative powers. No doubt by the traditional theory, as it exists in all the books, the goodness of our consti-

70

tution consists in the entire separation of the legislative and executive authorities, but in truth its merit consists in their singular approximation. The connecting link is the *Cabinet*. By that new word we mean a committee of the legislative body selected to be the executive body.

Bagehot *The English Constitution*

According to constitutional theory it is of course the Queen who chooses her Prime Minister, and through him her other ministers. But in fact, Bagehot says, as a rule this is not so. Effectively we have a Prime Minister and an executive chosen by the House of Commons. And so, Bagehot went on, in words that must have sounded very odd to some of his readers, 'We have in England an elective first magistrate as truly as the Americans have an elective first magistrate'. To understand how revolutionary this must have sounded, we have to remind ourselves again what the standard theory of the English Constitution was. As I have said, it was supposedly divided into two branches, the executive and the legislature. The legislature is Parliament. On the other hand there is the executive, in which the monarch deputes the powers of government to his or her ministers. Bagehot calmly sweeps all this into the dustbin. The real situation now is that the executive and legislature are combined. The Cabinet, the executive, is a committee of the legislature which essentially means the House of Commons.

What, then, of the Queen and the House of Lords? Have they not in fact simply become redundant? No, says Bagehot. Because he too has his own division of the constitution into two parts, quite different from the traditional one. Instead of dividing it into executive and legislature he divides it into what he calls the 'efficient' and the 'dignified' parts. The Queen and the House of Lords are the dignified part. Each part has its own head: the Prime Minister is head of the efficient part, the Queen is head of the dignified part. But does all this not mean that the dignified part has no function at all? Not at all, says Bagehot. The dignified part *does* have a function. But its function lies not in the realm of business but in that other realm which always fascinated Bagehot, that of psychology.

24 'The dignified part' of the English constitution – Queen Victoria opening Parliament in 1856

It is the dull, traditional habit of mankind that guides most men's actions. And all this traditional part of human nature is most easily impressed by that which is handed down. The characteristic merit of the English constitution is, that its dignified parts are very complicated and somewhat imposing, very old and rather venerable; while its efficient part is decidedly simple and rather modern. We have made, or rather stumbled upon a constitution which has two capital merits: it contains a simple efficient part and it contains likewise historical, complex, august theatrical parts, which it has inherited from long past – which *take* the multitude – which guide by an omnipotent influence the associations of its subjects.

The English Constitution

No one can deny that *The English Constitution* is a very clever book, which can still be read for interest and enjoyment and instruction. But when he qualified his Liberalism by such an emphatic belief in the need to maintain stability and deference by appealing to the irrational in men's natures, was Bagehot being cynical, or timid, or just realistic? We shall each answer, I suspect, according to our own political inclinations. Bagehot, we know, thought that the multitude were incapable of understanding the abstract ideas of a republican constitution; they needed the concrete symbol of a monarch. A constitutional monarchy, he said, unlike a republic, 'has a comprehensible element for the vacant many, as well as complex laws and notions for the enquiring few'. No one, I suppose, would write like that now, and fear of the multitude was a common enough feeling among Liberals in Bagehot's time. But when all the allowances have been made for the differences between his time and ours, what do we make of Bagehot himself? What, in particular, do we make of that typical tone of his, and that condescending, ironical, yet somehow passionate defence of practicality and ordinariness. Was he really perhaps a complacent mid-Victorian philistine, who enjoyed being cleverer than most and who perversely made it part of his cleverness to defend what he called stupidity? Let me end by seeing what can be said in his defence.

We know from his contemporaries that Bagehot was a brisk, fresh-faced, companionable man. Lord Bryce said of him:

> Bagehot was always cheerful, natural, spontaneous, unaffected. You felt he was hunting for truth, and you enjoyed the sense that he allowed you to be his companion in the chase.
>
> Alastair Buchan *The Spare Chancellor*

We know that he was outward-going, humourous and capable. Some of this we could have guessed anyway from his writings. But what more? We know, for example, that he thought of himself as a religious man, but the outlines of what he believed seem to have been indistinct even to himself. His father was a Unitarian and his mother an Anglican, and there is evidence that Bagehot himself had an affection for Roman Catholicism. With considerable self-knowledge he wrote to his future wife:

> What I have made out is a good deal of my own doing. I have always had an indistinct feeling that my inner life has been too harsh and vacant to give me an abiding hold of some parts of religion.
>
> Mrs Russell Barrington (ed.) *Love Letters of Walter Bagehot and Eliza Wilson*

He was very fond of poetry, which he called 'a deep thing, a teaching thing, the most surely and wisely elevating of human

25 Sketch from memory of Eliza Wilson, Bagehot's wife, by her sister Emilie

things'. And in his biographical and literary studies we have a clue perhaps to how we should take Bagehot's half-ironical celebrations of mundane practicality and ordinariness. There was one type of man he always felt to be alien to him, and that was the doctrinaire, the man of abstract certainties, the man with a closed mind.

> A man of this sort is a curious mental phenomenon. He appears to get early – perhaps to be born with, a kind of dry schedule or catalogue of the universe; he has a ledger in his head, and has a title to which he can refer any transaction; nothing puzzles him, nothing comes amiss to him, but he is not the least the wiser for anything.
>
> Bagehot *Collected Works*

The opposite of this is what Bagehot called 'the experiencing nature', which he found in its highest form in Shakespeare. The way Bagehot presented this kind of mentality sounds almost like a profession of faith. Discussing whether Shakespeare was a religious man, Bagehot says:

> If the underlying and almighty essence of this world be good, then it is likely that the writer who most deeply approached to that essence will himself be good. There is a religion of weekdays as well as of Sundays, of 'cakes and ale' as well as pews and altar cloths.
>
> *Collected Works*

It is in the light of this 'religion', if we can call it that, that we should perhaps set some of Bagehot's references to humdrum existence and enjoyment and the practical doings of ordinary men. However stolid and limited, they share some fragment of what was experienced and comprehended, in Bagehot's view, by the greatest of poets. Practical knowledge and mundane enjoyment are the ways the experiencing nature expresses itself at its lower levels, just as Shakespeare represents its highest expression. Both, for Bagehot, have something which men of abstract systems with ledgers in their heads could never have.

J. W. Burrow

BAGEHOT, W. *The English Constitution* O.U.P., 1928; C. A. Watts, 1962; Fontana, 1963.
Historical essays Dobson, 1971.
Physics and politics Beacon Press, 1956; Gregg International, n.e. of 1872 edn., 1971.
Collected works Economist newspaper, 4 vols. 1966-8.
BUCHAN, A. *The spare Chancellor: the life of Walter Bagehot* Chatto and Windus, 1959.
IRVINE, W. *Walter Bagehot* Hamden, C. T.: Shoe String Press, reprint of 1939 edn. 1970.
ST JOHN STEVAS, N. ed. *Walter Bagehot: a study of his life and thought together with a selection from his political writings* Eyre and Spottiswoode, 1959.

THOMAS COOK

In 1891 the firm Thomas Cook and Son celebrated its Jubilee and in the course of that single year confirmed its acknowledged dominance of the world of travel by selling well over three million tickets. The following year, 1892, Thomas Cook himself died and *The Times* in its coverage of the death described him and his son as:

> the Julius and Augustus Caesar of modern travel. Their offices are as ubiquitous as the Flag in Mr Kipling's poems. The land of the Midnight Sun knows them as well as the Sahara and it is only the absence of a railway that prevents them from issuing tourist tickets to the moon.

The imperial tone of this late-Victorian plaudit is far removed from the mid-century world of temperance reforming enthusiasm which inspired Thomas Cook's first experience of the travel business.

26 Thomas Cook (1808–92)

This Victorian inventor of the package-holiday was born in 1808 in the small Derbyshire town of Melbourne – which is just under the flight path of aircraft leaving Castle Donnington filled with the modern beneficiaries of the package-holiday. Cook's early life was hard but it gave experience of both organization and selling and provided opportunities for the expression of his improving temperament. He was sent to work as a gardener at the age of ten, for 6d a week – his father had died when he was four. He was soon selling vegetables from a stall in Derby market. But in his fourteenth year he became apprenticed as a wood turner. His grandfather had been co-pastor of Melbourne General Baptist Church for thirty years and the story goes that the young Cook used to steal into the Baptist Chapel at night to play preachers and congregations with a friend. By the time he was twenty, he had left his trade to become a professional village missionary and tract distributor in Northamptonshire. This work entailed travelling and it is said that in 1829 he covered 2692 miles, 2106 of them by foot. In 1833 he was back as a woodturner, married, in business at Market Harborough and espousing a new cause, temperance. Cook's speaking ability and his missionary experience put him at the centre of the move to establish the South Midland Temperance Association in 1838 and, despite the existence of a notorious and riotous anti-teetotal mob in Market Harborough, the town became both the centre of the Association's activities and the location of its new tract depot, which Cook managed on commission. He soon began to undertake publishing and editorial responsibility for a wide variety of temperance periodicals and tracts which included at this time *The Monthly Temperance Messenger* and *The Children's Temperance Magazine for Little Teetotallers*.

Cook quickly brought this enterprise under his personal ownership as the Midlands Temperance Press and, with a move to Leicester, he began his career as a campaigning publisher. He even extended his temperance scruples to smoking and published *The Anti-Smoker*. Cook himself described how he achieved an instant conversion where so many Victorian conversions took place – in a railway carriage. Two young men were smoking in the seat opposite.

> It occurred to me that I had under the seat a parcel containing a quantity of the Tract – *Friendly Advice on the Use of Tobacco*. I opened the parcel and drew out one of the tracts, which I placed in the hand of the young man who sat nearest to me. I simply asked him to read. He read the title and turned it to the next page, after reading a few lines of which he hastily took his pipe from his mouth and flung it away. After reading a few pages further, he drew from his waistcoat pocket a paper containing his stock of tobacco, which he vehemently cast away, declaring that he had 'done with that', and, turning to his companion said, 'Come, down with that cigar – and the snuff-box must go too.'
> This pleasing instance of the powerful operations of simple truth, administered in a kind of manner, was particularly gratifying and encouraging.
>
> T. Cook *The Anti-Smoker and Progressive Temperance Reformer* 1842

Thus Thomas Cook appears early as a tireless publicist and campaigner on the side of abstinence and self-improvement in that great Victorian struggle over the proper use of leisure time and the proper exercise of consumer responsibility.

The growth of urban-industrial society brought to the nineteenth century the modern distinction between work and leisure. This development involved the decay of an earlier world in which work and play formed a closely interwoven pattern of life, based on local community, the rhythm of which was set by the season of the agricultural year. Only the leisure class survived from that era and Thomas Cook was later to provide many services for its late-Victorian representatives. Of those who 'needed' to work, many did not accept the 'gospel of work' and chose an irregular life of intermittent paid employment, which seemed to some to threaten stable social progress and even social order. Others saw work as the way to earn leisure time and, in return for hard regular work, sought and received both increased remuneration and regular 'time-off' in the form of Saturday afternoons or annual holidays. The ways in which this 'time-off' was spent became a major social issue of the period. Some shared the optimism of the Inspectors of Factories in 1859.

> A still greater boon is the distinction at last made clear between the worker's own time and his master's. The worker knows now when that which he sells is ended, and when his own begins; and, by possessing a sure fore-knowledge of this, is enabled to prearrange his own minutes for his own purposes. This, it is, which has given the impetus to so many institutions for mutual improvement that have sprung up so rapidly of late years in almost every hamlet of our industrial districts.
>
> Reports of the Inspectors of Factories *Parliamentary Papers* 1860

But others saw free-time, linked with increased income or not, as a temptation to drink and self indulgence in brutalising pastimes. Society divided from top to bottom on this issue. The temperance movement itself affords good examples of support and co-operation from all levels of society and the same is true of other movements for mental and physical improvement and all forms of 'rational' recreation. And of course, 'sensual' recreation in general and the drink interest in particular, also found advocates from all ranks in society.

Thomas Cook was quick to appreciate the significance of the railway as a weapon in the struggle for 'respectability' and when walking from Market Harborough to Leicester for a temperance meeting in 1841, he conceived his first project as a travel agent.

> About midway between Harborough and Leicester – my mind's eye has often reverted to the spot – a thought flashed through my brain – what a glorious thing it would be if the newly developed powers of railways and locomotion could be made subservient to the promotion of temperance! That thought grew upon me as I travelled over the last six or eight miles. I carried it up to the platform, and strong in the confidence of the sympathy of the Chairman, I broached the idea of engaging a special train to carry the friends of temperance from Leicester to Loughborough and back, to attend a quarterly delegate meeting appointed to be held there in two or three weeks following. The Chairman approved, the meeting roared with excitement, and early next day I proposed my grand scheme to John Fox Bell, the resident secretary of the Midland Counties Railway.
>
> Cook *Cook's Scottish Tourist Official Directory* 1861

Cook hired a train and offered a reduced fare, one shilling the trip. Tea, music, games and speeches at Loughborough were all included in the arrangements, carefully made by Cook himself. 570 people travelled that day.

27 and **28** 'The powerful operations of simple truth' – Temperance and Intemperance contrasted

Cook's first excursion was no prototype – trips of this kind had been organised for at least two years before, even by temperance organizations – but it was a great success. He followed it with excursions to other Midland towns as well as places of natural beauty. In 1843, he took 3,000 children from Leicester to Derby to protect them from the 'sensual' temptations of Leicester on race day. Although this excursion traffic soon lost its specifically temperance character, Cook continued to stress its educative value. It took Cook's particular entrepreneurial flair to start 'moonlight trips' in 1856. On these excursions travelling was confined to night when the journey would interfere least with the working day and the excursionist could spend as much of the day-light as possible at Scarborough or at the Manchester Fine Art Treasures Exhibition or at some other chosen resort. Also by making use at night of spare transport capacity, Cook was able to reduce fares to the very minimum.

The Great Exhibition of 1851 marked a high point in Cook's early career in Britain. Such was his established reputation and the strength of his temperance connections in high places that he was engaged by the Midland Railway to publicise and organise excursions from the whole of the southern part of its network. This was not a sub-contracting arrangement – he simply took commission on each passenger – and after a bold piece of price cutting, every train at the Company's command, except the day-expresses, had to be made available for him. One of his ploys was to organise savings clubs of workmen to help them accumulate the cost of a ticket. In all, Thomas Cook moved 165,000 people to London for the Exhibition – that is roughly 3 per cent of the total number attending.

After this great success in 1851, it is hardly surprising that the Midland Railway kept its exhibition traffic under its own management for the International Exhibition of 1862. But Cook's ingenuity proved equal to the occasion. For the period of the Exhibition he rented a new tenement building opposite the site and soon the *Excursionist* – his house publicity journal – was advertising combined rail and hotel tickets for visits to the Exhibition from Leicester and Northampton. He made peace with the Midland Railway and in 1868 he negotiated a ticket agency for all that company's excursion traffic.

Thomas Cook had organised his first purely 'pleasure tour' in 1845. It was to Liverpool with a supplement for those wishing to go on the Caernarvon. He prepared the ground thoroughly beforehand. He prospected for suitable hotels and compiled and published a small guide book for the tour. The tickets involved complicated negotiations for through-facilities from several railway and steamer companies. Cook himself acted as courier for the trip and agreed to pay all bills incurred en route. This pattern of arrangements formed the basis of his popular Scottish tours run from the following year, 1846, until 1863 and the careful shepherding, thoroughness of preparation and grasp of complex arrangements were the hallmarks of his later continental tours.

Cook took the strain out of travel, but who benefitted and in what way? He often claimed to be one of the principle civilisers of the English people. His patrons, he said, came from all classes:

> The trips to Edinburgh, and the shorter excursions in England attract tradesmen and their wives; merchants' clerks away for a week's holiday, roughing it with a knapsack; swart mechanics, who are by no means the worst informed and are generally the most interested about the places they visit.
>
> E. Yates *All the Year Round* Vol. xi 1864

As to the benefits, Cook reported appreciative words spoken to him by a poor man on York railway station.

> Oh, Mr Cook, I wish it was in my power to write an article for a newspaper, to tell how much we owe to you for these cheap Excursions. Only think, for a few shillings, I, a poor working man have been enabled to see the glories of this fine old city – the Minster, the city walls, the old gateways, the Flower Show, and many other objects that I could never have seen but for your special train from Nottingham today. I wish I could tell the world all I feel of what we working people owe to you.
>
> *Cook's Scottish Tourist Official Directory*

This same poor man might have enjoyed an open day organised by Cook at Chatsworth. Cook made high claims for the behaviour of the crowd at this type of event and for the power of example to improve.

> I stood at the gates and saw almost every man of them enter, and I marked their conduct in returning home. There was no rudeness, no damage done in house or gardens, not a drunken passenger to be seen as the party returned home. Total Abstinence, though with myself a practice of a quarter of a century, is never made a condition of any travelling privilege which I have to offer; nor do I often raise the question as one of discussion. But I have marked with pleasure the silent workings of example, and the generally abstemious habits of Tourists.
>
> *Cook's Scottish Tourist Official Directory*

Generalising again on the beneficial results of excursions and tours, Cook wrote in 1861.

> It is delightful to see, as we travel on, the breaking down of partition walls of prejudice, the subduing of evil passions and unhappy tempers, the expansion of the intellect, the grasping of information, the desire for books and the eagerness of their perusal, the benevolent sympathies excited by a more

extended knowledge of the circumstances and sufferings of fellow creatures, the improvement in health and prospects, the endurance of fatigue and the perseverance under difficulties; with numerous other indescribable influences of a happy and beneficial tendency. And all these results are best obtained by associated travel.

Cook's Scottish Tourist Official Directory

This was special pleading for group travel with Cook. There were, of course, numerous excursions and tours run by many other commercial and private organisations: the railway companies themselves, the pubs and chapels who arranged trips from northern communities, industrialists who laid on temperance excursions for their employees, and pressure groups like the National Sunday League. Much of this activity had a highly 'respectable' face. But the 'sensual' side showed itself too. Respectable residents of south coast towns shivered at the prospect of incursions from excursionists and the evidence presented to the *Select Committee on the Sale of Beer on the Lord's Day* in 1854 about the drunken condition in which the Brighton railway returned its excursionists to London casts strong doubt on the view that excursions in themselves were intrinsically improving experiences. In 1864 Edmund Yates prepared a balanced assessment for *All the Year Round* of Cook's achievement so far.

> Now surely this kind of thing is a good kind of thing, and ought to be encouraged. It is right that a hard-working man, labouring in one spot for fifty weeks in the year, should, in his fortnight's holiday, betake himself to some place as far away from and as different from his ordinary abode as is within the reach of his purse; and this he is only able to do by aid of such providers as my excursion agent (Thomas Cook). I think I have a right to claim for him a position, modest but useful, in that great army of civilisation which is marching through the world.

In 1854 Thomas Cook gave up his publishing firm and, with his first continental excursion in 1855 on the occasion of the Paris Exhibition, he began that most celebrated phase of his career, associated with the organising of foreign travel. In some ways this development was simply a logical extension of his organising enthusiasm. France, Switzerland and Italy presented challenging organisational problems which could only be solved with the co-operation of foreign railway companies and even foreign governments. Cook, as ever, was eager for work. But he was also pushed into foreign travel by the policies of the British railway companies. Many were beginning to appoint their own excursion managers – Cook's own son, John Mason Cook, held that post in the Midland Railway for a time. Even the Scottish companies were anxious to squeeze him out of the profitable tour market. Whatever the reason for this extension of his work, he brought to continental travel characteristic enthusiasm and daunting moral confidence.

> We would have every class of British subjects visit Paris, that they may emulate its excellences, and shun the vices and errors. In matters of taste and courtesy, we may learn much from Parisians; and on some questions of morality we may have right views strengthened. Give us a quiet Highland Sabbath in preference to the triviality, mirth and labour of a continental Sunday.
>
> Cook *Cook's Excursionist and International Tourist Advertiser* May 1863

Not all his first steps abroad were successful. He lost money, for example, arranging the travel to a working men's demonstration in Paris in 1861. But his French and Swiss guided-tours, the corner-stone of his business abroad, were soundly established in 1863 and the Italian tours followed in 1864. It was with another exhibition in Paris in 1867 that Cook got a great chance to display his powers of improvisation and organisation. He acted as excursion manager for the London, Brighton and South Coast Railway and with the support of the French government he took over a large empty building in the centre of Paris to house first-class travellers and built a temporary encampment at Passy for those excursionists who could not afford better. The minimum fare for the four days, all-in, was 36 shillings, roughly equivalent to an artisan's weekly wage. He carried 20,000 people to the Exhibition and housed 10,000 of them. Later for the 1878 Exhibition, Cook surpassed himself with 75,000 visitors.

By the late 1860s Cook had made an international reputation of which much the most impressive result was the creation of the famous 'coupon system'. The Cook agency began to issue coupons payed for in advance and exchangeable for hotel rooms on a particular journey. By the 1890s there were 1,200 hotels in the scheme, located throughout the world, giving accommodation and preferential treatment in return for coupons. In effect, it was an elaborate international credit system based on confidence in the firm of Cooks. John Mason Cook had travelled miles to make the arrangements but a man from Cooks was left in each major centre as a trouble-shooter. 'Coupons' combined with excursion tickets were a flexible and simple system for the traveller to use. It was also remunerative for Cook: the Swiss railways, for example, were prepared to give him 30 per cent off the tickets. One Scots traveller described the convenience of the arrangement:

> By Mr Cook's arrangement I travelled with comfort and economy such as I never accomplished before. All I had to do was to purchase tourists' tickets, and hotel *coupons*, and after purchasing these at a much cheaper rate than I could other-wise have done, I had the extreme satisfaction of travelling over the Continent without ever having to put my hand in

my pocket. You walk into a hotel; you say you are under the wing of Mr Cook, and everybody is ready to receive you and pay you all attention.

Cook *Dr W. H. Russell of London, Consul Lever of Trieste, and Cook's Tourists* 1870

By the 1870s few European cities did not know Cook's tourists and, when so many people new to foreign travel were rushed about Europe, it is hardly surprising that charges of vulgarity were commonly heard.

They never separate, and you see them forty in number pouring along a street with their director – now in front, now at the rear circling round them like a sheepdog – and really the process is as like herding as may be. I have already met three flocks, and anything so uncouth I never saw before. Take my word for it, if these excursionists go on, nothing short of another war, and another Wellington, will ever place us where we once were in the opinion of Europe.

C. O'Dowd *Blackwood's Magazine* February 1865

Cook admitted that:

The Whitsuntide trip has a good deal of the Cockney element in it, and is mostly composed of very high-spirited people whose greatest delight in life is 'having a fling' and who carry London everywhere about with them in dress, habits and conversation, and rush back, convinced they are great travellers. From these roisterers the July and September excursionists differ greatly; ushers and governesses, practical people from the provinces, and representatives of the better style of the London Mercantile community in all travel as if impressed with the notion that they are engaged in fulfilling the wishes of a lifetime, in a pleasant duty never to be repeated.

All the Year Round

And G. A. Sala reported:

I have met with many hundreds of Cook's Tourists in the course of my travels; and I never could discern any difference between them and other English travellers on the Continent, save that they were, as a rule, better behaved and more anxious to acquire information than are the general run of travelling gents of the 'stuck-up' order. I have been told that one of the most illustrious of English statesmen has been heard to say that he regards Mr Thomas Cook and Mr John Hullah as two of the most important social benefactors that this age has seen.

Illustrated London News September 1884

Except on special occasions, it was mainly the respectable middle-classes who patronised Cook's foreign tours and perhaps it is right

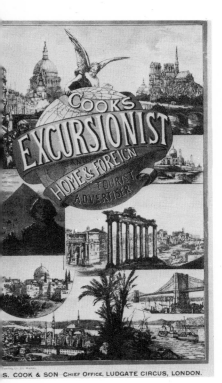

29 The front cover of Cook's *Excursionist,* established in 1851

to dismiss Cookophobia as one of the growing pains of middle-class Europe. But who can calculate the good he brought by showing Paris to English shopkeepers and Rome to English clerks? The firm continued the extension of its agency to the limits of the world – America, Greece, the Nile, Palestine – and when Cook returned successfully from a world tour in 1872 he was ready to issue 'coupons' to anyone who wanted to follow. The new tours he offered were grander and more exotic, but still bargains for those who could afford them. The list of notables who travelled with Cook got ever more impressive as the century progressed: Cook's servants were becoming relatively cheaper to travel with than one's own. The power of his organisation, the length of his connections, the ingenuity of his arrangements made it impossible not to use Cook. The British army used him; so did Queen Victoria. But when he took 20 Germans including the Emperor, 100 Turkish Pashas and 25 journalists round the Holy Land under canvas, it was only the Germans, sceptical of British tent technology, who shipped prefabricated asbestos hutments for their own use.

Thomas Cook could still bring enthusiastic seriousness to his tours of the Holy Land.

> There is one predominant feeling of interest that underlies all our visits to these lands and waters of biblical history. That is, the abiding impression that we are travelling amongst and gazing on a scene with which we have been familiarised from our earliest recollections.
>
> Cook. Letter to *Stamford Mercury* April 1872

But Cookite seriousness had a limited appeal even amongst those who could afford £140 and 75 days for a tour of the Nile and the

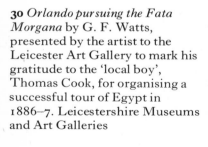

30 *Orlando pursuing the Fata Morgana* by G. F. Watts, presented by the artist to the Leicester Art Gallery to mark his gratitude to the 'local boy', Thomas Cook, for organising a successful tour of Egypt in 1886–7. Leicestershire Museums and Art Galleries

31 Cook with a tourist party at Pompeii

32 The office of Thomas Cook and Son in Alexandria

Holy Land. Historical monuments, archaeological sites, the life of the natives and even natural beauty did not necessarily attract the bulk of the leisure class who found their foreign pleasures by preference in the lazy life of the new playgrounds of Europe.

The temperance business connection in the nineteenth century produced many modern household names – Horniman for tea, Barlow for cotton, Cassell, Chambers and Collins for books. There was even another temperance travel agent – John Frame. That Cook's organisation enjoyed the greatest success of them all was partly due to the fact that it was early into a new field. He himself commanded unusual business drive and his commercial judgement matched his clever understanding of his clients' needs. He had the imagination to foresee the interest that opening up the Near East would evoke. He could improvise in an emergency and his powers of negotiation and persuasion were indispensable when teaching the directors of railway companies in Germany, for example, new excursionist ideas. His new ventures were always thoroughly prepared and his mastery of detail was crucial when control of such a disparate organisation was required over such long distances. He was cautious always to avoid fixed capital commitments. His tardiness in opening a London office showed this and for years he worked from the conservatory of his wife's British Museum Temperance Hotel. Egypt, where he controlled nine-tenths of the market, was the only place in which he went into ownership of steamers and hotels. Where complex arrangements and long distance credit transactions are the essence of a business, reputation and confidence, as in banking, are the name of the game. Probity and temperance enthusiasm, for this reason, if for no other were business assets. Although the wine cellars on his Nile steamers were advertised as first quality, Cook relished refusing drink and the grander the occasion the more he enjoyed sporting his abstinence. Cook took his temperance to the grave but he left behind a temperance hall in Leicester and Baptist almshouses in Melbourne.

Thomas Cook taught two generations of consumers how to spend their money on improving travel. In a materialist world of factories and physical goods he developed a business based on offices, hotels and invisible services. At a time when German and American imports seemed to threaten British prosperity, he led the world in a new type of business enterprise. It may be true, as *The Times* argued, that Cook failed in his endeavour to save the world by issuing tourist tickets to the Holy Land. But who can challenge that enthusiastic correspondent who argued that the unification of modern Italy owed less to political forces than to Thomas Cook and the introduction of the railway circular tourist ticket?

John Myerscough

HARRISON, B. *Drink and the Victorians* Faber, 1971.
PIMLOTT, J. A. R. *The Englishman's holiday* Faber, 1947.

JOSEPHINE BUTLER

33 Josephine Butler (1828–1906)

So far, no Victorian women have been featured. If we have to choose a single individual to represent them, there is a lot to be said for choosing a social reformer, because Victorian women energetically carried forward the great tradition of moral and social reform begun by Hannah More and Elizabeth Fry. Besides, womens' reforming activities help to clarify the overall situation of their sex, because reforming crusades brought the woman reformer up against all the barriers which limited women's social role. Josephine Butler is a reformer particularly worth discussing, because (unlike all the other Victorians studied in this series) she had an aristocratic upbringing. Any setbacks *she* suffered can be attributed primarily to her sex, for she never lacked social status.

She was born a Grey, a member of the distinguished Northumberland family which produced a great prime minister, Lord Grey of the Reform Bill, and a famous Edwardian foreign secretary, Sir Edward Grey. She had a happy childhood, which gave her a lifelong nostalgia for the wild moors of the Border country, a lifelong respect for the ideal of an affectionate and united family life, and a lifelong admiration for the evangelical simplicity and integrity of her father, John Grey of Dilston, whose favourite daughter she was. Josephine was soon happily married to a kindly and Liberal clergyman, George Butler, and during the 1850s she concentrated on bringing up her young family while he taught undergraduates in Oxford. She was then, and long remained, a strikingly beautiful woman, but she was not very happy in such a masculine and academic world. She later recalled how she had listened in silence to the dons' flippant, often cynical and anti-feminist talk, and had privately taken refuge in the passionate prayers she had engaged in since the days of her teenage religious crisis. But it took a family tragedy to propel her into working outside the family circle – the death in 1864 of her youngest child and only daughter, Eva. While running to greet her parents who had just returned home, the little girl fell down from the first-floor banisters and died shortly afterwards. Josephine described the incident some weeks later, in a letter to a friend.

Never can I lose that memory, – the fall, the sudden cry, and then the silence! It was pitiful to see her, helpless in her father's arms, her little drooping head resting on his shoulder, and her beautiful golden hair, all stained with blood, falling over his arm! Would to God that I had died that death for her! If we had been permitted, I thought, to have one look, one word of farewell, one moment of recognition! But though life flickered for an hour, she never recognised the father and mother whom she loved so dearly. We called her by her name, but there was no answer. She was our only daughter, the light and joy of our lives. She flitted in and out like a butterfly all day.

Josephine Butler *Recollections of George Butler*

For a long time, Josephine was prostrated by the grief and self-reproach which any mother would feel in such circumstances. But her distinctively Victorian quality emerges from the fact that this family tragedy provoked a religious crisis. How *could* she be expected to love and respect a God, Josephine asked herself, if he allowed an innocent child to suffer in such a way? Yet she did not respond by abandoning her faith. Like several of her contemporaries, she sought simultaneous consolation for suffering and reinforcement of her faith through practical activity in social work. This was in Liverpool, where the Butlers had recently moved when George became headmaster of Liverpool College, the well-known secondary school for boys. Josephine explained her frame of mind at this time in the biography she later wrote of her husband:

I suffered much during the first months in our new home. I did not exaggerate my own trial; I only knew that my heart ached night and day, and that the only solace possible would seem to be to find other hearts which ached night and day, and with more reason than mine. I had no clear idea beyond that, no plan for helping others; my sole wish was to plunge into the heart of some human misery, and to say (as I now knew I could) to afflicted people, 'I understand. I, too, have suffered'.

Recollections of George Butler

34 George Butler, husband of Josephine

Her explanation movingly illustrates Josephine's strongly emotional nature and the limited scope it could enjoy in an ordinary middle-class household. But it also brings out a striking quality which many middle-class Victorian women possessed – a deep preoccupation with the intense suffering they saw in the cruel society which surrounded their comfortable and sheltered homes. This strange combination of selfish and selfless considerations impelled Josephine Butler, as it had already impelled Florence Nightingale, into a reforming career which was far from comfortable and sheltered. Josephine began by visiting a Liverpool workhouse and reading to the young women she found there. The courage a religious, middle-class and respectable woman required for such work needs to be imagined: the dirt, the bad language, the disease, the fleas, the ugliness, the misery would soon have repelled a more squeamish and less profoundly religious woman. Suffering people are not always pleasant. Yet Josephine went further, and began reclaiming Liverpool prostitutes. The saintliness of her husband, and the strength of his love for her, emerge from the fact that he allowed Josephine to bring several diseased prostitutes into their home to die. Her charity was never a cold institutional thing, safely insulated from her family circle; it involved warm, deeply emotional and intensely religious relationships which transcended social class, disrupted her personal life and even threatened her husband's career.

Inevitably these experiences fired her with indignation at the social conditions which could force so many women into prostitution. She was then, in fact, on the point of becoming the figure who has fascinated and bewildered biographers and historians ever since.

It is worth having a closer look at her state of mind at this crucial moment. She had not lost her religious doubts, as we can see from her conversations with several young men she influenced in the 1860s. The future art historian J. A. Symonds, then an Oxford undergraduate, described how she visited him one day and

> . . . talked vehemently of how she suffered in her mind. As she lay there exquisitely slender and mobile, full length on the sofa, she did look torn by demons. She told me the torture of her thought, how religious, social, political doubt weighed on her. She never lost her feeling for God, but could not help thinking of Him as a tyrant. Sympathised with me, when I said such thoughts goaded one on to suicide as a means of finding out the truth.
>
> Phyllis Grosskurth *John Addington Symonds. A Biography*

So much for the notion which so easily comes to us now, that well-to-do Victorians had a pleasantly untroubled life! Their religious and social concerns often in fact tormented them. Their respectability may have given them privacy, and their servants may have given them leisure, but this often freed them only to brood on the physical and psychological sufferings of themselves and of others. In addition to her religious doubts, Josephine in the late 1860s became almost obsessed with the sufferings she had observed – as reformers often do just before breaking out into their initial crusade. She wrote about this in a letter during May 1868:

> In my delirium I used to cry out for some way of escape for starving women, and saw thousands of them being swept up with a broom and hidden like ashes under a huge grate, by political economists, and I kept saying 'O take care they are tenderer than you. They feel more.'
>
> Josephine Butler to Mr Rutson

Once again, though, it took unexpected developments to push Josephine into taking a major step. If it had not been for the introduction during the 1860s of what were called the Contagious Diseases Acts, Josephine might have remained a respected but obscurely provincial doer of good works, operating on a purely individual and non-political basis. As it was, towards the end of 1869, her increased understanding of these Acts redirected her life into channels one would not have predicted for an aristocrat's daughter and a happily-married schoolmaster's wife – transformed her into a fiery crusader who tore aside the hypocrisies covering the lax morality of the governing class, and who denounced the compromises with Christian principle which even Victorian politicians had to make.

The Contagious Diseases Acts were smuggled through parliament with the aim of reducing the very high level of venereal disease in the army and navy. Building on the prior experience of colonial and European régimes, a group of English doctors and statesmen introduced a system of state-regulated prostitution to several garrison and seaport towns, and hoped to extend it later perhaps to the whole country. The Acts empowered the police in these areas to arrest women suspected of being prostitutes, to have them medically inspected, and to require them (if found to be infected) to remain in hospital till cured. The women could then be released, but if they wished to continue as prostitutes they had to join an official prostitutes' register and submit to periodic government inspection.

For several reasons the Acts worried the group of Christians, many of them Quakers, who eventually persuaded Josephine to launch her crusade in 1869. By greatly increasing police powers, the Acts seemed to infringe the Englishman's traditional liberties. They seemed to sanction a double standard of morality, by requiring the prostitute to be inspected but not her male customer. They also increased the difficulty of reclaiming prostitutes, because they seemed to give prostitution an official sanction. They encouraged the arrogance of doctors by allowing their pursuit of public health to ride roughshod over traditionally Christian attitudes to public morals. And, lastly, they clashed with the idea that government should be run on the Christian principles which were supposed to inspire the individual citizen.

Yet the Acts were no fit subject for a middle-class woman to campaign against: they were not even talked about by decent people. Women were not supposed to speak in public at all, let alone on a topic like this. Not surprisingly, Josephine at first tried to back out of her historic role. As she later recalled:

> The toils and conflicts of the years that followed were light in comparison with the anguish of that first plunge into the full realisation of the villainy there is in the world, and the dread of being called to oppose it.
>
> *Recollections of George Butler*

88

Her crusade against the Contagious Diseases Acts is, in fact, as important for the fact that it happened at all, as for the impact it actually made on English politics. For in the long term, the women's movement gained much from the fact that a woman, through an organisation specifically designed for women (the Ladies' National Association), could speak on topics of great importance to women but which had hitherto been taboo, and could eventually force statesmen and public officials to listen to her.

35 Josephine Butler's ladies campaigning in 1880 against the Contagious Diseases Acts

36 Mrs Butler's periodical, *The Shield,* January 25th, 1878, carried a report of her meeting with the TUC delegates in Leeds, including 'our own good friend Mr Howell', secretary to the Congress

THE SHIELD:

ESTABLISHED TO PROMOTE
THE REPEAL OF THE CONTAGIOUS DISEASES ACTS.
(PUBLISHED EVERY SATURDAY.)

No. 148.—Vol. IV.] SATURDAY, JANUARY 25, 1879. [PRICE ONE PENNY.

Contents.

———◇———

There will be no debate until the second reading takes place. Our Secretary will send a special circular on this question to all friends.

THE TRADES' UNION CONGRESS AND REPEAL.

MRS. BUTLER AND OUR ASSOCIATIONS AT LEEDS.
(BY AN EYE WITNESS.)

YOU will be glad, I know, to hear of the really great work achieved by Mrs. Butler and our Associations, during the Trades' Union Congress in this town. You are probably aware

Apart from her beauty, her capacity for public speaking, and her husband's loyal support, Josephine could draw on two important strengths: on her religious resources, and on the Liberal political traditions of the Grey family. The Bible was one source of inspiration. Take her comment on Jesus' attitude to women, written in 1869, just before she began the crusade:

> Search throughout the Gospel history, and observe his conduct in regard to women, and it will be found that the word liberation expresses, above all others, the act which changed the whole life and character and position of the women dealt with, and which ought to have changed the character of men's treatment of women from that time forward.
>
> Josephine Butler (Ed.) *Woman's Work and Woman's Culture* 1869

Prayer was another of Josephine's resources. It enabled her to escape from the distracting turmoil of agitation and to focus her mind on priorities. It was no coincidence that she wrote a biography of St Catharine of Siena, for Josephine was a sort of Victorian saint, who held to the early Christian belief in miracles which her contemporaries had already begun to shake off. In her biography of St Catharine, Josephine describes, for the benefit of sceptical nineteenth-century readers, the saint's experience of direct communication with God:

> Those who have any experience of real prayer know full well that in the pause of the soul before God, after it has uttered its complaint, made known its desires, or sought guidance in perplexity, there comes the clearer vision of duty, and the still small voice of guidance is heard, rectifying the judgment, strengthening the resolve, and consoling the spirit.
>
> *Catharine of Siena. A Biography* 1878

This is the aspect of Josephine which we now find least familiar, but there is no doubt that her faith gave her the courage to fight – even to affront – the powers that be. There is a curious interrelation, which none of Josephine's biographers has so far adequately explained, between her psychological and her physical condition. The suffering which surrounded her tended to make her ill, but nothing enabled her to recover more quickly than mounting an agitation against it. This was in fact the situation in 1869, at the beginning of her great crusade. The campaign's early stages acted as a tonic, but her increased contact with suffering in the course of the agitation eventually caused her illness to return. Her career in fact involved a continuous alternation between exhilarated activity and profound depression.

Add to Josephine's religious motives the humanitarian and libertarian attitudes inherited through her father, John Grey, and reinforced by her contacts with Mazzini – and you have her two major sources of stability amid the bewilderments and corruptions of public agitation. She felt inspired by the anti-slavery movement, which her father had been keen on, and also by the Englishman's long-continued fight for individual liberty, which the Victorian Liberal historians celebrated. Her heroes were the decent and courageous individualists who dared to stand out against contemporary opinion and against those high in authority – the men who had secured Magna Carta, and the unassuming men of principle from Wat Tyler, through Hampden, to her own father.

> Men of great integrity and purity of life, who have no thought of pushing into any ambitious sphere, but only of doing with all their might the work which their hand finds to do, are the salt of society, the strength of a nation, and it is not well that such should be forgot.
> Josephine Butler *Memoir of John Grey of Dilston* revised edn. 1874

Her biography of her father was published just before she began her crusade. And indeed, all six of Josephine's biographies – of her father, her husband, her sister Mme Meuricoffre, Rebecca Jarrett, Catharine of Siena and Pastor Oberlin – describe simple, pure-minded, and energetic Christians, far removed from, and suspicious of, the Scribes and the Pharisees. But the trouble with people of this sort (perhaps also with Jesus himself) is that they do not usually have to balance off conflicting priorities as politicians must do: and, as private citizens, they do not have to work continuously with people whose motives are (to say the least of it) 'mixed'.

The political disadvantages involved in modelling oneself on such characters soon became clear. For as soon as the indignation of Josephine's movement had forced the government into appointing a royal commission on the Acts in 1871, her blazing commitment to principle seriously complicated the task of getting them abolished. Take, for instance, the exchange between Josephine and a member of the royal commission, Mr Rylands:

> *Rylands:* In your experience of these fallen women have you found in practice that they have been utterly degraded, and have lost all womanly feelings?
> *Josephine Butler:* I have not found loss of womanly feelings in one, except in garrison towns, and that is lately. I am astonished that such a question should be asked me – a woman.
> *Rylands:* You think even those in the most degraded positions are always open to the sympathy of those of their own sex?
> *Josephine Butler:* They are always open to the sympathy of those who are gifted by Providence and nature with the art of reaching hearts; but in the matter of these women they are very like the story of the chameleon, one says it is green, and another red. To one class of persons these women appear like devils; to another class they are their true selves; the image of God may be marred, but it never is wholly blotted out.

What we find attractive about her evidence, of course, is the extent of her compassion for society's outcasts. As she sat, nervous and ill-prepared, before the cold questioning of these men of the world – Josephine perhaps recalled to mind the Liverpool prostitutes who had died in her home only two or three years before.

The obverse of Josephine's compassion, though, was her angry indignation with men of the governing class, who had often themselves first led these women into their trade. So Josephine spoke in ways which were anything but politic. There is in her evidence a prickly concern for principle, and an airy unconcern for facts – which made her a very unsatisfactory witness, as she herself later realised. Two examples of her exchanges, first with the commission's chairman, Mr Massey, and later with another member, Mr Hastings, illustrate the point.

Massey : You have been about the country a great deal in connexion with this subject; are you acquainted with many of the institutions which are established in Portsmouth and Plymouth for the reception of fallen women?

Josephine Butler : I know nothing of those in Portsmouth and Plymouth at all. I know scarcely anything of the garrison towns. Of the operation of the Acts I neither can nor will speak, and I must decline to do so because I have no interest in the operation of the Acts. It is nothing to me whether they operate well or ill, but I will tell you what you wish to know as to my view of the principle of the Acts.

*

Hastings : With regard to reformatories, you are aware, of course, that there are a certain number of certified reformatories in this country to which girls convicted of felony can be sent?

Josephine Butler : I am.

Hastings : Are you aware that any one has yet been established by voluntary effort, to which girls can be sent, who, having been convicted of crime, are also on the streets?

Josephine Butler : No, I am not aware of that fact, but it may be so.

Hastings : That being the fact, do you not think it is some proof that the voluntary system has a tendency to be ineffective?

Josephine Butler : Decidedly, for this reason, that people are not sufficiently imbued with the spirit of Christ, and with sound views as to political economy. That is the reason; but that does not prove that therefore the State would do the thing better, or that State measures would be more effective. It only requires more voluntary agency, and a fuller measure of the true spirit of charity and justice, and the thing is done.

This was little more than 'bearing witness', and was certainly not the most effective way of getting a favourable report. Politicians could not afford to remain so ignorant of the actual localities where the Acts were applied, nor could they accept Josephine's purely long-term solution for the evil. Josephine even told the commissioners that she and her supporters considered it

> an absurdity, a mockery, that any tribunal of gentlemen, however wise and conscientious, should be set to inquire into a moral question like this. We have the Word of God in our hands – the law of God in our consciences. We hold that the practical working of an Act, which is vicious in principle, is no fit subject for an inquiry. You may be sure that our action in this matter will continue to be exactly the same, even if the Commission pronounce the Acts highly moral.

In Josephine Butler's career, tragedy runs at more than one level, for the influences which lent her courage also led her to adopt an outlook and strategy which to some extent made her efforts self-frustrating. So all that her agitation achieved at this stage was the government's abandonment, for the time being, of any plans for extending the Acts to other places. What was really needed, if the Acts were to be abolished, was the direction of the campaign against them by an experienced politician – perhaps with a rather lighter, but more empirical, touch – who would use arguments which could carry weight in Westminster and Whitehall. Despite her aristocratic and Anglican background, Josephine (as she herself admitted) was always distant from such groups:

37 Josephine Butler in later life

> I have lived among the middle and lower classes. I know nothing of fashionable society or aristocracy or grand London people. The few times I have been among them, I found they did not understand my language, nor I theirs.

> Josephine Butler to Mr Rutson, May 1868

When James Stansfeld (a former Liberal cabinet minister) took over the leadership of the crusade in 1874, Josephine moved increasingly into international work – opposing state-regulated prostitution overseas. Stansfeld organised a successful parliamentary inquiry which ultimately got the Acts suspended in 1883, and abolished in 1886. There is no doubt that Josephine Butler's idealism and energy were essential to get the crusade moving. But before success could be complete, her unusual qualities needed to be supplemented by a leadership with rather different skills.

So what are we to make of this remarkable woman? Our own generation is becoming almost as preoccupied as hers was with the state's threats to individual liberty, and we share her concern for women's rights. We too are preoccupied with the search for satisfactory relations between the sexes, and so in some ways we find in her a precursor – a pioneer of new and more enlightened attitudes to women's social role. This is particularly so with her insistence on promoting women's emancipation only through encouraging co-operation rather than antagonism between the sexes.

On the other hand, we are brought up short by her mystical visions and voices, by her intense hostility to birth-control, and by her insistence that when considerations of health and morality conflict, it is health which must give way. And we find in her career – as in that of many Victorian reformers – an uncongenial and ruthless preparedness to divide humanity into black and white, sheep and goats. William James, in his *Varieties of Religious Experience*, described how 'sensitiveness and narrowness, when they occur together, as they often do, require above all things a simplified world to dwell in'. Young radicals of the 1970s may find some of Josephine's political attitudes congenial. Yet they will be more repelled than most by some of her attitudes on other questions. For example, one of the commissioners in 1871 suggested to her that the Contagious Diseases Acts were necessary if only to protect innocent offspring from venereal disease, however sinful the parents might have been. Who would now acquiesce in her reply?

> It is the law of nature that children should suffer for the sins of their parents, and I do not think that we can venture by legislative measures to interfere with that law, but that we may very much prevent the sufferings of infants by moral influences exercised on those who transmit to them this evil.

This was an individualism at least as doctrinaire as that of John Stuart Mill, who also testified against the Acts before the 1871 commission. It was not, of course, a policy which a practical politician could endorse. R. A. Butler, the Conservative politician, comes from the same family as Josephine and greatly admired her. But he admits in his autobiography that practical considerations forced him – when drafting his Street Offences Act as Home Secretary in 1959 – to repudiate her rigid insistence on the equal treatment of the prostitute and her male client.

So our assessment of Josephine Butler must inevitably be complex. She was 'eminently Victorian' in some respects, but in other ways she seems decidedly modern. Her various preoccupations pull us in contrary directions. But we can all agree that she was a remarkably interesting and courageous woman – and in the context of this series, a fitting representative of her sex.

Brian Harrison

BUTLER, J. *Personal reminiscences of a great crusade* H. Marshall, 1896.
BUTLER, J. *Recollections of George Butler* Bristol: J. W. Arrowsmith, n.d.
BUTLER, J. ed. *Woman's work and woman's culture : a series of essays* Macmillan, 1869.
ACTON, W. *Prostitution* John Churchill, 1857; F. Cass, n.e. of 1870 edition 1972.
BELL, E. M. *Josephine Butler* Constable, 1962.
PETRIE, G. *A singular iniquity : the campaigns of Josephine Butler* Macmillan, 1871.

GEORGE HOWELL

As a young man George Howell had three ambitions: to speak in the Exeter Hall; to write a book: and to become a Member of Parliament. Despite his lowly origins he achieved them all.

George was born in Somerset in 1833. His father was a sub-contractor employed in great construction projects carried on in the west country at the end of the industrial revolution. It was a hard life and one haunted by fear of severe poverty if trade should fall away or sickness come. Like many early Victorian families it was easier to classify the Howells by their standards – which were firmly maintained – than by their social location – which was fluid and uncertain. George used to recall his years on the construction sites with a mix of filial piety and of self-congratulation:

38 George Howell (1833–1910)

> With all my experience during these years, I was spared that villainous knowledge which depraves. Scenes of revelry and riot, of debauchery and vice, filthy language, ribaldry, and coarse oaths I seldom heard, and then only with disgust – as foreign to my nature and to my bringing up. All this I owe to my home influence and perhaps to my own innate nature.
>
> F. M. Leventhal *Respectable Radical : George Howell and the Working Class Politics*

Howell senior's health broke down. Young George struck out on his own and paid his first visit to London in 1851. He attended Evangelical gatherings in the Exeter Hall, but most of his spare time was spent at the Great Exhibition. The attractions of London proved irresistible. He settled there in 1854 in search of fame through self-improvement. He attended lectures by T. H. Huxley and other 'advanced' men. He had already exchanged Anglicanism for Wesleyan Methodism; in London he discarded Methodism in favour of secularism and positivism. He supported himself, by working as a bricklayer. If the Chapel was weak in London, so was the trade union lodge. But in 1859 a great struggle began in the London building trade which had an immense importance for the subsequent history of British labour, and for the career of George Howell.

The building workers demanded the nine hour day. The Master Builders replied by locking out the men and insisting that they should sign 'the document' – a pledge not to join a trade union. The Masters appealed to public opinion.

> The men who have been in our employ have been applying the wages which we pay to treacherously supply the mutiny against us. They keep pickets in their nightly pay whose task it is to threaten, to intimidate and to spy. These pickets send reports to a central inquisition which deals out vengeance and engages in other un-English practices. Under these circumstances we have no choice but to stop all employment until the men give up their absurd and ruinous demands and promise to renounce the conspiracy in which they are engaged. If we are cruel, we would be cruel only to be kind.
> *Reynolds News* August 1859

Under altered forms the struggle in the London building trades lasted for nearly three years. It ended in strengthening trade unionism at every point. The builders followed the example of the engineers and adopted the principles of a 'new model'. Unions were to be national rather than local. A heavy emphasis was to be placed upon their function as friendly societies. The subscription was high, but so were the out of work, sickness and other benefits. The trade policy was based on restricting the supply of labour by limiting the number of apprentices: by opposing systematic over-time: by trying to shorten the working day: by controlling work load and by encouraging emigration. It asked the employers to recognise the union in the interests of industrial order and progress. It was not a school of war, but a school in which workmen might listen to the words of the lecturer and become respectful and respected. Industry, chastity and sobriety were insisted upon. George Howell was closely identified with the spirit and the practice of this 'new model'. He was perfectly qualified by character and training to serve as one of the great men of business who now emerged as the first established bureaucracy in the history of world labour. Unfortunately for him, the bricklayers found a very adequate full-time officer in Edwin Coulson. There were no jobs to be had on the new Labour paper, the *Bee-hive*. Howell did, indeed, manage to gain office in the newly established London Trades Council, but this was a part-time appointment and he was forced to relinquish it when he was victimised by the Master Builders. Bitterly disappointed in all his hopes, Howell was effectively driven out of the metropolis. But new movements and new institutions soon created opportunities which allowed him to return. The new model unionism peculiarly belonged to the 'pompous trades and proud mechanics', but these aristocrats of labour had more generosity and more vision than is sometimes suggested. In the early sixties they showed a sincere interest in the fate of democracy and nationality in Poland, Italy and the United States. The American Civil War was fought vicariously in England – with the bulk of the upper and middle classes favouring the Confederacy while the workers increasingly identified with Abraham Lincoln. In March, 1863, Howell was called back to London to share the platform with John Bright at a great meeting at the St James' Hall in support of the American Union and the emancipation of the slaves. Bright, from the chair, delivered the keynote speech.

> Now take the two sections of the country which are engaged in this fearful struggle. In the one labour is honoured more than elsewhere in the world. In the other it is degraded. The labourer is made a chattel. He is no more his own than the horse that drags a carriage through the next street: nor is his wife, nor is his child, nor is anything that is his, his own.
>
> You wish the freedom of your country. You wish it for yourselves. You strive for it in many ways. Do not then give the hand of fellowship to the worst foes of freedom that the world has ever seen, and do not, I beseech you, bring down a curse upon your cause which no after penitence can ever lift from it. You will not do this. I have faith in you. Impartial history will tell that, when your statesmen were hostile or coldly neutral, when many of your rich men were corrupt, when your press – which ought to have instructed and de-fended – was mainly written to betray, the fate of a Contin-ent and its vast population being in peril, you clung to free-dom with an unfaltering trust that God in His infinite mercy will make it the heritage of all his children.
>
> G. M. Trevelyan *John Bright*

Howell recalled this meeting as a great turning point in the history of English Labour and of English democracy. He wrote to Bright:

> Your presence with us on the American question gave a great impetus to the political tendencies of the Unions, and aided us in our endeavours to bring them into the political arena.

Among those in the great audience at the St James' Hall was Karl Marx. Like Howell, Marx welcomed the entry of the trade unions into the political arena. But what he dreaded was that they would subordinate themselves to Bright, the 'umble and 'omely hero of middle class radicalism. A year later the International Work-ing Men's Association was founded. Howell joined its General Council. Marx drafted its rules and its inaugural address.

> To conquer political power has become the great duty of the working classes. They seem to have comprehended this, for in England, Germany, Italy and France there have taken place simultaneous revivals, and simultaneous efforts are being made at the political reorganisation of the working man's party.

39 Manhood Suffrage (*Punch* cartoon, 1866). Mr Punch, addressing a labour aristocrat: 'Do you mean to say, my friend, that *that* is the sort of manhood you wish to be mixed up with?'

This became Howell's opportunity. In 1865 he became full-time Secretary of the newly established Reform League. The League reduced the People's Charter to two points: universal manhood suffrage and vote by ballot. In the event, the Reform League failed to give complete satisfaction either to Bright or to Marx. As against Bright, it insisted on maintaining its programmatic and organisational independence. Howell and his friends would not agree to replace the demand for manhood suffrage with the more modest claim for household suffrage. They could not see their way to entering Brights' middle class Reform Union, but like the Chartists before them they felt the need to maintain their class identity. However, the League was not independent enough to suit Marx. His anxieties were understandable. While Howell and Marx agreed that the great task was 'the conquest of political power by the working class' that did not understand each other, Howell gave sincere assurances that he wanted to have nothing to do with dictatorship of the proletariat.

> I have never been, and never shall be, an advocate for merely changing our masters. I want neither aristocratic rule, nor the rule of the middle classes, nor the rule of the working classes. I want a government of the entire people – where wealth and intellect will have its fair share of power – no more.
>
> Howell to W. Morrison MP, November 1868

One of Howell's first tasks as Secretary of the Reform League was to draft an Appeal to Trade Unionists.

> Let us once be able to maintain by the force of intellect and truth our right as workmen in that House, and depend upon it we shall rise in the social scale.
>
> R. Harrison *Before the Socialists*

The better organised and more politically conscious workmen of mid-Victorian England had given up the millennial hopes of Robert Owen and the fierce language of Chartists who thought, not of rising in the social scale, but having done with the social scale altogether. No such vengeful thoughts crossed the mind of George Howell or his supporters as they crowded the Theatre Royal to hear Miss Nellie Nesbitt in 1866 giving her rendering of 'Don't Stop, Let "Progress" be the Word'!

> For Queen and for Country together we'll stand
> And you'll find us both loyal and true,
> And if any danger should threaten our land,
> As of old we shall know what to do:—
>
> We'll follow the plough or we'll follow the drum,
> But don't try to fetter our will,
> For no matter how good the time that has come
> We mean to have a better time still.
>
> *Before the Socialists*

'For Queen and for Country together we'll stand . . . but don't try to fetter our will'. This was a mix which was at once reassuring and frightening to the ruling classes. If the workmen had no intention of using the vote to hit property on the head, they might become very ugly indeed if their claim to political equality was too long defied. In July 1866 the Government had to appeal to Howell and his friends to help restore order in Hyde Park after a crowd had broken down the railings. In February 1867, the Government announced that it would be unable to maintain order if Howell organised a monster demonstration. Accordingly the Reform League began to organise its own constabulary. Finally, in May 1867 the Government was foolish enough to once more deny the League. It announced that it would resist the holding of a demonstration in Hyde Park. On the morning of 6 May 1867, *The Times* commented:

> Today more than on any other occasion since the pitiable episode of 1848 . . .

(the reference is to the celebrated failure of the Chartist demonstration of 10 April in that year.)

> . . . the working men of London are on trial. They are invited to band themselves together and offer a public defiance

40 'Vox Populi (?)' or, A Bully that must be put down. Cartoon from *The Tomahawk,* 1867, satirising the urban workman demanding enfranchisement

VOX POPULI

to the constitutional authorities, to violate the law, and the plainly defined rights of the Crown, to insult the House of Commons, to annoy and outrage the upper and middle classes, and to jeopardise the peace of the Metropolis.

But it was all to no avail. If there were 10,000 police and military around the Park there were 100,000 working class reformers converging upon it. It was left to the President of the Reform League to sum up and in doing so to disclose what it was that had induced such eminently respectable and well disposed citizens as Howell and himself to risk a collision with authority. Howell, as Secretary, recorded his President's remarks in the Minutes, 8 May 1867.

> The Government gave them all to understand that they had an enormous array of military force – infantry, cavalry, and artillery (laughter) – yes, artillery at the railway stations – cutlasses without end at Scotland Yard, batons fabricated at Woolwich and special constables (great laughter) – ridiculous and absurd as they were, sworn in all directions. Supposing he had given way and issued an address requesting the men of London, in consequence of the powerful appeal of Mr Gladstone on Friday, not to go to the Park. Many of them would not have gone, but many of them would, in bad temper, under the impression that they had been doubly dealt with, and that there had been something in the shade of treachery, and riot and tumult would have inevitably occurred. It was impossible to conceive a more marked contrast than was presented last Monday between the feebly insulting conduct of the Government and the ruling classes, and the admirable, orderly, peaceable, self-possessed, and dignified conduct of the people. (Loud cheers.) It was a great moral triumph – a triumph greater than any language of his could express.

And so it was! Within a few days Mr Disraeli had accepted an amendment which doubled the number to be enfranchised. By August the Reform Bill had become law.

The question now was what would the newly enfranchised workers do with the votes which they had won? They had numbers – although not overwhelming numbers. They had grievances: notably with respect to the law relating to trade unions. They had, in the Reform League, the most perfect political organisation yet created by working people. But Howell, as Secretary of the League, found that funds were low. Wealthy middle class sympathisers no longer opened their purses. At first he complained bitterly about what he termed the 'iron power' of capital. Then he secretly agreed to manage a special fund provided for the League by Samuel Morley, a great textile manufacturer, and Liberal MP. Under conditions of secrecy, Morley gave Howell £1,900 to try and wrest small boroughs from the Tories. Labour issues were to be given no special prominence and Labour candidates who threatened to split the anti-Tory vote were to be discouraged and put down. It worked splendidly for Mr Gladstone. It helped to give him such a large majority that he became more than usually insensitive to the claims of organised Labour!

At the last moment Howell offered himself as a candidate in the improbable constituency of Aylesbury. True to his agreement with Morley his election address made no reference to the grievances of trade unions. He favoured, so he said, every effort to economise on national expenditure. He invited the Whig, Rothschild, to run with him in a double member constituency instead of making a compact with the Tory. Rothschild refused to do so. The Liberal Whip, Glyn, a banker and railway magnate, told Mr Gladstone

> Howell had no chance at Aylesbury, but I am very much disappointed at the line Rothschild has taken. He has refused today to combine or act and in strong terms. I have done all I can. Howell is a true man and has been of great use to me. He has unfortunately chosen the wrong place and went to Aylesbury against my advice – a stranger cannot win there and Rothschild's treatment has done harm and will create bad feeling.

In November 1868 the satirical journal *Judy* published a cartoon entitled: 'The underground railway to Westminster'. The station master announced to a crowd of carpenters and bricklayers:

> No third class can travel! Why must I repeat?
> Some Lord or some swell has bespoke every seat.
> So 'step it' my hearties! Pack off with your tools.
> Directors have power to alter their rules.

41 'No third class!' Cartoon from *Judy* (short-lived sister magazine of *Punch*), 1868

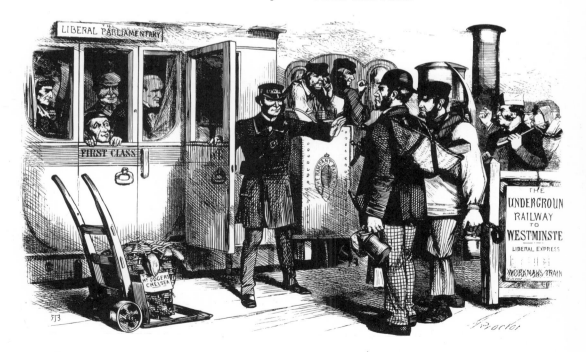

The Liberal victory in the General Election of 1868 left Howell in a grave dilemma. Samuel Morley and other parliamentarians came to his aid. They set him up as an election agent. Unfortunately, the organised workers were, by 1869, committed to Labour representation and refused to interest themselves in merely registering Liberal voters. Howell proposed to his patrons:

> that the gentlemen who have been generous enough to give me this start should consent that I should have the remainder of the money to purchase a little business. I own I don't like trusting entirely to politics for one's bread. It lessens a man's influence and independence – I don't want to be a mere political hack open to every engagement, if only it brings in money.
>
> Howell to J. Stansfeld MP November 1869

But what exactly did Howell understand by 'independence' and by 'influence'? In the same letter he continued:

> If the money is placed at my disposal I will as truly and fairly try to carry out to the very letter the original intention of the *subscribers*. I hope, sir, neither you nor Mr Morley nor Mr Glyn will feel offended at this request. It is not because I want to handle the money, but because I think that by this means I may be still more useful.
>
> I want to be independent amongst my own class and I can be if this is done. For I cannot always lend myself to all the foolish movements of working men.

Mr Morley was ready to give Howell £350 for this purpose. What he would not agree to was that Howell should adopt a superior person attitude to 'all the foolish movements of working men'. Howell would be no use to the 'subscriber' if he did that! On the contrary, when workmen quarrelled with the Liberal Government over its failure to recognise the legality of trade unionism, and its failure to afford protection to trade unions against actions for damages by employers and dishonest dealings by officials, Howell was not expected to distance himself from his fellow workmen. Quite the reverse! He was expected to secure a leading position the better to moderate working class demands. And at first he succeeded brilliantly. In 1869 he was appointed the first Secretary of the newly established Trades Union Congress. And so it was, that in 1871 he found himself on the one hand accountable to the TUC and expected to get rid of repressive legislation, and on the other in honour bound to the Liberal Government which had introduced the very legislation of which the TUC complained!

Instead of obeying his instructions and organising mass demonstrations against the Administration, he engaged in private discussions with the law officers of the Crown.

I find that I win respect from such men as Vernon Harcourt and Henry James by the way which I meet them even in the discussion of law and discuss some of its abstract principles.

Alas the TUC was not interested in the command which its secretary showed of law and 'its abstract principles'. Its concern was with the fact that the wives of agricultural labourers were being sent to prison for saying 'boo' to a blackleg. It insisted that Howell's amending measure, supported by 'advanced' and 'well-disposed' Liberals, failed to legalise peaceful picketing. It ordered Howell as Secretary of the Parliamentary Committee, to stop intriguing in the lobbies and to mobilise mass pressure upon Mr Gladstone and his colleagues. Howell had to obey. The opposition of organised Labour to the Liberals was certainly one factor in the fall of Gladstone in 1874 and the advent of Disraeli's second administration. Disraeli promptly acknowledged the power and importance of trade union opinion by meeting all the essential demands of the TUC. Paradoxically this removed the one obstacle in the way of Howell making an honest man of himself. Disraeli demolished the barrier which separated organised Labour from the Liberal parliamentarians. Howell resigned his secretaryship of the TUC and devoted himself to writing potted histories of the Labour Movement and digests of the Labour laws. Having established his claim to literary fame, he offered his services to constituencies as a Liberal-Labour candidate. After some disappointments, he stood in North East Bethnal Green in 1885. The result of the poll was announced in late November.

Howell, George	(Liberal)	3095
Mayne, George Dawson	(Con.)	1844
	Liberal majority	1251

Howell had now achieved his third and greatest ambition, but it brought him little comfort. He might be a recognised Labour leader, but members of the newly established socialist organisations recalled Marx's observation:

It is an honour *not* to be a recognised Labour leader. Almost all the recognised English labour leaders are sold to Gladstone, Dilke and Morley.

Howell might up-stage his socialist critics by reminding them that he had known Marx and had actually worked with him in the International. But he had not been a socialist in those days; and he was decidedly anti-socialist now. A champion of the old aristocratic craft unions, he despised and feared the new unionism of the unskilled which arose in the late eighteen eighties. He opposed the demand for the legal limitation of the working day to eight hours.

I hold that it would be impracticable; that it would be a repressive and inconvenient restraint upon liberty; that it would lead to a dictatorship of inspectors of factories, offices and workshops; and that, if it did not, it would be inoperative. The demand for more law indicates a decadence of manhood, an absence of self-restraint. It marks an epoch of dependence, the sure precursor of decay in men and nations.

Howell 'Liberty for Labour' in *A Plea for Liberty* 1891, T. Mackay (ed.)

Howell had always believed that liberty was the absence of restraint by the state. It was his sincere conviction about such matters which helped to make possible his secret dealings with great employers and Liberal politicians.

In 1895 Howell lost Bethnal Green to an Indian standing as a Conservative. To his best friend he wrote:

After ten years hard labour in Parliament I was kicked out by a black man, a stranger from India, one not known in the constituency or in public life.

Respectable Radical

If being 'eminently Victorian' means exhibiting attitudes which belong exclusively to Victorian times, then George Howell is not a man of the required type. The problem of securing a satisfactory legal status for trade unionism, which Howell and his generation thought they had solved, has re-emerged. The TUC still has very much the same structure as it had a hundred years ago. And some of Howell's successors have spoken and behaved much as he did. But the Victorian quality of Howell's life can be pointed out by noticing how he extends the ideals or enriches the insights of other of his contemporaries who have been studied in this series. In the new model union, for example, one finds Samuel Smiles gospel of self-help restated in collective rather than personal terms. Again Howell's political behaviour suggests that Walter Bagehot may have over-worked the idea of deference as the key to incorporating workmen within the English Constitution. Workmen might be active and not just passive citizens without any risk to the political culture. This was possible in Victorian Britain so long as they were ready to adopt middle class aspirations for themselves and their children: to seek progress, in other words, but only within the conditions of order.

Royden Harrison

COLLINS, H. and ABRAMSKY, C. *Karl Marx and the British Labour Movement* Macmillan, 1965.

HANHAM, H. J. *Elections and party management* Longman, 1959.

HARRISON, R. *Before the Socialists* Routledge and Kegan Paul, 1965.

LEVENTHAL, F. M. *Respectable Radical: George Howell and Victorian working class politics* Weidenfeld and Nicolson, 1971.

2

ARTISTS OF THE AGE

by Basil Taylor

The following text is a revised version of the material contained in the earlier, smaller BBC publication *Artists of the Victorian Age,* written by Basil Taylor to accompany the original broadcasts. It does not attempt to provide a comprehensive conspectus of painting of the period, but rather, concentrates on ten well-known artists of the age.

The pairing of the artists has been influenced by varying considerations. Frith and Watts, for instance, exemplify the contrast between two different areas of nineteenth-century art and taste. Rossetti and Burne-Jones, so distinct in their personalities and modes of life, developed similar subjects and interests along quite different channels.

A PERIOD OF CHANGE

The word Victorian cannot as a historical definition be usefully applied to painting so as to indicate or even suggest a compatibility of style, subject and artistic purpose, for in the sixty-five year span of the Queen's reign, Turner made his last works, Holman Hunt painted *The Scapegoat* (**59**), and Whistler composed his *Arrangement in Grey and Black, No. 1* (**105**). The word can be used to define a term of years, but there was a period of little more than fifteen years between 1850 and 1865 when the art of a majority of the most talented painters showed a sufficient community of method and aim to be called Victorian in a qualitative sense.

One reason for the extraordinary variety of pictorial style and subject of the painting in the Queen's reign is simply the unprecedented social and cultural complexity which developed in the nineteenth century. The period witnessed a change which necessarily occurs in a human population, not only when it expands so dynamically, but when the occupations, experience and environment of its members become more diverse, when social and political institutions are rapidly democratised, and the spread of general education creates a large, literate, but still unsophisticated class. With respect to the history of painting, what mattered was not just the qualities of this social change, but the simple fact that an increasing ratio of the population could become consumers of art. (The development in the technology of communications, especially through the camera, and the scope of pictorial reproduction, also had a most important effect in enlarging public response to the visual arts.)

To take a familiar example, Frith's prosperity and fame as a painter of modern life, only rivalled in the eighteenth century by the success of Hogarth and his 'modern moral' prints, was advanced not only by the innumerable reproductions of his pictures such as *Derby Day* (**66**) and *The Railway Station* (**82**), but by the fact that these went into so many families which before would have not had such a contact with the work of a living and eminent painter.

Despite the differences of purpose and style which are exemplified in Holman Hunt's image of a goat on the shore of the Dead Sea, Frith's record of holidaymakers on Ramsgate beach, some earnest allegory by Watts, or Beardsley's *Lacedaemonian Ambassadors,* there were certain prevalent convictions which often, if not always, went together, such as a devotion to the historical past and the pursuit of natural truth.

A great body of Victorian art was, to use an approximate term, naturalistic. The determination of so many artists scrupulously to be guided by the appearance of nature and its physical form, and to represent things accurately, seeking likeness to life, was also a criterion constantly and earnestly invoked by most Victorian critics, and with a most elaborate justification and passionate eloquence by Ruskin. In his writings, as in the pictures of Holman Hunt, for instance, the ideal of truth to nature was pursued with an unshakeable moral certitude. There is a parallel to be followed between pictorial naturalism in its various manifestations and the pursuit of exact, verifiable knowledge and information in other spheres of Victorian culture, such as the prevailing confidence in scientific method and benefit, the developing mastery of technology, and the acceptance by many of the prospect of human perfectibility within a general pattern of progress. Ruskin certainly believed, not only that art had, like everything, been subject to continuous improvement, but that artistic perfection was within sight and grasp. History was among the fields of study to which a scientific, or quasi-scientific, method was applied, supported by a wider passion for the past, and the tendency among educated people to think historically about all matters of concern. This obsessive concern with history, one of the most obvious marks of the period's intellectual activity, accounts for the abundance of both pictures and literature in which the physical attributes of another age are carefully detailed. It was possible for a Victorian painter, as it never has been since 1900, to be in the avant garde *and* to take his style, subjects and imagery from a past time. No artist in this country, not even Whistler, stated anything like the absolute demand made by Courbet in France that the artist should fix his attention upon the present and paint only what nineteenth-century eyes could see.

Life and work in the painters' studios did not, perhaps, change very much in essence from what it had commonly been for several centuries, except that the life-style of a few exceptionally prosperous Victorian artists, Leighton for example, was as unprecedented in its luxurious grandeur as was the quality of their public reputation. However, the conditions which surrounded and supported the painter's practice, the professional ambience, changed profoundly, and within a few decades, during the nineteenth century. As late as 1830 sophisticated and advanced training in the visual arts was still only to be had in one national school, the Royal Academy, and from a few private sources. By 1880 there was a network of art schools, headed by the institution since known as the Royal College of Art, hardly different in its extent from the system in being today, and the study of drawing had also been generally introduced into schools of elementary education. The methods of imitative drawing which were in all fields of teaching orthodox in mid-Victorian England had a great, if informal and indeterminate, influence upon the appreciation of pictorial and ornamental art.

There was a proliferation of exhibiting societies to serve the needs and aspirations of a relatively enlarged population of painters, sculptors and graphic artists, and an equally significant increase in the number of art dealers conducting their affairs much as they do today. In 1830 the only national collection of art accessible to everyone was the British Museum; by the end of the century nearly all our great public museums and galleries were in being, and with numerous new provincial museums enabled the entire populace to be educated and refined by art, as a Ruskin or a Watts believed they should be. The number of professional critics writing with some specialised knowledge and experience about the visual arts was greater than before and, indeed, more space was given in newspapers and magazines for reviews than their successors enjoy nowadays. There was a large and developing literature of painting and by the end of the century several art magazines with impressive circulations serving the interests of artists and laymen. The academic study of art history was not, in all respects, the creation of this time, but the academic pursuit of it and much of its basic methodology was a nineteenth-century product. This literary and scholarly activity was fostered by, and could hardly have developed without the invention and refinement of photography and the development of photo-mechanical techniques which made cheap and effective reproduction commonplace, enormously enriching the visual experience even of those people with modest means.

With a characteristic energy and conviction the Victorians created what we would call 'the art world', and constructed it in very much the same shape that it possesses today. It was not merely to exploit, communicate and interpret the art of painting, but quite fundamentally influence the painter's practice and bring the experience of art with a new sense of purpose into the social fabric.

GAUNT, W. *The aesthetic adventure* Cape, 1945. o.p.

GAUNT, W. *The pre-Raphaelite tragedy* Cape, 1942. o.p.

GAUNT, W. *The restless century : painting in Britain 1800-1900* Phaidon Press, 1972.

HUBBARD, H. *A hundred years of British painting 1851-1951* Longman, 1951. o.p.

HUNT, J. D. *The pre-Raphaelite imagination 1848-1900* Routledge and Kegan Paul, 1968.

IRONSIDE, R. and GERE, J. *Pre-Raphaelite painters* Phaidon, 1948. o.p.

MAAS, J. *Victorian painters* Barrie and Rockliff, 1969.

REYNOLDS, G. *Painters of the Victorian scene* Batsford, 1953. o.p.

REYNOLDS, G. *Victorian painting* Studio Vista, 1966. o.p.

ROTHENSTEIN, J. *Artists of the 1890's* Routledge and Kegan Paul, 1928. o.p.

STALEY, A. *The pre-Raphaelite landscape* Clarendon Press, 1973.

For further reading see also books listed under individual artists on pages 110-21.

William Mulready (1786–1863)

Daniel Maclise (1806–70)

These painters were both firmly established in their practice and in public esteem before the accession of the Queen in 1837; Mulready had been elected RA in 1816, and Maclise became an associate member of the Academy in 1835. Although they produced thereafter pictures which, in style and content, seem to typify very exactly the most popular and acceptable art of mid-Victorian England, their work also demonstrates that such painting was an extension of various traditions stretching back over three or four generations into the eighteenth century. And the professional problems and hazards which faced two individuals, so different in temperament and aspiration, were, no less, the same as those their predecessors had encountered.

Having started as a landscape painter, Mulready was to limit himself, with an occasional excursion into subjects taken from literature, to modest and familiar domestic themes involving equally familiar sentiments or moral ideas similar to those treated earlier by Francis Wheatley and George Morland. Even the sentiment or the moral was reticently expressed, and Ruskin criticised him on one occasion for being a painter of 'Nothing', of insufficiently important matters. The latter acknowledged, nevertheless, Mulready's mastery of a naturalistic style, that conscientious and disciplined naturalism which is to be found as often in his penetrating, sensitive drawings as in pictures such as *Choosing the Wedding Gown* (**69**), or *Train up a child in the way he should go. . . .* (**56**). He is one of those artists who show that the Pre-Raphaelite naturalism of Holman Hunt and Millais had been anticipated by older painters, and was more original and individual for its technique than for its pursuit of factual accuracy. Mulready studied the structure of a chair or a tree, or the physical actions of the human body, with a concentration and sympathy which made him not only one of the most penetrating and sensitive English draughtsmen, but an important teacher and consultant for many younger artists.

By contrast with Mulready's uneventful and unspectacular life, Maclise pursued his practice as the type of public figure which Millais and Leighton were subsequently to be, and which Reynolds had been in the eighteenth century. Like Reynolds, Maclise was dissatisfied not simply with the achievement of English art, but with the insufficient opportunities provided by patronage here for those painters with the ambition to work in the highest reaches of art. Like Reynolds, he quickly found an entry into high society, as well as enjoying the company and support of writers and intellectuals: Dickens and Thackeray, the actor Macready, Bulwer

Lytton, politician as well as novelist, and the hostess Lady Blessington, were among his wide company of friends. He applied a remarkable technical facility to the most demanding subjects, choosing them from passages in literature and from events in the Bible and history which involved a complex of human action and moments of the greatest dramatic or emotional tension – *The Play Scene in Hamlet* (**53**), for example, and *The Death of Nelson* (**54**) – one of the two vast compositions which he made for the new Palace of Westminster. Maclise's art provides one of the most obvious instances of a problem which commonly faced the artists of this period – a struggle to reconcile three demands, all of which seemed so important: the compulsion to be truthful, in terms of a naturalistic style, to the facts of the physical world and of all that could be discovered by conscientious research about the events of history; a desire to achieve the artistic grandeur and dignity of the masters of the past, and the conviction that art should be a source of moral and spiritual enlightenment.

Mulready first studied art with the sculptor Thomas Banks and in 1800 entered the Royal Academy schools, where in later years he was himself to become one of its most conscientious and admired teachers. He was also instructed by the water-colour painter John Varley, whose sister he married, and who encouraged him in his early practice as a landscape painter. By 1810 he was exhibiting the general subjects with which his name was chiefly associated, and thereafter he was only occasionally to depart from this type of subject into the treatment of subjects taken from literature, such as *The Seven Ages of Man* (**57**). In 1840 he designed for Rowland Hill the first penny postage decorative envelope. He was awarded the Legion of Honour for a group of works he exhibited in Paris in 1855.

STEPHENS, F. G. *Memorials of William Mulready* (Illustrated biographies of the great artists) Sampson Low, 1867.
VICTORIA AND ALBERT MUSEUM *Drawings by William Mulready* ed. Anne Rorimer. Victoria and Albert Museum, 1972.

Maclise was born and educated in Cork, coming to London in 1827 and entering the Royal Academy schools a year later. He first exhibited portrait drawings as well as history pictures. Two years before becoming a Royal Academician, he was introduced to Dickens, who remained a devoted friend for the rest of his life; Maclise illustrated *The Cricket on the Hearth* and *The Chimes*. In 1844 he visited Paris, this being the first of several expeditions into Europe which had a strong influence upon his artistic ideas as well as his practice. His part in the decoration of the new Palace of Westminster began about 1845, and five years later he started work on

42 *William Mulready* (detail) by John Linnell. National Portrait Gallery, London

43 *Daniel Maclise* (detail) by Edward Matthew Ward. National Portrait Gallery, London

the two frescoes devoted to Waterloo and Trafalgar, which were finished in 1861 and 1865 respectively, and which were to be not only his largest and most elaborate compositions, but the maturing of those artistic principles which he had developed earlier in subjects drawn from a wide range of literary, biblical and historical sources. In his later years, and under the pressure of hypochondria, he withdrew into a more secluded and inactive life.

ARTS COUNCIL OF GREAT BRITAIN *Daniel Maclise 1806-1870: catalogue of an exhibition held at the National Portrait Gallery, London, 3 March – 16 April 1972*. Arts Council, 1972.

O'DRISCOLL, W. J. *A memoir of Daniel Maclise, R. A.* Longman, Green, 1871.

William Holman Hunt (1827–1910)

John Everett Millais (1829–96)

These painters were, with Rossetti, the chief members of the Pre-Raphaelite Brotherhood, that company of seven young men who, in 1848, formed a partnership dedicated to the reform and renewal of English art, believing that it had declined into a state of aesthetic and spiritual triviality. Until his death, Hunt was the one member of the group whose work retained the most distinctive characteristics of Pre-Raphaelite style. He remained faithful to the avowed principles which the Brotherhood had striven to promote in the five years of its collective existence, not only in his practice, but by defending his own interpretation of their ideals against what he considered to have been the defection of former colleagues, and artistic challenges from other directions, such as impressionism. It is characteristic of Hunt that he should have called his autobiography *Pre-Raphaelitism and the Pre-Raphaelite Brotherhood*, and that the book should not only be an apology for his own art, but a latterday manifesto for a campaign fought fifty years before. By temperament and experience he was always an outsider, and it was the obstinate intensity of his convictions, especially his determination to 'paint scrupulously from nature', which gave his best pictures their enduring force. He also stuck to the Brotherhood's original will to paint subjects of the most serious significance, and in these pictures to seek the spiritual centre of the subject. In his major paintings, whether they dealt with modern life, like *The*

Awakening Conscience (**63**), or treated Biblical themes, like *The Light of the World* (**62**) and *The Scapegoat* (**59**), or were derived from literature, as in a scene from Bulwer Lytton's *Rienzi*, Hunt constructed an elaborate body of symbols and treated these symbolic elements with that fastidious naturalism, which seemed to him, as it did to Ruskin, not only ethically desirable, but to be an artistic expression of the modern spirit in an age committed to exact observation in the scrutiny of nature or the study of the past. (The most obvious sign of this faith was his decision to paint his Biblical subjects whenever possible at the original sites in the Holy Land, so as to ensure their spiritual depth and authenticity.) Hunt was never a fluent, confident, or indeed a productive artist. His sense of 'a want of masterliness' which he experienced in his youth remained with him to the end of his active life and perhaps helped to provoke those technical problems and crises which so often hindered his progress.

Millais, by contrast, is one of the striking instances in the history of art of precocious talent and technical facility, for he achieved immediately that skill with which he managed the intricate details of his *Ophelia* (**68**) or the *Christ in the House of His Parents* (**72**). After the critical assaults upon his work in the first years of the Brotherhood, the advance of his success was never stayed. By 1860 he had abandoned both the pictorial style and the working methods of his Pre-Raphaelite pictures. Thereafter his pictures were no less dependent than before upon an appeal to sentiment and nostalgia, but his expression of human feeling and the spirit of historical times became increasingly broad and vulgar, and was matched by a coarse exploitation of his technical virtuosity. Works such as *The Boyhood of Raleigh* and *Bubbles* brought him not only a financial fortune but a fame and reputation unmatched by any of his contemporaries.

44 *William Holman Hunt* (detail) by Sir William Blake Richmond. National Portrait Gallery, London

Hunt was born in London in modest circumstances, and having first combined the part-time study of drawing with work as a clerk, he entered the Royal Academy schools in 1844, the same year in which he met Millais and four years later Ford Madox Brown and Rossetti. From these associations the Pre-Raphaelite Brotherhood came secretly into being at the end of 1848. The trials and adversities of the next few years encouraged him to consider abandoning art, but by 1852 the sale of *The Hireling Shepherd* (**58**) and *The Light of the World* (**62**) had brought an encouraging change in his fortune. In 1854 he made the first of several visits to the Middle East where, in the Holy Land, *The Scapegoat* (**59**) was started that year, being the first of the Biblical subjects, of which others were *The Finding of the Saviour in the Temple*, *The Shadow of Death* and *The Triumph of the Innocents*. By 1900 his eyesight began to fail, and before his death he had to abandon painting. He never became a Royal Academician, but in 1905, the year he published his autobiography, he was awarded the Order of Merit.

HUNT, H. *Pre-Raphaelitism and the Pre-Raphaelite Brotherhood* Chapman and Hall, 1913.

WALKER ART GALLERY *William Holman Hunt: an exhibition arranged by the Walker Art Gallery, Liverpool, March – April 1969* Walker Art Gallery, 1969.

45 *Sir John Everett Millais* (detail) by William Holman Hunt. National Portrait Gallery, London

Millais entered the Royal Academy schools at the age of eleven and besides winning medals for drawing while still a child, he exhibited his first large composition at the age of sixteen. He was the first member of the Brotherhood to gain public honour, being elected an associate of the Royal Academy in 1853, in spite of the furious criticism of his *Christ in the House of His Parents* (**72**), exhibited there in 1851. In 1853 he visited Scotland with John Ruskin whose wife, Effie, he was to marry two years later. His painting, *The Black Brunswicker*, shown in 1860, finally demonstrated his abandonment of Pre-Raphaelite disciplines. In the 1860s he was to become one of the most prolific book illustrators of that period, providing drawings for novels by Trollope and the poetry of Tennyson. In 1885 he was created a Baronet and, in the last year of his life, served as President of the Royal Academy. Apart from the familiar subject pictures of his later years, he painted portraits of many of his most eminent contemporaries, and also landscapes marked by an intricate, unselective naturalism.

MILLAIS, J. G. *The life and letters of John Everett Millais* Methuen, 1899.

William Powell Frith (1819–1909)

George Frederick Watts (1817–1904)

The work of these two men represents the ideological extremes of Victorian art in relation both to the pretensions of painting and the experience and expectations of the contemporary public.

Frith's career coincided almost exactly with the Queen's reign, for he first exhibited a picture in the year after her accession, a scene from *Twelfth Night*. Like many other painters of the time he published his autobiography, and the book exactly expresses his progress and his identity as an artist. It is primarily a succession of genial anecdotes, simply recounted by an observer who shows little concern for, or curiosity about, the motives of human behaviour. In its description of his own career, Frith concentrates upon the practicalities, upon the means by which he shrewdly managed his affairs as a public entertainer, following the course prescribed for him by the general taste rather than by any compelling ideal. It was a life apparently without shadows or tensions.

He began by treating scenes from popular books and plays – *The Vicar of Wakefield* and *Roderick Random, Kenilworth* and *Barnaby Rudge*, for example – in a simple illustrative manner, literally representing the details of the text. This was a tradition which had emerged in English art during the first half of the eighteenth century and had been developing strongly during the years of Frith's youth as a counterpart to the growing appetite for book illustration in novels, volumes of poetry and periodicals. In the year of the Great Exhibition, 1851, he happened upon the first of those modern subjects with which his name is primarily associated. His discovery, while on holiday, of 'the variety of characters on Ramsgate sands, all sorts and conditions of men and women' led to the picture entitled *Ramsgate Sands : Life at the Seaside* (**80**), which was shown with acclaim at the Academy and eventually acquired by the Queen. From that moment the painter concentrated upon scenes of contemporary life. His *Derby Day* (**66**) of 1856, and *The Railway Station* (**82**) of 1862, were so successful that barriers had to be erected before them in the exhibition to protect the canvases from the press of inquisitive spectators. Like Hogarth, in his modern moral subjects, Frith had realised the simple appeal of the act of recognition, of finding in a picture an image of actuality. He not only acknowledged the priority of his great predecessor, but acknowledged that he lacked one of Hogarth's major talents, for when he described the series of works which he devoted to a gambler's progress, called *The Road to Ruin*, he decided to avoid 'the satirical vein of Hogarth for which I knew myself to be unfitted'. His modest purpose was to show, but not to teach.

For Watts, the painter's purpose was quite simply to 'paint a range of ideas', to enlighten, to educate his fellows, and indeed to seek to improve society's condition by furnishing works of an exemplary nature which would inspire men to live and act virtuously. 'My intention,' he wrote, 'has not been so much to paint pictures that charm the eye as to suggest great thoughts that will appeal to the imagination and the heart and kindle all that is best and noblest in humanity . . . demanding noble aspirations, condemning in the most trenchant manner prevalent vices, and warning in deep tones against lapses from morals and duties.' His picture of *The Good Samaritan,* exhibited in 1850, was painted as an expression of the artist's admiration and respect for a Manchester philanthropist, Thomas Wright, and he offered to provide, without payment to himself, a series of monumental decorations illustrating 'The Progress of the Cosmos' for one of the great public buildings of the Victorian age, Euston Station.

The mode in which this high purpose was to be achieved was allegory; the chief vehicle of his allegorical programmes was the human figure, symbolising, for example, Hope or Time, Love and Death, two of his obsessive themes; the chief artistic inspiration and source for his idealised rendering of the human figure was the art of the High Renaissance, those masters whom he revered and whose vision he re-created in an eclectic style combining Florentine form with Venetian colour. The other side of Watts' achievement, apart from sculpture, was his portraits, and the list of his sitters, most of them men, reads like a roll call of the most eminent Victorians: Lord Shaftesbury, Cardinal Manning, Tennyson, Browning, Carlyle, John Stuart Mill, Matthew Arnold, William Morris...

Frith, who was encouraged by his father to become a painter, was first a student in the private school of Henry Sass and then at the Royal Academy. When he was elected to membership in 1853 he filled the vacancy created by the death of Turner. Thereafter his life was an unbroken thread of success, Dickens being one of his most eminent friends, and the Queen one of his patrons. Although his most successful and famous works had modern themes, he continued until the end of his life to paint the illustrative paintings taken from literature with which his career had begun.

FRITH, W. P. *My autobiography and reminiscences* Bentley and Son, 1887.

46 *Self-portrait* (detail) by William Powell Frith. National Portrait Gallery, London

47 George Frederick Watts

Watts, who said, 'I belong to a family that has gone down in the world', was admitted to the Royal Academy schools at the age of eighteen. A prize he won in 1843 for a design of a work intended for the new Palace of Westminster helped him to spend the next three years in Italy. There he enjoyed the patronage of Lord Holland who, with his wife, became the artist's most ardent and influential supporter. Later, in London, he painted decorations for their residence, Holland House. After failing in his project for the decoration of Euston Station in 1852, he persuaded the benchers of Lincoln's Inn to allow him to embellish their Hall with a fresco, entitled *Justice – A Hemicycle of Law Givers*, these being Moses, Mahomet, Alfred, Charlemagne and Justinian. His most ambitious project was a building, to be called The House of Life, furnished with a vast sequence of frescoes symbolising the history of man and civilisation. Although it was never achieved, many of his oil paintings treat subjects intended for this cycle of works. In the 1860s, the decade in which he gained membership of the Academy, he also began to produce sculpture, his most ambitious work being the equestrian monument called *Physical Energy* which was eventually to go to Cape Town as a memorial to Cecil Rhodes. In the

1880s Watts decided to present a large body of his work to the nation, including a sequence of his portraits, and these were installed during his lifetime in the Tate Gallery and the National Portrait Gallery. The marriage to his first wife, the actress Ellen Terry, was dissolved. He was one of the first individuals to receive the Order of Merit when it was instituted in 1902.

CHAPMAN, R. *The laurel and the thorn – a study of G. F. Watts* Faber, 1945.
WATTS, M. S. *George Frederick Watts : annals of an artist's life* 3 vols. Macmillan, 1912.

Dante Gabriel Rossetti (1828–82)

Edward Burne-Jones (1833–98)

Rossetti, after the uncertainties of a difficult childhood, found in the Pre-Raphaelite Brotherhood an emotional refuge, a company where a freedom and independence prevailed, and where his conviction that 'This is not a religious age. Only the material, the immediately practical, not the divine and spiritual, is important' would have been sympathetically understood and supported. If he was the dominant voice and chief source of imaginative vitality in their enterprise, he was also separated from his comrades by his essentially visionary nature and wayward temperament. In only one or two works, such as *The Girlhood of Mary Virgin*, did he seek to emulate the naturalism of Hunt and Millais, and within a few years he had begun to make his most symbolic works. His refusal to compromise with contemporary realism led him not merely to form images of past times and other worlds – many of his contemporaries did that also in response to the intense historical curiosity of the age – but out of his devotion to the Middle Ages and the ideals of chivalry and romantic love he constructed a dreamland. The legends of the Arthurian court, themes from Dante's writings, and above all that poet's relationship with Beatrice Portinari, took possession of Rossetti both as a painter and as a poet, for, born into a family of poets, the forms and images to be found in his pictures and poems were, like Blake's, inseparable. Into the passionate and yearning relationship of Dante with Beatrice, Rossetti projected his own emotions and imaginings, and the spirit of that romance certainly influenced the tenor of his association with the two women, Elizabeth Siddal and Jane, the wife of William Morris, whom he painted so often as themselves and in the role of various saints and goddesses.

Of all the members of the Brotherhood, Rossetti was to have the strongest and most enduring influence upon the art of the nineteenth century. When in 1857 he gathered around him another group of young men, Morris among them, in order to decorate the Debating Chamber of the new Oxford Union, he gave a fundamental and lasting inspiration to a group who, with their own later associates and disciples, were to be a most powerful force in architecture, decorative design and craftsmanship here and in Europe. His influence was not just to affect those who responded directly to his imagery and sense of Romance, for both Whistler and Beardsley were among his later admirers, and that rigorous critic of Victorian culture, Roger Fry, found in his work a forerunner of the twentieth-century art, because Rossetti, he said, 'possessed the gift of expressive design'.

Burne-Jones was an Oxford disciple of Rossetti who, with Morris, was the most important contemporary influence upon him. A self-taught painter, Burne-Jones 'found himself at five and twenty where he ought to have been at fifteen'. His unwavering refusal to look at the sights and subjects of his own time is explained by his avowal that 'I mean by a picture a beautiful romantic dream of something that never was, never will be – in a light better than any light that ever shone – in a land no one can define or remember, only desire – and the forms divinely beautiful . . .' The numerous decorative designs which he made for the firm of designers and craftsmen which William Morris founded in 1861 not only encouraged the decorative qualities so evident in his later work, but encouraged him to paint on a larger scale than he had done when directly under the influence of Rossetti. He educated himself profoundly in everything which was to bear upon his art, in the literature of the classical, mediaeval and renaissance world, and in the art of those periods, especially of fifteenth and sixteenth-century Italy.

48 *Self-portrait* (detail) by Dante Gabriel Rossetti. National Portrait Gallery, London

Rossetti was born in London, the son of an Italian poet and political refugee. He studied discontentedly at the Royal Academy schools between 1846 and 1848 and thereafter shared a studio with Holman Hunt. His brother, William Michael, who became a critic of art and literature, was also a member of the Pre-Raphaelite Brotherhood. In 1851 he began his association with Elizabeth Siddal which was ended by her death from an overdose of laudanum two years after their marriage in 1862. After the dissolution of the Brotherhood in 1853 he was invited by Ruskin to teach at the recently founded Working Men's College. There and at Oxford he became the leader of another group of young men, and in 1857 he initiated the decoration of the Oxford Union Debating Hall. The association he then formed with William Morris led to his making stained glass designs for the latter's firm, and more importantly to his devoted liaison with Jane Morris. A year later he was commissioned to paint a triptych for Llandaff Cathedral, the subject being *The Seed of David*. His later years were marked by a complex of emotional crises and anxieties; recourse to drugs, shortage of money and the chaos of his domestic affairs. A vicious attack upon his 1871 volume of poems by the critic Robert Williams Buchanan, published under the title 'The Fleshly School of Poetry', led to an attempt at suicide in 1872, and after a brief recovery, a further decline followed in spite of the continuing success of his painting.

DOUGHTY, O. ed. *Poems* Dent, 1957.
DOUGHTY, O. *A Victorian romantic: Dante Gabriel Rossetti* Muller, 1949.
SURTEES, V. *The paintings and drawings of Dante Gabriel Rossetti 1828–1882: a catalogue raisonné* 2 vols. Oxford University Press, 1973.

49 *Sir Edward Burne-Jones* (detail) by Philip Burne-Jones. National Portrait Gallery, London

Burne-Jones was originally destined for a career in the Church and went to Oxford in 1853, where he formed his lifelong association with William Morris, but left three years later without taking his degree. Soon after his first meeting with Rossetti, and under the latter's guidance, he began his career as an artist. In 1857 he was one of those involved in painting the decorations at the Oxford Union. In 1859 he visited Italy for the first time and from that time the impact of Italian art of the fifteenth and sixteenth centuries began to replace the influence of Rossetti. The foundation of Morris's company, Morris, Marshall, Faulkner and Co., initiated him into the field of decorative design, where he was to exercise his inventiveness in a wide variety of products and fields of craftsmanship. As such he was the most talented of Morris's associates and later contributed illustrations to the books published at the Kelmscott Press by his friend. He became an Associate Member of the Royal Academy in 1886 but resigned from it seven years later. He was made a Baronet in 1894.

BURNE-JONES, G. *Memorials of Edward Burne-Jones* Macmillan, 1904
HARRISON, M. *Burne-Jones* Barrie and Jenkins, 1973.

James McNeill Whistler (1834–1903)

Aubrey Beardsley (1872–98)

The contest of Whistler and Ruskin at the trial of 1878, when the painter sued the critic for libel, was an event of symbolic importance in the history of nineteenth-century painting, as well as being a crucial episode in the lives of the two men. The defendant represented the claims of naturalism and the significance of a picture's subject as the vehicle of great ideas; the plaintiff asserted the claim of what a later critic was to call 'significant form'. For Whistler the painter was, as another artist put it, a man with a box of colours, and any works by him primarily arrangements of those colours comparable in their expressive effect with the structure of tones which form a musical composition, a symphony, a nocturne or variations, the very words which he was already using in his titles, whether the theme be the moonlit Thames, a firework display, or Thomas Carlyle. 'Nature,' he was to say, 'is usually wrong and seldom succeeds in producing art'.

By his work, his spirited and often arrogant advocacy of it, and the magnetism of his personality he was the most influential liberating force for those younger artists of independent thought who emerged in the last quarter of the nineteenth century. Being an emigré and an instinctive cosmopolitan, he moved freely between England and France, having studios, schools and a circle of friends in both capitals. Here he was the connecting personality between the Aesthetic Movement and the different tendency towards an art of modern life represented by his pupil Sickert and other members of the New English Art Club founded in 1886. His taste in the art of the past was fastidious and advanced; he was among those who were rediscovering Velasquez and collecting the decorative art of Japan and Japanese prints. The butterfly which he adopted as his device and 'signature' was an appropriate symbol of his free impulsive movement through the artistic world of his time, and of the elegance and fragility of his art. In spite of his association with both movements, he cannot rightly be described as an impressionist or as a symbolist.

By the time Beardsley encountered Whistler, whose work so strongly appealed to him, the latter was an accepted master and it was the younger man who was soon to epitomise the radicalism of the nineties. It was not, however, the form and style of his work which offended conservative susceptibilities, for his technical brilliance as an illustrator and designer could be accepted, but rather the ironical irreverence of his vision, and his attachment to everything in life and art that critics of the age regarded as being morally and artistically decadent. He spoke of his talent for the grotesque as being primary in his art. The trial of his friend Oscar Wilde in 1896, a trial which for so many dramatically symbolized the 'modern iniquities' of the time, dragged him into disrepute and adversity. Beardsley was forced to recognise, even in childhood, that the lease of his life was bound to be short and the scale of his work, limited to small designs in black and white, was conditioned by his physical frailty. In his brief career he submitted in rapid succession to one pictorial or literary influence after another, encouraged by his great appetite for reading, falling under the sway of Rossetti, for example, Japanese prints, the masters of English literary satire, the writings of Huysmans and other contemporary symbolists. On account of that he was an eclectic, as well as sharing with others the habits of drawing and design we associate with the Art Nouveau, but both his imagery and his treatment of pattern and arabesque, especially in his later work, has such uniqueness as to place him among the truly original artists of the nineteenth century.

50 *James McNeill Whistler* (detail) by Walter Greaves. National Portrait Gallery, London

Whistler was born in Massachusetts in 1834, the son of a civil engineer. He first studied art in Russia where his father was temporarily employed. In 1851 he entered West Point, but after failing his examinations and giving up his first job as a cartographic draughtsman, he decided to become a painter. He lived in Paris from 1856 to 1859 and there became acquainted with Courbet and other French painters of his generation. His first important composition, *At the Piano*, was rejected by the Salon but accepted and welcomed at the Royal Academy immediately thereafter. During the next years, he divided his time between Paris and London. In 1871 he started his sequence of Thames nocturnes and not long afterwards began to give his work 'musical' titles. In 1876 he began to create the Peacock Room in the Kensington house of F. R. Leyland. The libel action against Ruskin which brought him only a farthing's damages also had an adverse influence upon his career. In 1872 the portrait of his mother, later acquired by the French Government, was exhibited at the Salon. After the Ruskin trial and his subsequent bankruptcy, Whistler spent a period in Venice and there made some of his finest etchings, a technique in which he had already proved himself a master. In 1888 Monet introduced him to the poet Mallarmé, who was to become an intimate friend. The breadth of his artistic affiliations at this time is shown by the fact that he was the President of the Royal Society of British Artists, and exhibiting in Paris with such artists as Pissarro, Sisley, Renoir and Rodin. In 1890 he published the collection of his writings known as *The Gentle Art of Making Enemies*. A retrospective exhibition of 1892, and its reception, proved how effectively his reputation had recovered, and at his death he was treated as one of the masters of nineteenth-century art.

LAVER, J. *Whistler* Faber, 1930.
SUTTON, D. *James McNeill Whistler: paintings, etchings, pastels and watercolours* Phaidon Press, 1966.

SUTTON, D. *Nocturne, the art of James McNeill Whistler* Country Life, 1963.

WHISTLER, J. M. *The gentle art of making enemies* Heinemann, 1890.

Beardsley was born at Brighton and was precocious in both mind and imagination, as well as showing very early his independence of will. His tuberculosis was diagnosed at the age of seven. Having left school at sixteen he worked until 1891 as a clerk and then, under the influence of Burne-Jones and Whistler particularly, he committed himself to art. In 1892 he was commissioned by the publisher John Dent to illustrate an edition of Malory's *Le Morte D'Arthur* and in the following year began to design illustrations for Oscar Wilde's play *Salome*. The first period of his career culminated with his work for *The Yellow Book,* of which he was co-founder and art editor. He was also at this time busily employed by commissions for posters and other graphic work. After the crisis in his affairs caused by the Wilde trial, which led to his dismissal from *The Yellow Book*, he found a new employer in Leonard Smithers, creator of the magazine *The Savoy*, to which Beardsley was appointed adviser; for the same publisher he made his illustrations for *The Rape of the Lock* and the *Lysistrata* of Aristophanes. In *The Savoy* appeared parts of his unfinished literary work, 'The Story of Venus and Tannhauser,' there called *Under the Hill*. At the time of his death at Menton he was engaged upon his designs for Jonson's *Volpone*.

51 *Aubrey Beardsley* (detail) by J. E. Blanche. National Portrait Gallery, London

READE, B. *Beardsley* Studio Vista, 1967.

WEINTRAUB, S. *Beardsley* Penguin Books, rev. edn. 1972.

The following selection of examples of works by the ten Victorian artists discussed above, and certain of their contemporaries, includes many of the illustrations contained in the earlier publication *Artists of the Victorian Age*. As a commentary on the illustrations, Basil Taylor has selected suitable extracts from the broadcasts.

52 Daniel Maclise: *Caxton's Printing Office,* 1849–51, 86 × 112 inches, Knebworth House collection

Maclise was essentially a painter of history and scenes from literature with a historical bias. His subjects ranged from Moses, Hercules and Alfred the Great, through the Norman Conquest and Robin Hood to Henry VIII, Charles I and Peter the Great of Russia. His choice of literary sources was equally ambitious: Shakespeare – whether *Twelfth Night* and *A Midsummer Night's Dream*, or *Macbeth* and *Othello* – Lesage's *Gil Blas*, Milton, Goldsmith, Scott, Thomas Moore, both Moore's Irish Melodies and his picturesque oriental poem *Lalla Rookh*. To each he gave their authentic costume and properties,

as authentic a view at any rate as contemporary knowledge could afford. One could obtain a faint impression of what these pictures were like, if one could not see them, by reading the elaborate historical novels of Harrison Ainsworth or Bulwer Lytton. The picture of Caxton was painted for Lytton and inspired by Lytton's novel of mediaeval chivalry, *The Last of the Barons*. Here is the abundant documentary detail carefully contrived from the available historical evidence. He found a printing press to copy which was at least very old, if not one of Caxton's. There is the crowd of figures filling the space,

or that part which is not reserved for other diverting objects. There is the compulsion to make history instructive. He said the occasion – Caxton showing a proof to the King and his family – was memorable in the history of English literature and civilisation. The picture is a large illustration, the concept and composition of it, and the behaviour of the figures, might first have been conceived by a writer, a historical novelist concerned to take his readers from one incident to another. A writer could explain the motives and feelings of his characters, and Maclise confidently attempts to do the same.

53 Daniel Maclise: *The Play Scene in 'Hamlet'*, 1842, 60 × 108 inches, Tate Gallery, London

We can see in the *Play Scene from 'Hamlet'* the rich congested abundance of materials that Maclise enjoyed imitating and the dramatic lighting of them, which complicated the problem of rendering their textures. This picture and others still sparkle like a Christmas tree. Ruskin called the *Hamlet* picture a 'glittering and grinning fantasy' – disliked the application of such virtuosity to a serious subject, a noble tragedy. Elsewhere he wrote: 'I cannot refrain from beseeching Mr Maclise to devote his vivid imagination and vigorous powers of hand to creations of more tenderness, repose and dignity; and above all not condescend, capable as he is of kindling his canvas with life and stamping it with character, to spend his time in imitating the sparkle of wine glasses and elaborating the fractures of nutshells.' When Maclise died, Dickens honoured his friend with heart-felt respect, spoke of his 'prodigious fertility of mind and wonderful wealth of intellect', said that 'they would have made him if he had been so minded at least as great a writer as he was a painter'.

54 Daniel Maclise: *Death of Nelson*, 1863–5, 132 × 544 inches, Royal Gallery, Palace of Westminster, London

When, in 1858, Maclise began to work on his two chief subjects for the new Palace of Westminster – *The Death of Nelson*, and *The Meeting of Wellington and Blucher* – he was still under the obligation to use fresco. The conditions in the building, the position of the wall in relation to the light, above all his conception of the subject, all went against using the method and he asked to be relieved of the commission. The Prince Consort intervened, not simply with persuasion, but with practical advice. Use instead, he suggested, not the oil colours which Maclise would have liked, but a method based upon water glass, the same

stuff that people once used to preserve eggs. That would enable the design to be painted directly on the wall, not on canvas, would make the surface non-reflecting, and in theory make it durable. The technique had been developed particularly in Germany. So Maclise agreed to go there to study. He spent several months in Berlin, Dresden and Munich, wrote a report on his observations and tests and, back in London, started again. At the end of 1861 the Waterloo subject was finished, and two years after the Trafalgar one was begun in 1863, that was completed too. He worked continually on a daily basis to the

exclusion of almost everything else, and worked under the kind of conditions which exacerbated his tendency to hypochondria and melancholy. He told the art critic Frederick Stephens: 'There never was a hall so badly calculated for the exhibition of paintings'. He complained of water dripping down the wall, light reflected from it, the damp of wet clothes and umbrellas, 'thousands of them', he said, and the dust and the noise of workmen engaged on other tasks. 'Royal Gallery,' he said, 'Royal Lumber Room is a fitter name for it.'

The designs show to an extreme Maclise's obsession with

historical fact. The great German historian Ranke said that the historian's task was to establish exactly what had occurred. That was a good motto for the inspiration behind the most serious historical writing and study of the nineteenth century, and it is a suitable motto for Maclise's endeavours too. He sought to recover every scrap of first-hand information about the two events – interviewed survivors, consulted eye-witness records, looked for and found actual items of uniform worn during the battles. And those who were his sponsors supported and believed in his research, because they shared the same historical outlook. The paintings have nothing glittering or grinning about them. They are powerful, strange, even eccentric images. They are almost unbearably intricate. Although as compositions of a myriad of parts they are most carefully and rationally constructed, they are also congested, they provoke a sense of claustrophobia. And that comes from the artist's determination to include everything from the smallest rivet to the most impassioned expression of anxiety in a human countenance. Quality and truth seem to be equated with completeness.

The world which Mulready's paintings show is a small one, and his compositions are sparsely populated too. With few exceptions, which would include some excellent early landscapes, they are best described by the word 'genre', scenes of domestic life, most often contemporary, sometimes taken from literature.

In *The Sonnet*, a young man has written a poem for his girl and is anxiously watching her response to it. In the picture whose full title is *Train up a child in the way he should go and when he is old he should not depart from it,* a child is frightened by the beggars to whom his mother is urging him to give a coin; they are black men. In another work, called *The Convalescent from Waterloo* (in the Victoria and Albert Museum), a soldier recovering from wounds is thoughtfully watching some small boys fighting. The dramatic centre of these pictures is not simply, as in two cases, a point of moral implication – ideas of charity in one instance, of human conflict in the other – but each one also offers a moment of psychological crisis, however slight it may be, of exactly the same kind we expect to find in nineteenth-century novels, and in modern ones too. A writer such as George Eliot or Emily Brontë brought the crises of high tragedy out of the sphere of the great figures who had populated high tragedy before, into the sphere of ordinary life. So Mulready, in his grave, serious pictures, brought similar crises out of high art into the field of genre. Perhaps Mulready's biographer, Frederick Stephens, meant that when he said that he 'imparted philosophy to his works', and that 'their human sympathy was characteristically modern', by which, of course, he meant Victorian.

55 William Mulready: *The Sonnet,* 1839, 14 × 12 inches, Victoria and Albert Museum, London

56 William Mulready: *Train up a Child,* 1841, 25½ × 31 inches, Collection of John Avery

57 William Mulready: *The Seven Ages*, 1837, 35½ × 45 inches, Victoria and Albert Museum, London

Ruskin said that the subject of
Mulready's *Seven Ages of Man*,
based on the speech of Jacques in
As You Like It, could not and
should not be painted, that the
words could not be translated into
images. 'In the written passage,
the thoughts are progressive and
connected; in the picture they
must be coexistent and yet
separate; nor can all the
characters of the painting be
rendered in painting at all. One
may represent the soldier at the
cannon's mouth, but one cannot
paint the "bubble reputation"
which he seeks.'

Hunt wrote this about *The Hireling Shepherd*. 'My first object was to paint a real shepherd and a real shepherdess in full sunlight with all the colour of luscious summer, without the faintest fear of precedents of any landscape painter who had rendered Nature before.' With the same conviction he was to want the real light of the Holy Land to shine out from his Biblical pictures, one important reason why he painted them there, spent so much time in the Middle East.

The most distinctive part of Pre-Raphaelitism, Hunt's painting as a whole, and Millais' Pre-Raphaelite ones, the aspect of them which seemed most unconventional in 1850, was the particular quality of their naturalism, their pictorial form and style. And it is important not to think of this simply as a matter of trying to render every detail –

that certainly, but in Hunt's case especially there was an intention more important and original than that, a way of understanding and rendering light and colour. The first principle was to set up the canvas in front of the subject, whatever it might be, and to represent it directly on the canvas, not, if avoidable, work in the studio from drawn studies which had been made elsewhere. In one of his writings about the movement, Ruskin insisted upon the particular point which distinguished true Pre-Raphaelitism from false imitations of its effects by other artists. 'The true work,' Ruskin said, 'represents all objects exactly as they would appear in nature, in the position and at the distance which the arrangement of the picture supposes.' He meant by that the distance from the painter's viewpoint. The distinction which Ruskin was making he also

considered elsewhere. If you are walking along the shore, he suggested, and see a boat on the horizon, you know that it has portholes along its side, although you cannot see them. So do not put them in. Paint what the eye sees, not what it tells you is there. Painting what the eye sees means of course painting things under the conditions of natural light, painting light and colour as you see them. At the end of his life, in the preface to his autobiography, Hunt made this significant observation: 'The source of all colour is light,' and he referred to scientific research as a confirmation of that Newtonian concept. Many years before, his friend Frederick Stephens had said that Hunt had 'observed the relationship between light and colour more accurately, truthfully than any artist before him, had perceived the true colours to be observed in shadows.'

58 William Holman Hunt: *The Hireling Shepherd*, 1851, 30 × 42½ inches, City of Manchester Art Galleries

In both Hunt's *Hireling Shepherd* and Millais' *Ophelia* (**68**) the landscape was painted first and the figures added afterwards, also, of course, painted from life. The two painters found the landscape settings they needed for these subjects in the countryside near Ewell. And the girl in the *Hireling Shepherd* came from an estate at Ewell. For several months she stayed in London and posed for the picture. Ophelia was the shop girl, Elizabeth Siddal, whom Rossetti was to marry, and Millais had her lie in a bath of water warmed by lamps placed underneath so as to get the authentic appearance of the wet draperies. In some parts of these pictures certainly, perhaps over the whole of them, Hunt and Millais used a method which they devised to give a maximum brilliance of colour. They had first prepared a solid hard, white ground. I use Hunt's own words to indicate what followed: 'Upon this surface complete with exactness the outline of the part in hand. On the morning for the painting, with fresh white, spread a coat very evenly over the part for the day's work, of such consistency that the drawing should faintly show through. Over this wet ground the colour should be laid, the touches made so tenderly that the ground below shall not be worked up.' So the picture developed piece by piece like a jigsaw, and as an intricate composition of small coloured touches, the colour being determined by an assiduous observation of what the eye perceived.

59 William Holman Hunt: *The Scapegoat*, 1854, $33\frac{3}{4} \times 54\frac{1}{2}$ inches,
The Trustees of the Lady Lever Art Gallery, Port Sunlight

The Scapegoat was the first
picture which reflects Hunt's
determination to make his Biblical
pictures in the Holy Land, in the
settings, and under the light, of
their original localities. The
subject derives from the Hebrew
ritual connected with the Day of
Atonement, when one of two
goats is sacrificed and the other,
the scapegoat, the bearer of
mankind's sins, is driven out into
the wilderness. Hunt's serio-
comic adventures in making the
picture – tethering a goat on the
barren shores of the Dead Sea, the
death of one animal, the encoun-
ters with inquisitive and perhaps
unfriendly Arabs – all the
consequences of pushing his
austere convictions to the limit –

have become a familiar episode in
the history of Victorian earnestness. But when the picture was
shown in 1856, one critic stated a
general objection quite unequi-
vocally. 'The question,' he said,
'is simply this – here is a dying goat
which as a mere goat has no more
interest for us than the sheep
which furnished our yesterday's
dinner. 'But it is the type of the
Saviour', says Mr Hunt. Here we
join issue, for it is impossible to
paint a goat, though its eyes were
upturned with human passion,
that could explain any allegory or
hidden type.' Here is one literal,
fact-finding Victorian mind
confronting another, equally
devoted to the facts. Later Hunt
took to publishing pamphlets in

explanation of his pictures,
explaining their purpose and
symbolic detail.

John Brett (1830–1902) was one of
several artists who, although not
members of the Pre-Raphaelite
Brotherhood, were strongly
influenced by their work as well
as by the writings of Ruskin in
defence of naturalism. The work
(top right) painted at Box Hill,
Surrey, established Brett's
reputation. His meticulous
method was also a product of his
interests as an enthusiastic
amateur scientist.

60 John Brett: *The Stonebreaker*, 1858, 19½ × 26½ inches, Walker Art Gallery, Liverpool

61 John William Waterhouse: *The Lady of Shalott* 1888, 60¼ × 78¾ inches, Tate Gallery, London

This picture, made at the same time as Holman Hunt was working on his version of Tennyson's poem, provides an interesting contrast with it, the one so imaginative a reconstruction of the legend, the other so literal an illustration of it. See also note to plate **64**.

62 William Holman Hunt: *The Light of the World,*
1853, 49⅜ × 23½ inches, Keble College, Oxford

The painting called *The Awakening Conscience* was intended to be a secular counterpart of *The Light of the World*, in so far as it shows a human soul being enlightened by the voice of conscience and thus by Godly inspiration. Of the two quotations which he put into the catalogue of the Academy exhibition where it was shown, one is from Isaiah, the words, 'Strengthen ye the feeble hands and confirm ye the tottering knees; say ye to the faint hearted, be ye strong, fear ye not, behold your God'. The picture shows a girl in the house of the man whose mistress she is. On the frame Hunt had incised the words from Proverbs, 'As he that taketh away a garment in cold weather, so is he that sings songs to a heavy heart'. Hunt said that these words had led him to see how 'the companion of the girl's fall might himself be the unconscious utterer of a divine message. I arranged the two figures to present the woman recalling the memory of her childish home and breaking away from her gilded cage with a startled holy resolve, while her shallow companion still sings on, ignorantly intensifying her repentant purpose'. The picture is filled with symbolic details and some of them must have been, perhaps they still are, somewhat inscrutable, because they are so intimately a part of the setting. The meaning of the cat tormenting the bird in its gilded cage is evident. The design on the wallpaper not so, although no less intentionally symbolic, birds feeding on corn and grapes in the presence of sleeping bird-scarers. Ruskin even found the furniture meaningful, 'the terrible lustre of it, its fatal newness', he said.

63 William Holman Hunt: *The Awakening Conscience*, 1853, 29¼ × 21¾ inches, Trustees of Sir Colin and Lady Anderson

64 William Holman Hunt:
The Lady of Shalott, 1887–1905,
74 × 57½ inches, Wadsworth
Atheneum, Hartford, Connecticut,
The Ella Gallup Sumner and
Mary Catlin Sumner Collection

When he painted *The Lady of
Shalott* after Tennyson's poem,
Hunt converted the writer's
Arthurian invention into
something more portentous.
He found the story a parable,
which 'veiled from the casual
reader,' he said, 'the severer
philosophic purpose, the failure
of the human soul towards its
accepted responsibility'. Hunt's
responsibility was to art and to
nature. So the Lady's mirror in
the lonely tower became a
metaphor of art, the breaking of
the mirror a rejection of artistic
responsibility. (See also plate **61**.)

65 Sir Edward Burne-Jones:
*Perseus Receiving the Mirror
from Athena,* one of a series of
ten Perseus subjects commissioned
in 1875, 60 × 50 inches,
The Southampton Art Gallery

One of the most characteristic
features of Burne-Jones' work is
that sinuous languid line which
prevails in all his compositions,
and a languorous mood which
goes with it. The colour, too, was
often that softened, diminished
colour which, although by no
means confined to greens and
yellows, is nevertheless invoked
by that famous term 'greenery-
yallery', which occurs in Gilbert
and Sullivan's operetta, *Iolanthe,*
which satirised the Aesthetic
Movement.

Frith moved from *Ramsgate Sands* (**80**) to a more elaborate picture of the same kind and an even more successful one, *Derby Day*. He wrote in his diary for 3 May 1856: 'Opening day of the exhibition. Never such a crowd seen round a picture. The Secretary obliged to get a policeman to keep the people off'. Two days later the man who had bought the picture in advance found the people, as he said, 'smelling the picture like bloodhounds'. He demanded that a rail should be put in front to protect his property and he told the painter that 'it required a close inspection to read, mark, learn and inwardly digest it'. Frith had sold separately to a dealer the copyright in the engraving for £1500. Part of its success was no doubt due to the fact that he had not only chosen such a universally appealing

66 William Powell Frith: *Derby Day,* 1856, 40 × 88 inches, Tate Gallery, London

occasion, but put into the crowd of figures even more picturesque incidents.

Only one other picture in the history of the Royal Academy exhibitions prior to the showing of the *Derby Day* had had to be protected from public curiosity, as that one was. That had been Wilkie's picture called *The Chelsea Pensioners,* also a modern subject – the pensioners were shown at Chelsea Hospital receiving the news of Waterloo – also in a descriptive naturalistic style.

It would be a mistake to think of Frith's pictures as being narratives. They provide instead an archipelago of anecdotes connected by the event or the place in which they are located, Ramsgate, Epsom race course, Paddington Station. And in a visual sense each event or figure claims as much attention as any other, and there is nothing but a general bustle to unite them. They appealed to that sense of simple recognition to which so much popular Victorian art, books and pictures made *their* appeal. If Frith did experience intensities of joy, sadness, surprise, disappointments and self-fulfilment, he hardly communicates them.

67 James McNeill Whistler: *Nocturne – Black and Gold : The Fire Wheel,*
c. 1870, 21 × 29¾ inches, Tate Gallery, London

In 1885 Whistler first gave the
lecture which was known as
Mr Whistler's Ten O'Clock, a
confession of his mature artistic
faith. 'That Nature is always
right,' he said, 'is an assertion,
artistically as untrue, as it is one
whose truth is universally taken
for granted. Nature is very rarely
right, to such an extent even, that
it might also be said that Nature
is usually wrong.'

The most thorough and
original working out of Whistler's
ideals came in those pictures of the
1870s known as Nocturnes,
paintings of the Thames at night,
the dark, still, greasy water,
dappled with the riverside lights,
the waterside buildings and the
bridges in simplest silhouette;
sometimes the fireworks spring up
from the pleasure gardens of
Cremorne in plumes of flame or
flocks of sparkling light. Whistler
would sit out the night in a hired
boat filling his visual memory
with effects such as these. Then
in the studio with a small reper-
toire of carefully prepared
colours, what he called his
'sauce', he would try to fix the
poetic atmosphere of the subjects
as simply and spontaneously as he
could manage.

There was a passage in his Ten
O'Clock lecture which exactly
conveys their spirit. 'When the
evening mist clothes the riverside
with poetry, as with a veil, and the
poor buildings lose themselves in
the dim sky and the tall chimneys
become campanili, and the warehouses are palaces in the night,
and the whole city hangs in the
heavens and fairy land is before
us – then the wayfarer hastens
home and Nature who for once

68 Sir John Everett Millais: *Ophelia,* 1851–2, 30 × 40 inches, Tate Gallery, London (See note to plate **58**)

has sung in tune sings her exquisite song to the artist, alone her son and master.'

It was a work similar to the present one which caused Ruskin to write that he 'never expected to hear a coxcomb ask two hundred guineas for flinging a pot of paint in the public's face'. So when the action for libel instituted by Whistler came to court, there was a significant interchange between Whistler and Ruskin's counsel. 'Did it take much time to paint the *Nocturne in Black and Gold?*' he was asked, 'How soon did you knock it off?' 'I knocked it off possibly in a couple of days, one day to do the work and another to finish it.' 'And that was the labour for which you asked two hundred guineas?' 'No, it was for the knowledge gained through a lifetime.' Thus did Whistler challenge a common Victorian assumption; that the value of a work was directly related to the amount of hard labour that had gone into the making of it.

69 William Mulready: *Choosing the Wedding Gown*, 1845, 21 × 17¾ inches,
Victoria and Albert Museum, London

70 William Mulready: '*Yes, she is gone off with two gentlemen in a postchaise, and one of them kissed her, and said he would die for her.*' Preliminary sketch for a set of illustrations for *The Vicar of Wakefield*, by Oliver Goldsmith. Victoria and Albert Museum, London.

As a book illustrator, the best of Mulready's drawings are those he made for Oliver Goldsmith's novel *The Vicar of Wakefield*. The picture known as *Choosing the Wedding Gown* also takes a scene from that novel. It proves the fine simplicity of Mulready's best work, his virile, sensitive drawing, and his appreciation of human behaviour and feeling, which could be tender, not sentimental. His sympathetic treatment of scenes from the book points to what he enjoyed painting, and the historical sources and background of his art. Goldsmith's novel was one of the most popular 'classics' in the Victorian period, and it is not difficult to understand why. It is a story of middle-class life and its common, domestic enjoyments and crises, presented with light, agreeable undertones of humour and sentiment, qualities also found in some Victorian fiction – in *Cranford*, for instance, and the slighter novels of Trollope. And there had been eighteenth-century counterparts of Goldsmith's book in painting too, at least in terms of sentiment and comedy; such artists as Francis Wheatley, George Morland, and William Redmore Bigg.

71 Sir John Everett Millais: *The Return of the Dove to the Ark,* 1851, $34\frac{1}{2} \times 21\frac{1}{2}$ inches, Ashmolean Museum, Oxford

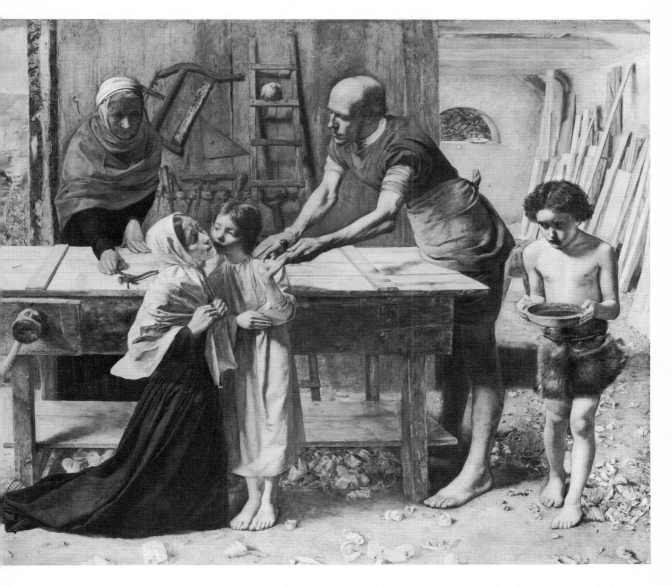

72 Sir John Everett Millais: *Christ in the House of His Parents*, 1849, 34 × 55 inches, Tate Gallery, London

Millais' *Christ in the House of His Parents* is for all its skill a simple, plain-speaking picture, by contrast even with Holman Hunt's *The Light of the World* (**62**). The only element of symbolism in it is the wound in the Christ child's hand. Although he did paint the setting in a real carpenter's shop, he did not have Hunt's zeal for historical reconstruction. If you disregard some elements in the costume this might be a nineteenth-century occasion. That was one reason why it provoked such hostile criticism. Dickens called it 'mean, odious, revolting and repulsive', and the *Times* critic, 'an attempt to associate the Holy Family with the meanest details of a carpenter's shop . . . disgusting'.

73 Sir John Everett Millais: *Lorenzo and Isabella,* 1849, 40½ × 56¼ inches, Walker Art Gallery, Liverpool

74 Sir John Everett Millais: *Accepted,* 1853, 10 × 7 inches, Private Collection

One theme more than any other occupied Millais' attention in his larger pictures of the 1850s and 60s – the relationship between people in love, lovers' meetings and partings and yearnings, the remembrance of love lost or removed by fate – a theme we can also apply as a touchstone for interpreting the identity of other Victorian painters. As far as Millais is concerned, the subject shows itself first in his picture of *Lorenzo and Isabella,* illustrating Keats' 'Isabella: or The Pot of Basil'. The concentration there of the lovers' two heads together was artfully contrasted by the painter with the detachment of all the other faces in the design. One of Millais' most admired pictures, the one called *The Order of Release,* shows a Scottish soldier, released from prison, being restored to his wife.

This was one of a succession of lovers' meetings and partings put into a historical context: a Roman soldier parting from his British girl as the legions sail away; a Huguenot parting from his Roman Catholic girl on the eve of the St Bartholomew's Day massacre; a meeting between a cavalier officer and his beloved in a wood, the man peeping

75 Arthur Hughes: *The Long Engagement,*
1859, 41½ × 21½ inches,
Birmingham Museum and Art Gallery

76 William Powell Frith: *The Proposal,*
1877, 23¾ × 19½ inches,
Private Collection

anxiously out from his hiding
place inside a tree. All these
pictures, and others like them,
touch upon – one cannot say more
than that – touch upon passions
which in mid-Victorian England
were subject to strong social and
moral restraints. Millais made
these passions respectable by
putting them inside fancy dress
and into remote times. It is
significant that when he did come
nearer to the realities of modern
love, to the sort of crisis of feeling
which he had experienced when
he married Ruskin's former wife,
Effie, he did so in some little
drawings, such as *Accepted*, not

intended for public display.
   Elsewhere in the art of the time,
in painting as well as in innumerable poems and novels, we find
other artists coming closer to the
emotional realities. Arthur
Hughes, for example, who was a
disciple of Millais – it is an
interesting coincidence that he
should have posed for the figure
of the anxious royalist lover in the
tree, referred to above. Not long
afterwards he painted the picture
reproduced here, called *The Long
Engagement*. It started as a scene
from *As You Like It*, but became
a very intense image of intense,
pent up feeling, of emotional

suspense and frustration in
secret seclusion. There are other
pictures by Hughes with the same
spirit. One called *April Love* was
accompanied by a quotation from
Tennyson which puts all the
anguishing insecurity into words:

Love is hurt with jar and fret,
Love is made a vague regret,
Eyes with idle tears are wet,
Idle habits link us yet.
What is love? For we forget.
Ah, no, no.

*The Miller's
Daughter*

77 Sir Hubert von Herkomer:
On Strike, 1891, 89¾ × 49¾
inches, Royal Academy of Arts,
London

Although such modern subjects
treating matters of serious
concern were never as common or
popular in Victorian art as those
taken from history, literature or
the imagination, they might be
justified by the elements of
narrative and pathos which these
contain. Warmly received when
exhibited at the Royal
Academy, they show the influence
of just those realistic tendencies in
French art which Whistler
experienced at first hand during
his early years in Paris and which
he later rejected.

78 Frank Bramley: *A Hopeless Dawn*, 1888, $47\frac{1}{2} \times 65\frac{1}{2}$ inches, Tate Gallery, London

79 Sir Hubert von Herkomer: *Hard Times*, 1885, $33\frac{1}{2} \times 43\frac{1}{2}$ inches, City of Manchester Art Galleries

80 William Powell Frith: *Ramsgate Sands : Life at the Seaside,* 1852–4, 30 × 60½ inches, reproduced by gracious permission of Her Majesty the Queen

Ramsgate Sands, or *Life at the Seaside* is a picture of what people commonly do when they spend their holiday at the seaside. It was not only *the* success of the 1854 Academy exhibition; it transformed the career of an artist who already knew what it was to be, as he said, 'overwhelmed by commissions'. Before the exhibition he had already sold the painting to a dealer for a thousand guineas. The Queen, seeing it at the Academy, wanted to buy it, and ultimately did so from the dealer, who reserved the right to keep the picture long enough for it to be engraved. He sold the engraver's plate to the Art Union of London, a body founded in the 1840s to support contemporary artists and to provide people of modest income with the opportunity to acquire works of art. It was a lottery with art prizes, in fact.

In the previous fourteen years since Frith first sent a work to the Academy, he had concentrated mainly upon scenes from literature – familiar scenes from popular classics. Writing of this period in his autobiography, he said, 'fear of modern life subjects still possessed me. The hat and trousers pictures that I had seen attempted had all been dismal failures and I felt sure, or thought I did, that unless a subject of tremendous human interest could be found, such an interest as would make the spectator forget the dresses of the actors in it – modern life was impossible.' In 1851, still conscious of 'the drawbacks of unpicturesque modern dress', he was converted by the sights he saw while on holiday at Ramsgate.

81 William Dyce: *Pegwell Bay,*
1859–60, 24¾ × 35 inches,
Tate Gallery, London

William Dyce (1806–64) was a
precursor of the Pre-Raphaelites,
and best known for his religious
and subject pictures, and as one
of the first to revive fresco painting
in England. The present work
includes a comet which appeared
in 1858.

82 William Powell Frith: *The Railway Station*, 1862,
46 × 101 inches, Royal Holloway College, University of London

The circumstances which attended the appearance of *A Railway Station* – Paddington Station, in fact – not only suggest Frith's uncommon talent for business, but typify the new Victorian art world. Frith sold the picture to a dealer with copyright for £4500, reserving for himself the right to show it at the Academy. That right he later forfeited for a further £750. When the painting was put on view by itself, apart from the sketch for it, on the dealer's premises, 21,000 people paid to see it.

84 George Frederick Watts: *Love and Life,* c. 1884–5, $87\frac{1}{2} \times 48$ inches, Tate Gallery, London

83 George Frederick Watts:
Love and Death, c. 1885–7,
$97\frac{1}{2} \times 46$ inches, Tate Gallery, London

Watts described the picture *Love and Life* in these terms: 'I would suggest frail and feeble human existence aided to ascend from the lower to the higher plane by love with his wide wings of sympathy, charity, tenderness and human affection. Love is not intended to be either personal or carnal. . . .' Watts confessed to Ruskin that 'My instincts cause me to strive after things that are hardly within the province of art.' The vehicle of his ideas and visions was the human figure. 'I have used the human form', he said, 'because there are no others by which it would be at all possible to suggest ideas belonging to human conditions, but I have purposely abstained from any attempt to make the figure seem real . . . knowing that familiarity produces a sense of the commonplace.' Watts believed with an unshakeable earnestness that the painter had a responsibility to *influence* the conduct of man. No painter in the history of English art has had such a strong and obsessive sense of mission, not even Benjamin Robert Haydon, who was, like Watts, an apostle of High Art, of the Grand Manner of artistic idealism. I can communicate Watts' purpose best by putting together some of his opinions as his widow recorded them in her three-volume study of him: 'The greatest works of art of all times have been idealistic . . . Art must be allowed the same range as poetry and literature – the graceful, the sentimental, the historical, the ethical, the religious . . . I cannot claim more for my pictures than that they are thoughts, attempts to embody visionary ideas . . . The greatest art, whether plastic or graphic, will be devoted to those ideas and emotions that excite enthusiasm and inspire devotion . . . A great work of high art is a noble theme

85 George Frederick Watts: *Orpheus and Eurydice*, first exhibited 1869, $27\frac{1}{2} \times 18$ inches, Aberdeen Art Gallery

treated in a noble manner, awakening our best and most reverential feelings, touching our generosity, our tenderness, or disposing us generally to seriousness – a subject of human endurance, of human justice, of human aspiration and hope depicted worthily by the special means that art has in her power to use.' Watts hoped to be able to translate his ideas into a vast apparatus of frescoes to be housed in a building constructed to hold them and to be called The House of Life. The House of Life was to embody in its symbolism the form of the universe, the life and progress of mankind and the civilisations which man had created. The project was of course never realised, but many of Watts' works from 1870 onwards were the product of his thinking about it, and of his hope that if the frescoes could never be created, at least somewhere an assembly of the relevant oil paintings might be formed so as to provide at least an outline of his vision.

86 George Frederick Watts: *Alfred Tennyson*,
1873, 23½ × 19½ inches,
National Portrait Gallery, London

Watts' portraits, so many of them depicting the most famous men of his time, were also to a great degree neither personal nor carnal. They are, rather, differentiated symbols of the same sort of grave eminence. They do not have the physical and psychological particularities of the individuals they celebrate, that quality which is so impressive in the portraits of Holbein, for example, or Ingres. They also betray the lack of pictorial invention, the lack of pictorial imagination indeed, which characterises the rest of Watts' work, in spite of its visionary pretensions. In form and composition they are as much stereotypes as the Kitcat club portraits by Sir Godfrey Kneller.

The Last of England might be called a poetic documentary. It deals with the fact of emigration. The man staring out from the stern of the retreating ship is the Pre-Raphaelite sculptor Thomas Woolner who went away to Australia in 1852. This is a picture which, whether Madox Brown was conscious of it or not, conveys most powerfully senti-ments which were strongly present at every level of mid-Victorian society, a feeling that the world was poised between past and future, between regret for what was passing and expec-tations for the future, a compound of sadness and hope. Brown, who was a close friend of all the Pre-Raphaelite painters, wrote of this picture: 'The minuteness of detail which would be visible under such conditions of broad daylight I have thought necessary to imitate, as bringing the pathos of the subject home to the beholder.'

87 Ford Madox Brown: *The Last of England*, 1855, 32½ × 29½ inches, City of Manchester Art Galleries

88 Ford Madox Brown: *Work,*
1852–65, $54\frac{1}{2} \times 77\frac{1}{8}$ inches,
City of Manchester Art Galleries

This picture, a strange compound
of naturalism and symbolism, of
didacticism and a minute observation of the natural world, was
intended by the artist to be an
image of 'Work as it now exists'.
In the suburb of Hampstead
various figures typifying aspects
of labour are brought together –
they include two eloquent
apostles of a work ethic, Thomas
Carlyle and the Christian
Socialist F. D. Maurice; a navvy –
according to Brown, 'the British
excavator . . . the outward and
visible type of Work', a beggar, a
group of the rich, and others.

Elizabeth Siddal's death marked a turning point in the character of Rossetti's painting, in the way that he embodied pictorially his dreams of romance and his obsession with the female identity. In his earlier works he had expressed his dreams and visions through the lives of other people and other worlds, removed from him and his Victorian environment, both in time and in culture, the world of fourteenth century Florence or the Arthurian Court, as transformed by Rossetti's visionary wishfulness.

The picture called *Beata Beatrix* was perhaps the first sign of what these later works were to be like. It was begun before Elizabeth Siddal's death. Using her both as model and inspiration it is a vision of Dante's Beatrice, poised between life and death, earth and heaven, the picture itself similarly poised between the painter's personal experience and the chief historical symbol of his feelings, the Dante-Beatrice relationship.

In the 1860s and 70s his paintings became physically larger and more substantial, usually made in oil colours. Like the *Beata Beatrix* they were almost always transformations of his favourite sitters, the women with whom he formed intense or casual relationships, and were thus dramatised portraits. Within their narrow compass they vary in the emphasis that Rossetti put upon the two elements the works contain, the sense of actuality represented by the sitter, and the poetic idea which the women impersonate. The picture called *The Blue Bower* is not much more than a sensuous, decorative image of the girl Fanny Cornforth who satisfied the physical part of

89 Dante Gabriel Rossetti: *Beata Beatrix*, c. 1863, 34 × 26 inches, Tate Gallery, London
90 Dante Gabriel Rossetti: *Astarte Syriaca*, 1877, 72 × 42 inches, City of Manchester Art Galleries

Rossetti's needs. Swinburne called her a bitch and said that by comparison with Elizabeth Siddal 'she stood at the other pole of the sex'. The work called *Astarte Syriaca*, by comparison, was one of numerous expressions of his feelings for Janey Morris, and is marked by that disembodiment of the human form which can also be found in the pictures of Burne-Jones, and more sententiously in the work of Watts. The anguished reverence for female beauty which the painting communicates is also to be found in a poem describing the picture which Rossetti wrote a year before his death:

Mystery; lo! betwixt the sun and moon
Astarte of the Syrians: Venus Queen
Ere Aphrodite was. In silver sheen
Her two fold girdle clasps the infinite boon
Of bliss whereof the heaven and earth consume:
And from her neck's inclining flower-stem lean
Love freighted lips and absolute eyes that wean
The pulse of hearts to the sphere's dominant tune.

Torch-bearing, her sweet ministers compel
All thrones of light beyond the sky and sea
The witnesses of Beauty's face to be:
That face, of loves all penetrative spell
Amulet, talisman and oracle, —
Betwixt the sun and moon a mystery.

91 Dante Gabriel Rossetti: *The Blue Bower*, 1865, $35\frac{1}{2} \times 27\frac{1}{4}$ inches, The Barber Institute of Fine Arts, University of Birmingham

92 Dante Gabriel Rossetti: *The Bower Meadow*, 1872, $33\frac{1}{2} \times 26\frac{1}{2}$ inches, City of Manchester Art Galleries

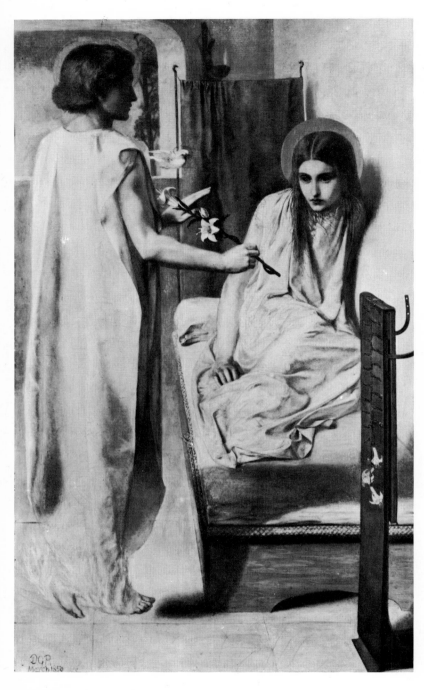

93 Dante Gabriel Rossetti: *The Annunciation*, 1850,
28½ × 17 inches, Tate Gallery, London

Rossetti's two pictures, *The
Girlhood of Mary Virgin* and
The Annunciation, which he
exhibited elsewhere than the
Royal Academy, were generally
better received by the critics
than the other early Pre-
Raphaelite paintings. *The Times*
referred to *The Annunciation* as
'the work of a poet'.

Rossetti was less inclined than
Hunt or Millais to submit to the
discipline of painting laboriously
from nature, or to treat subjects
with a didactic theme. The one
picture, *Found*, which combined
both these attributes, shows a
prodigal country girl being
rescued from the city streets by a
boy from home. It was begun in
1853, but it remained unfinished,
although still in progress, at
Rossetti's death nearly thirty
years later.

94 Dante Gabriel Rossetti: *Found,* 1853–82, 36 × 31½ inches, Samuel and Mary Bancroft Collection, The Delaware Art Museum, Wilmington, Delaware, USA

95 Dante Gabriel Rossetti: *King Arthur's Tomb,* replica by Elizabeth Siddal,
1855–60, 9¼ × 14½ inches, Tate Gallery, London

Rossetti's paintings in the first half of the 1850s, from which he earned a small and inconsistent income, were made in water-colours; they were small compositions, their subjects being taken from the life and work of Dante, from the *Vita Nuova,* for example, and from Malory. In some of these pictures, such as the *Dante's Dream,* the figures were quite solidly realised and stand in a spacious setting, even if the depth of the space is limited. But in other cases, the image is more abstract, the forms flatter, the space more constricted, the effect of tightly wrought pattern more intense. They combine the quality of early mediaeval illuminations with the radiance of stained glass and the formality of heraldic painting. Rossetti's main intention was to achieve an expressive effect of colour. This is what he said about it to one of those who bought his water-colours in the 1850s, a business man called Francis Macracken. 'I believe colour today to be a

96 Dante Gabriel Rossetti: *Dante's Dream at the Time of the Death of Beatrice,*
1856, 18½ × 25¾ inches, Tate Gallery, London

quite indispensable quality in the
highest art, and that no picture
ever belonged to the highest order
without it. Colour is the physiog-
nomy of the picture, and like the
shape of the human forehead it
cannot be perfectly beautiful
without proving goodness and
greatness. Other qualities are its
life exercised, but this is the body
of its life, by which we love it at
first sight.' And the pictures do
indeed fulfil this description.

97 Dante Gabriel Rossetti:
How they met themselves, 1851–60,
10¾ × 8¾ inches,
Fitzwilliam Museum, Cambridge

The last twenty years of Rossetti's
life were passed in the shadow of
Elizabeth Siddal's death in 1862.
Whether she committed suicide
or whether her death was the
climax of a chronic sickness of
body and mind, complicated by
the drugs she took to assuage it,
the events created in Rossetti's
consciousness a nexus of mental
and emotional disturbance from
which he never liberated himself.
In the composition called *How
they met themselves* he had already
prefigured the fateful quality of
the relationship. Two lovers
walking in a wood encounter the
ghosts of their own selves. The
ghost of their relationship
continued to haunt him.

98 Sir Edward Burne-Jones:
The Beguiling of Merlin,
1874, 73 × 43½ inches,
The Trustees of the Lady Lever
Art Gallery, Port Sunlight

'I mean by a picture,' Burne-Jones
said, 'a romantic dream of
something that never was, never
will be, in a light better than any
light that ever shone – and a land
no-one can define or remember,
only desire.' He wrote of 'living
deep down in what was essential
to life'.

99 Sir Edward Burne-Jones: *The Mill,* 1870, 35¾ × 77¾ inches, Victoria and Albert Museum, London

100 Sir Frank Dicksee: *Harmony,* 1877, 62 × 37 inches, Tate Gallery, London

Sir Frank Dicksee (1852–1928) was among those Victorian painters whose romantic subject pictures were much influenced by the Pre-Raphaelite spirit and iconography. The present picture established the artist's reputation when it was shown at the Academy in 1877.

Until 1865 Burne-Jones' inspiration was chiefly mediaeval, but gradually thereafter he became increasingly influenced by the art of the High Renaissance, by Michelangelo, Raphael and Leonardo, and among Italian artists of the previous generation, Botticelli particularly. The scale of their work was anyway more appropriate to his designs and to his desire to make oil paintings on a large scale. From Renaissance art came those compositions of figures in which the theme of the work is conveyed by the postures of the body. Figures emphatically muscled when they were male, with flowing, sinuous outlines when they were female, dressed, when they were so, in draperies which were decorative and formalised. Although so many of his designs were applied, translated by the processes of craftsmanship and by other workers, Burne-Jones, even as a decorative artist, belonged to the world of Fine Art which had the Renaissance as its chief historical source.

One of the artist's most familiar and popular subjects was the story of King Cophetua and the Beggar Maid, which Tennyson had used for a poem. The theme is that of a lowly creature, a beggar maid, redeemed as it were by physical and spiritual beauty. The king is shown abstractedly and ardently contemplating the girl, who represents for him a perfect union of nature and spirit, which he had sought so long. In Tennyson's poem Cophetua says at the end, 'This beggar maid shall be my queen'.

101 Sir Edward Burne-Jones: *King Cophetua and the Beggar Maid*, 1884, 115½ × 53½ inches, Tate Gallery, London

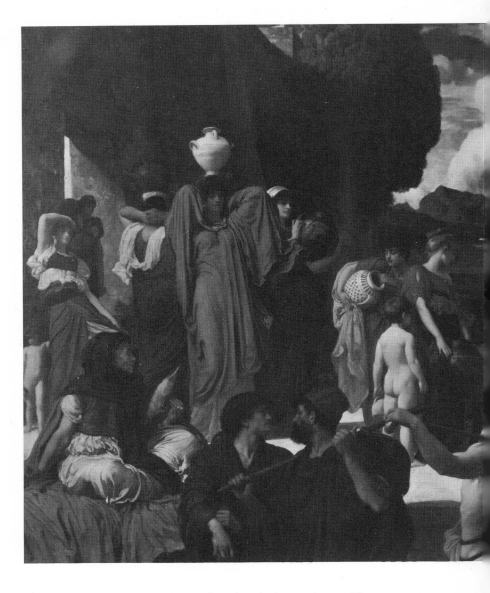

102 Frederick, Lord Leighton: *Captive Andromache*, c. 1887,
77 × 160 inches, City of Manchester Art Galleries

Leighton (1830–96) can be
regarded as the most striking
instance of the success, fame and
prosperity which a painter might
achieve in Victorian society when
great productive energy, intellectual sophistication and social ease
were, as in his case, combined
with an earnest sense of the
accepted history and traditions of
art, an obvious concern with the
ideal of beauty, and the capacity
for skilful imitation joined to a
feeling for decorative design.

103 Sir Edward Poynter: *Israel into Egypt,* 1867, 54 × 125 inches, Guildhall Library, City of London

Sir Edward Poynter (1836–1919)
who followed Leighton and
Millais as President of the Royal
Academy was, with Alma
Tadema, the most highly
esteemed painter of historical
subjects in his generation –
paintings which were influenced
by the will to achieve a physical
accuracy comparable with that
obtained through the researches
of professional historians.

In 1867 Whistler began to give his pictures those distinctive titles that we associate with them, *Symphony in White No. 1, Arrangement in Grey and Black, Caprice in Purple and Gold, Arrangement in Pink and Purple, Harmony in Grey and Green, Nocturne in Blue and Gold*. The words are immediately suggestive of musical form and composition. The *Symphony in White No. 1* was the title later given to a picture painted in 1862 of his mistress Jo standing before a white curtain in a white dress with a white flower in her left hand and with her long auburn hair flowing in Pre-Raphaelite manner

over her shoulders. The *Caprice in Purple and Gold* was the title later given to another portrait of Jo, and painted two years later. She sits on the floor in front of a Japanese screen, in Japanese costume, and with a scattering of Japanese prints before her. The decorative arrangement of all these things is much stronger than the presence or the characterisation of the figure.

Japanese prints and Oriental porcelain were an important influence upon Whistler's art. The taste for these things in particular, and Oriental art in general, which was to have such a great effect on European art,

had begun to emerge in the 1850s. An exhibition of Japanese applied art was held in London as early as 1854. It was a taste taken up by people whose artistic interests and convictions were otherwise very different. Rossetti was one of the first to form a collection of Oriental blue and white china, and Whistler may indeed have been influenced by him to collect the same thing. Japanese objects, with their simple shapes, strong colours, ornament in which flat bold planes predominated, not only began to appear in people's houses as decorative features, but influenced the design and ornament of European furnishings.

104 James McNeill Whistler: *Caprice in Purple and Gold, No. 2 : The Golden Screen,* 1864, 19¾ × 27 inches. Courtesy of the Smithsonian Institution, Freer Gallery of Art, Washington, DC, USA

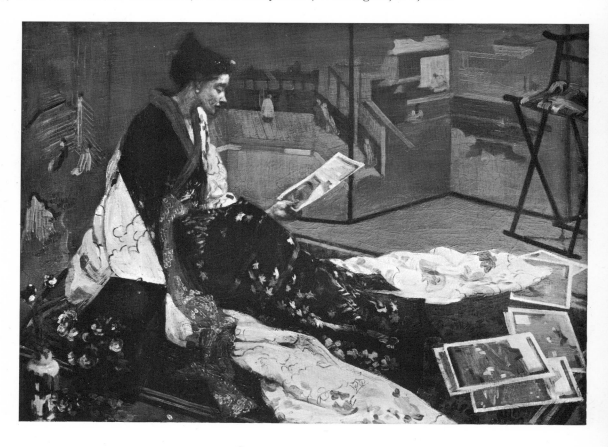

105 James McNeill Whistler: *Arrangement in Grey and Black, No. 1 : Portrait of the Artist's Mother*, 1872, 56 × 64 inches, Louvre, Paris

Whistler's portraits, the portraits of his mother and Thomas Carlyle (**106**) for example, those two *Arrangements in Grey and Black,* are works of fastidious design, in which the placing of simply framed pictures on a plain wall, the imprinting of Whistler's butterfly signature, the placing of a hat and cane, the position of white lace or a white collar, are the expressive gestures of a serious refinement. 'Take the picture of my mother,' wrote Whistler, 'exhibited at the Royal Academy as an *Arrangement in Grey and Black*. Now that is what it is. To me it is interesting as a picture of my mother ; but what can the public care about the identity of the portrait ? Art should appeal to the artistic sense of eye or ear without confounding this with emotions entirely foreign to it, as devotion, pity, love, patriotism and the like.'

106 James McNeill Whistler:
*Arrangement in Grey and Black,
No. 2 : Portrait of Thomas
Carlyle,* 1872–3,
$67\frac{3}{8} \times 56\frac{1}{2}$ inches,
Glasgow Art Gallery and Museum

For Whistler, as for so many other
artists in modern times, music,
not literature, was the art with
which painting should ally itself.
In the Ten O'Clock lecture he said
that 'Nature contains the
elements in colour and form of all
pictures, as the keyboard contains
the notes of all music.' And
elsewhere he put the point even
more directly. 'As the music is the
poetry of sound, so is painting the
poetry of sight and the subject
matter has nothing to do with
harmony of sound or of colour.
The imitator is a poor kind of
creature.'

107 Albert Joseph Moore: *Beads,*
$11\frac{3}{4} \times 20\frac{1}{4}$ inches,
National Gallery of Scotland,
Edinburgh

Albert Moore (1841–93) was a
friend of Whistler, who admired
his essentially decorative
compositions of classical figures
which made the artist a leading
figure in the Aesthetic Movement.

108 Sir William Quiller Orchardson: *The First Cloud*, 1887, $32\frac{3}{4} \times 47\frac{3}{4}$ inches, Tate Gallery, London

Although the subject pictures by Orchardson (1832–1910) invariably involved a strong historical or contemporary theme, they show a concern comparable with Whistler's work for fastidious composition and tonality.

109 Aubrey Beardsley: *How Morgan le Fay Gave a Shield to Sir Tristram*. Drawing for illustration to *Le Morte d'Arthur*, Fitzwilliam Museum, Cambridge

Beardsley's first important commission offered him in 1891 was to provide illustrations for a new edition of Malory's *Morte d'Arthur*, one of the chief source books of Pre-Raphaelitism, for Rossetti, Morris and Burne-Jones. The illustrations Beardsley made are marked by his own particular qualities and extravagances of design, but they are indebted all the same to the artists I have mentioned, might have been produced by an eccentric follower of Burne-Jones for a book produced by Morris's Kelmscott Press. Yet only three years later he was to say that a new magazine with which he was then associated, *The Savoy*, should 'attack untiringly and unflinchingly the Burne-Jones and Morrisian mediaeval business'.

HOW. MORGAN. LE FAY. GAVE. A. SHIELD. TO. SIR. TRISTRAM.

110 Aubrey Beardsley: *The Eyes of Herod.* Drawing for illustration to *Salome,* Grenville L. Winthrop Bequest, Fogg Art Museum, Harvard University, Massachusetts

111 Aubrey Beardsley: Front cover of *The Yellow Book*

The Yellow Book, the most famous artistic periodical of the 1890s, was founded in January 1884 by Beardsley and the writer Henry Harland, the former being art-editor. Beardsley was dismissed by its publisher John Lane after the conviction of Oscar Wilde, and before the appearance of the fifth number.

Before the *Morte d' Arthur* edition was published, Beardsley was working on another project with a very different source and character. Oscar Wilde's *Salome* was published in Paris in its original French version at the beginning of 1893. Beardsley made a drawing of Salome with the head of John the Baptist, which came to the attention not only of the author, but of the publisher of the English version, John Lane, and Beardsley was commissioned to make designs for that English edition. Not of course a mediaeval subject, but Beardsley's embodiment of the story does not have much to do with first-century Palestine either. The images are extremely eclectic in character, with elements from Japanese prints, out of the wall paintings in Whistler's Peacock Room, and the sort of decorative motifs found in the products of the Aesthetic Movement – sinuous plant forms and furniture with simple profiles, and attenuated parts and strange proportions of structure.

Under the Hill was the expurgated
version of Beardsley's Story of
Venus and Tannhauser, and was
published in the periodical,
The Savoy, edited by Arthur
Symons and founded by Leonard
Smithers.

112 Aubrey Beardsley: *The Abbé.*
Drawing for illustration to
Under the Hill, R. A. Harari, London

113 David Roberts *Gateway of the Great Temple at Baalbeck,* Royal Academy of Arts, London

3

PERCEPTIONS IN POETRY

by Isobel Armstrong

PAST OR PRESENT?

The Victorian fascination with a strange and exotic past is represented both in poetry and in painting. The painting by David Roberts, *Gateway of the Great Temple at Baalbek*, turns away from the Victorian scene to a magnificent and alien past. (See plate 113, preceding double spread.)

When I was first asked by the BBC to write a series of programmes on the response of the Victorian poets to contemporary life, my first reaction was to wonder why the poetry, rather than the novel, had been chosen to represent the age, for the novel is fairly close to ordinary life, whereas many of the Victorian poems one most immediately thinks of are not contemporary poems at all. In fact, you could easily make quite a substantial anthology of Victorian poems whose subjects seem to have no direct reference to the present.

Many of the most beautiful and profound of Tennyson's poems, such as *Oenone, The Lotos-Eaters* and *Ulysses*, take their subjects from classical sources and have a hauntingly distant, hazy quality, because the classical subject is seen through the rich golden haze of elegiac romantic feeling. Tennyson's later Arthurian poem, *The Idylls of the King*, turns away from modernity to legend. Browning's more robust energy, his intelligence and satirical bent suggest, perhaps, that he would have liked to take topical Victorian themes as the subjects of his poems, but his most well-known works are based on Renaissance figures, the artists and musicians in poems such as *Fra Lippo Lippi, Andrea del Sarto* and *Abt Vogler*. Matthew Arnold tried – vainly, I think – to recreate the epic in his Persian legend *Sohrab and Rustum*, a tragic story in which father and son fight one another unknowingly.

Among the major poets, only Clough stayed resolutely with the present, writing, for instance, about the social conscience, and the love affairs, of an undergraduate on a student reading party in Scotland *(The Bothie of Tober-Na-Vuolich)*, or about the love affair of a young man who found himself in Rome at the moment when the French besieged the city in 1848 *(Amours de Voyage)*. On the other hand, the less well-known poets follow the major poets in taking their subjects from myth or legend or history or even fairy story. There is Swinburne's classical *Atalanta in Calydon*, Morris' richly decorated interweaving of Norse and classical legend in *The Earthly Paradise*, Christina Rossetti's strange, sensuous fairy tale of temptation and trial, *Goblin Market*.

Confronted with so much poetry which seems to turn away deliberately from the Victorian present, a modern reader might be

THE ELECTRIC SHOCK

The Victorian poets and science

> . . . and here were telescopes
> For azure views; and there a group of girls
> In circle waited, whom the electric shock
> Dislink'd with shrieks and laughter: round the lake
> A little clock-work steamer paddling plied
> And shook the lilies: perch'd about the knolls
> A dozen angry models jetted steam:
> A petty railway ran: a fire-balloon
> Rose gem-like up before the dusky groves
> And dropt a fairy parachute and past:
> And there thro' twenty posts of telegraph
> They flash'd a saucy message to and fro
> Between the mimic stations; so that sport
> Went hand in hand with Science; otherwhere
> Pure sport: a herd of boys with clamour bowl'd
> And stump'd the wicket; babies roll'd about
> Like tumbled fruit in grass; and men and maids
> Arranged a country dance.

Tennyson *The Princess,* Prologue, lines 67 – 84

That account of a working-class holiday fête is by Tennyson, perhaps the best-known of all the Victorian poets. In this series of programmes I am going to talk about the various ways in which the Victorian poets responded to contemporary life – their attitudes to urban life, to social problems, to love, to religion and, in this programme, to science. The poem you have just heard comes from the prologue to Tennyson's *The Princess* and describes the meeting of a mechanics institute which he saw in 1842. The newspaper report of this festival tells us that eight hundred people sat down to tea, that there were two bands and that there was dancing and cricketing. But mechanics' institutes were founded to educate their members as well as to amuse them, and the giggling group of girls, described so vividly by Tennyson, were being instructed about electricity at the same time as they were being shocked by it. The miniature steamer, the train and the mock telegraph were all there to illustrate the wonders of the science which was the foundation of Victorian technology. 'Sport went hand in hand with Science', Tennyson

114 Science is domesticated as children gather for an informal lesson in Millais' *The Ornithologist*, Glasgow Art Gallery and Museum

116 (right) Educational festivals, fêtes and outings, such as that of the Mechanics' Institute in Tennyson's *The Princess,* abounded in the nineteenth century. Here a party of school children set out for pleasure and instruction

says, and his description catches some of the excitement, the sense of wonder and sheer enjoyment of the magical things that science was able to achieve. Indeed, many Victorians thought of science and magic together, and one often finds fairy stories like the Arabian Nights being invoked to describe the many excitements of science.

It is as well to remember this zestful response to scientific discovery, for it is easy, sometimes, to put too much emphasis on the misery which scientific discoveries created for the poets, particularly those of geologists and biologists. Obviously, scientific development helped to create the mood of doubt and depression expressed by some poets, and I will look at this in another programme. Even Tennyson wrote some agonised, horror-stricken poems about

115 The wonders of the age of machinery: spectators view the huge cogs of a sugar-cane crushing-mill at the Great Exhibition of 1851

the meaninglessness of a world in which the arbitrary forces of evolution were at work: *In Memoriam* has several such passages.

> 'So careful of the type'? but no.
>   From scarpèd cliff and quarried stone
>   She cries, 'A thousand types are gone:
> I care for nothing, all shall go.
>
> 'Thou makest thine appeal to me:
>   I bring to life, I bring to death:
>   The spirit does but mean the breath:
> I know no more.' And he, shall he,
>
> Man, her last work, who seem'd so fair,
>   Such splendid purpose in his eyes,
>   Who roll'd the psalm to wintry skies,
> Who built him fanes of fruitless prayer,
>
> Who trusted God was love indeed
>   And love Creation's final law —
>   Tho' Nature, red in tooth and claw
> With ravine, shriek'd against his creed —
>
> Who loved, who suffer'd countless ills,
>   Who battled for the True, the Just,
>   Be blown about the desert dust,
> Or seal'd within the iron hills?
>
> No more? A monster then, a dream,
>   A discord. Dragons of the prime,
>   That tare each other in their slime,
> Were mellow music match'd with him.
>
> O life as futile, then, as frail!
>   O for thy voice to soothe and bless!
>   What hope of answer, or redress?
> Behind the veil, behind the veil.
>
> Tennyson *In Memoriam*, LVI

The impersonal struggle for survival, 'Nature, red in tooth and claw', tearing creation to bits, seemed ruthlessly destructive and made it difficult to believe in a benevolent God. Charles Darwin's great work of evolutionary theory was published in 1859. Evolutionary theory had, in fact, been developed well before him, but Darwin transformed the theory by his concept of natural selection, which showed that some variations within a group of organisms make them fitter to survive and reproduce than others, so that modifications in favour of survival are passed on to later generations. Darwin, therefore, called his book *On the Origin of Species by means of Natural Selection, or the Preservation of Favoured Races in the Struggle for Life,* a title with a sinister ring. Tennyson, however, was more influenced by the work of geologists, such as Charles Lyell, and by the populariser of evolutionary ideas Robert Chambers, whose *Vestiges of Creation* was published in 1844. For Chambers, the great movement of creation in space and time suggested that natural law was the expression of God's will. The scale of God's creation is huge, he argued confidently, so:

> How can we suppose that the august Being, who brought all these countless worlds into form by the simple establishment of a natural principle flowing from his mind, was to interfere personally and specially on every occasion when a new shellfish or reptile was ushered into existence on *one* of these worlds?

> Chambers *Vestiges of Creation*

On the other hand, Tennyson at times thought that the loving Creator was now annihilated. A creation where 'not one life shall be destroyed', where 'nothing walks with aimless feet' and where 'not a worm is cloven in vain' was contradicted by evolutionary theory.

Not all the poets were so despairing. Arthur Hugh Clough builds an extraordinarily exuberant poem out of a moment of attraction to an unknown girl in a railway carriage. The sudden charged moment of sexual feeling is seen as part of the energy which drives even the smallest forms of organic life. Even mollusc and lichen depend on it to propagate and survive. Because humans have evolved through fish and reptile, the girl and the man hold within themselves the huge, slow, but vital, history of evolving life, the energies of the 'leopard lithe' and the inexorable life of the 'slow crustacea'.

> Ah no! – Yet owned we, fused in one,
>   The Power which e'en in stones and earths
> By blind elections felt, in forms
>   Organic breeds to myriad births;
> By lichen small on granite wall
>   Approved, its faintest feeblest stir
> Slow-spreading, strengthening long, at last
>   Vibrated full in me and her.
>   *
> Flashed flickering forth fantastic flies,
>   Big bees their burly bodies swung,
> Rooks roused with civic din the elms,
>   And lark its wild reveillez rung;
> In Libyan dell the light gazelle,
>   The leopard lithe in Indian glade,
> And dolphin, brightening tropic seas,
>   In us were living, leapt and played:
>
> Their shells did slow crustacea build,
>   Their gilded skins did snakes renew,
> While mightier spines for loftier kind
>   Their types in amplest limbs outgrew;
> Yea, close comprest in human breast,
>   What moss, and tree, and livelier thing,
> What Earth, Sun, Star of force possest,
>   Lay budding, burgeoning forth for Spring.

> Clough *Natura Naturans*, stanzas 6, 8, 9

Browning is another poet who responded zestfully to the possibilities which science opens up. One poem is spoken by an imagi-
nary Arab physician, Karshish, supposedly living just after the time
of Christ. He explores the way in which a rational, empirical,
'scientific' mind works, excluding all emotion and subjective feeling from his investigations. Karshish is, naturally, very limited. He
finds himself confronted by Lazarus, whom Christ had raised from
the dead, and he finds him quite inexplicable. And yet Browning is
fascinated by the tireless, imaginative energy of the man's research-
ing mind, its impassioned accuracy and perfectionism. As Karshish
moves impersonally from an account of blowing eye-drops up his
messenger's nose to a comment on the superior properties of
Judaean mucilage for drugs and an attempt to diagnose scalp disease, Browning finely renders the scientist's clinical use of terms
which, nevertheless, sound strange, exotic and beautiful – 'sublimate', 'gum-tragacanth', 'the pestle and the porphyry'.

And falling-sickness hath a happier cure
Than our school wots of: there's a spider here
Weaves no web, watches on the ledge of tombs,
Sprinkled with mottles on an ash-grey back;
Take five and drop them . . . but who knows his mind,
The Syrian runagate I trust this to?
His service payeth me a sublimate
Blown up his nose to help the ailing eye.
Best wait: I reach Jerusalem at morn,
There set in order my experiences,
Gather what most deserves, and give thee all –
Or I might add, Judaea's gum-tragacanth
Scales off in purer flakes, shines clearer-grained,
Cracks 'twixt the pestle and the porphyry,
In fine exceeds our produce. Scalp-disease
Confounds me, crossing so with leprosy –
Thou hadst admired one sort I gained at Zoar –
But zeal outruns discretion.

Browning *An Epistle, containing the strange medical
experience of Karshish, the Arab physician*, lines 44–61

Browning realised that science had literally changed the pers-
pectives of the world he inhabited. In *Mr Sludge, 'The Medium'* the
speaker, who is a trick medium, argues that the small signs he deals
with are as important as the great, and uses the discoveries of
science to support his argument. The telescope and the microscope
have changed our sense of the proportions of things; our notions of
the relations of things, of great and small, have become violently
unstable. Everything is relative. In a speech which throngs with
words of measurement – big, little, great, small – Sludge brings out
the full drama of an environment of ever-changing, ever-readjust-
ing size and proportion. The microscope makes the world full of
pullulating life and activity. Even a mite grows huge. God 'comes
close behind a stomach-cyst', a mere sac.

A mote of sand, you know, a blade of grass —
What was so despicable as mere grass,
Except perhaps the life o' the worm or fly
Which fed there? These were 'small' and men were great.
Well, sir, the old way's altered somewhat since,
And the world wears another aspect now:
Somebody turns our spyglass round, or else
Puts a new lens in it: grass, worm, fly grow big:
We find great things are made of little things,
And little things go lessening till at last
Comes God behind them. Talk of mountains now?
We talk of mould that heaps the mountain, mites
That throng the mould, and God that makes the mites.
The Name comes close behind a stomach-cyst,
The simplest of creations, just a sac
That's mouth, heart, legs and belly at once, yet lives
And feels, and could do neither, we conclude,
If simplified still further one degree:
The small becomes the dreadful and immense . . .

Browning *Mr Sludge, 'The Medium,'* lines 1112 – 30

Science gave the Victorians two kinds of space, two kinds of perspective. On the one hand there were the vast spaces of the universe and the slow processes of geological time, which seemed to diminish human activity almost to nothing. On the other hand there was the space directly around you, which thronged with minutely individualised forms of life, each with its particular organisation and qualities, each, whether it was the larva of an insect or the spawn of a frog, related in some way to the infinite series of differentiations and adaptations which had gone on throughout man's evolution. In *Vestiges of Creation* Chambers is fond of moving from the minute to the vast in order to show this drama.

> The tear that falls from childhood's cheek is globular, through the efficacy of that same law of mutual attraction of particles which made the sun and planets round . . . Two eddies in a stream . . . fall into a mutual revolution at a distance of a couple of inches, through the same cause which makes a pair of suns link in mutual revolution at the distance of millions of miles.

Chambers *Vestiges of Creation*

The Victorian poet had to find two different languages for these opposed kinds of space, for the two-inch-spaced eddies on a stream and for the millions of miles of space in which suns rotated.

Some poets transferred the close, scrupulous, minute observation of the botanist or the biologist to the world immediately around them. Their language strives for precise and accurate rendering of the smallest visual detail. There is a kind of scientific method in Tennyson's lyricism, for instance. He notices the tiny dews on furze and the wet spiders' webs, as well as the autumn trees of a

117 This meticulous botanical drawing of a foxglove suggests how science trained the Victorians in minute observation of detail

118 One of the characters in Mrs Gaskell's *Cranford* says that without Tennyson he would never have seen that the buds of the ash are black: the colours and fibres of each autumn leaf are reproduced in Millais' painting with the same accuracy. *Autumn Leaves*, City of Manchester Art Galleries

landscape. He notices the pink fringe at the tips of a daisy petal, the woolly breasts and beady eyes of bats. In the same way Browning noticed the intense red splashes on autumn leaves, the woolly exterior of the bud of a vine. Some poets were almost obsessed with the need for truthfulness and accuracy in description. It is as if they tried to protect themselves from the scientists' view that poetry was unnecessary and redundant.

In the nineteenth century the function of the arts was increasingly questioned. The age was practical and utilitarian in any case, and the achievements of science seemed to make poetry useless, a mere luxury. It was wasteful and self-indulgent and did not seem to have an immediate use or relevance to life. In the last resort people could do without it. And so the poets showed that they too could be as accurate as a scientist: they appropriated objectivity and detail for themselves. There is also something rather desperate about this. The scientists opened up a vast, shifting universe. By clinging to *things*, to minute detail and particular phenomena, you held on to what was real and concrete and defended yourself against a huge and alien universe.

Hopkins, who loathed Darwinian notions, interestingly enough comes closer than any of the Victorian poets to achieving this accuracy. Hopkins admired the work of Ruskin and learned a good deal from his close, painstaking observation of natural phenomena in *Modern Painters*. Ruskin tried to show that the phenomena of the sky and the earth could be recorded truthfully, almost with scientific accuracy. In a passage from the section of *Modern Painters* entitled 'Of Truth of Skies' Ruskin describes the effects of the interaction of vapour and light with precision and exactitude.

> The appearance of mist or whiteness in the blue of the sky is thus a circumstance which more or less accompanies sunshine, and which, supposing the quantity of vapour constant, is greatest in the brightest sunlight. When there are no clouds in the sky, the whiteness, as it affects the whole sky equally, is not particularly noticeable. But when there are clouds between us and the sun, the sun being low, those clouds cast shadows along and through the mass of suspended vapour. Within the space of these shadows, the vapour, as above stated, becomes transparent and invisible, and the sky appears of a pure blue. But where the sunbeams strike, the vapour becomes visible in the form of the beams, occasioning those radiating shafts of light which are one of the most valuable and constant accompaniments of a low sun. The denser the mist, the more distinct and sharp-edged will these rays be; when the air is very clear, they are mere vague, flushing, gradated passages of light; when it is very thick, they are keen-edged and decisive in a high degree.
>
> Ruskin *Modern Painters*, Part II, Sec. III, Chap. I, 'Of Truth of Skies'

The same precision of description is found in the accounts of landscape and sky in Hopkins' *Journals*, only it is far less sober. Hopkins transformed Ruskinian observation into impassioned objectivity, an extraordinarily strenuous way of looking at the world. His *Journals* are filled with minute and exquisite observation – of the formation of oak trees, the colour of a bluebell, the tiny surface creases which form on the skin of milk when it is just about to come to the boil, the exact colour and texture in the underside of the crest of a wave. Hopkins searched exhaustively for precisely the *right* descriptive word, sometimes reviving old words, sometimes inventing new ones. For instance, he writes of the surface of water in moonlight being made to look as if it is metallic. The uneven

119 Artists *and* scientists looked at the world above, as well as below and around them. Constable's clouds have the same impassioned observation that we find in Ruskin and Hopkins. Victoria and Albert Museum, London

surface is 'roughened, dinted, tooled'. He piles up adjectives, and chooses the word 'dinted' rather than the more orthodox 'dented', perhaps because it suggests some action very slightly lighter and less violent. The detail and particularity of things seem to burst from the page with an energy of their own – at one point in his *Journals* he even said that what you looked hard at, looked hard at you. Here he is looking hard at the sky:

July 13. Fine. All day faint long tails, getting thicker as the day went on, and at one time there were some like long ringlets, namely curls shaping out a hollow screw. Rows of cloud lay across sky at sunset, their lit parts yellow, below which was the curious opaque blue one sometimes sees with that colour.

Hopkins *Journals* (1866)

Hopkins' poems intensify this enraptured precision. In *Hurrahing in Harvest* Hopkins invents his own compound words to describe the shapes and behaviour of clouds – 'silk-sack clouds', 'meal-drift'.

> Summer ends now; now, barbarous in beauty, the stooks rise
> Around; up above, what wind-walks! what lovely behaviour
> Of silk-sack clouds! has wilder, wilful-wavier
> Meal-drift moulded ever and melted across skies?
>
> I walk, I lift up, I lift up heart, eyes,
> Down all that glory in the heavens to glean our Saviour;
> And, éyes, heárt, what looks, what lips yet gave you a
> Rapturous love's greeting of realer, of rounder replies?
>
> And the azurous hung hills are his world-wielding shoulder
> Majestic – as a stallion stalwart, very-violet-sweet! –
> These things, these things were here and but the beholder
> Wanting; which two when they once meet,
> The heart rears wings bold and bolder
> And hurls for him, O half hurls earth for him off under his feet.

Hopkins *Hurrahing in Harvest*

In the second space created by the scientists, the space of a vast universe and slow geological change, Hopkins was not at home. In fact he resolutely turned away from it. On the other hand Tennyson and Browning acknowledged the hypotheses of science and tried to find a language to express imaginatively their sense of living in a world shaped by huge cosmic forces. And so it would be right to argue, I think, that science gave the rhetoric of these poets its charged and expressive vocabulary. In this passage from *Paracelsus* Browning is fascinated by the massive energy which changes the structure of the world, the extreme transitions from molten fire and heat to cold, the gigantic eruptions which deposit melted ore in river beds and in mountains, where it 'Winds into the stone's heart'.

> The centre-fire heaves underneath the earth,
> And the earth changes like a human face;
> The molten ore bursts up among the rocks,
> Winds into the stone's heart, outbranches bright
> In hidden mines, spots barren river-beds,
> Crumbles into fine sand where sunbeams bask –
> God joys therein. The wroth sea's waves are edged
> With foam, white as the bitten lip of hate,
> When, in the solitary waste, strange groups
> Of young volcanos come up, cyclops-like,
> Staring together with their eyes on flame –
> God tastes a pleasure in their uncouth pride,
> Then all is still; earth is a wintry clod:
> But spring-wind, like a dancing psaltress, passes
> Over its breast to waken it, rare verdure

Buds tenderly upon rough banks, between
The withered tree-roots and the cracks of frost,
Like a smile striving with a wrinkled face;
The grass grows bright, the boughs are swoln with blooms
Like chrysalids impatient for the air,
The shining dorrs are busy, beetles run
Along the furrows, ants make their ado;
Above, birds fly in merry flocks, the lark
Soars up and up, shivering for very joy;
Afar the ocean sleeps; white fishing-gulls
Flit where the strand is purple with its tribe
Of nested limpets; savage creatures seek
Their loves in wood and plain – and God renews
His ancient rapture. Thus he dwells in all,
From life's minute beginnings, up at last
To man – the consummation of this scheme
Of being, the completion of this sphere
Of life: whose attributes had here and there
Been scattered o'er the visible world before,
Asking to be combined, dim fragments meant
To be united in some wondrous whole,
Imperfect qualities throughout creation,
Suggesting some one creature yet to make,
Some point where all those scattered rays should meet
Convergent in the faculties of man.

Browning *Paracelsus*, lines 653 – 92

The same vocabulary of heat and molten solids and giant energy is present in the more convincingly optimistic parts of Tennyson's *In Memoriam*, where these transformations can be accepted as sublime evidence of a shaping power.

Contemplate all this work of Time,
　　The giant labouring in his youth;
　　Nor dream of human love and truth,
As dying Nature's earth and lime;

But trust that those we call the dead
　　Are breathers of an ampler day
　　For ever nobler ends. They say
The solid earth whereon we tread

In tracts of fluent heat began,
　　And grew to seeming-random forms,
　　The seeming prey of cyclic storms,
Till at the last arose the man;

Who throve and branch'd from clime to clime,
　　The herald of a higher race,
　　And of himself in higher place,
If so he type this work of time

Within himself, from more to more;
　　Or, crown'd with attributes of woe

Like glories, move his course, and show
That life is not as idle ore,

But iron dug from central gloom,
And heated hot with burning fears,
And dipt in baths of hissing tears,
And batter'd with the shocks of doom

To shape and use. Arise and fly
The reeling Faun, the sensual feast;
Move upward, working out the beast,
And let the ape and tiger die.

Tennyson *In Memoriam,* CXVIII

In 1880 T. H. Huxley opened Sir Josiah Mason's Science College in Birmingham. He gave an address on the ends of education, attacking the exclusively literary and classical culture upon which the traditional notion of a liberal education depended. This speech was part of his running battle with Matthew Arnold, who seemed to Huxley to give no place to science and the thrusting new technology and industry which it supported. 'I venture to think' he said, 'that the pretension of our modern humanists to the possession of the monopoly of culture and to the exclusive inheritance of antiquity must be abated, if not abandoned'. The poets at any rate had conceded this point in a way, by allowing the concepts of science to penetrate their vocabulary.

And throughout the century evolutionary ideas were a fertile source of poetic imagery. In Swinburne's *Hertha* an incantatory quality is given to the notion of a world governed by an impersonal force of cyclic change, a world in constant movement from life to destruction.

I the grain and the furrow,
The plow-cloven clod
And the plowshare drawn thorough,
The germ and the sod,
The deed and the doer, the seed and the sower, the dust
which is God.

*

The storm-winds of ages
Blow through me and cease,
The war-wind that rages,
The spring-wind of peace,
Ere the breath of them roughen my tresses, ere one of my
blossoms increase.

All sounds of all changes,
All shadows and lights
On the world's mountain-ranges
And stream-riven heights,
Whose tongue is the wind's tongue and language of
storm-clouds on earth-shaking nights . . .

Swinburne *Hertha*, lines 36 – 40, 121 – 130

This pessimism about an unchanging world is absent from the poetry of Tennyson and Browning, and the later in the century they are, the more the poets use the vast aeons of evolutionary space and time to diminish the importance of life.

In the middle of the century the poets' response to science was mixed, sometimes distrustful, sometimes eager; and whatever their feelings about it, they made use of the vocabulary which science offered. But their views darken as the century moves on. Hardy's poem *Before Life and After*, which longs for a return to primordial unknowingness, is more terrible than anything in Tennyson's *In Memoriam* because it sees the evolution of consciousness itself as a corrupting state. Huxley was optimistic about a scientific culture. Hardy's poem is so despairing that Huxley could scarcely have begun to answer it.

> A Time there was – as one may guess
> And as, indeed, earth's testimonies tell –
> Before the birth of consciousness,
> When all went well.
>
> None suffered sickness, love, or loss,
> None knew regret, starved hope, or heart-burnings;
> None cared whatever crash or cross
> Brought wrack to things.
>
> If something ceased, no tongue bewailed,
> If something winced and waned, no heart was wrung;
> If brightness dimmed, and dark prevailed,
> No sense was stung.
>
> But the disease of feeling germed,
> And primal rightness took the tint of wrong;
> Ere nescience shall be reaffirmed
> How long, how long?

Hardy *Before Life and After*

120 Thomas Hardy

GOD'S IN HIS HEAVEN?

Doubt and consolation in Victorian poetry

> The year's at the spring
> And day's at the morn;
> Morning's at seven;
> The hill-side's dew-pearled;
> The lark's on the wing;
> The snail's on the thorn:
> God's in his heaven –
> All's right with the world!
>
> Browning *Pippa Passes*, lines 222 – 29

That song by Browning is part of a much larger poem, *Pippa Passes*, published in 1841; but many people know this poem out of its context and, to them, its apparently manly sentiments typify all that seems crudely self-satisfied in Victorian optimism. Yet it is deliberately naïve because it is sung by a simple factory girl from the silk-mills at Asolo in Northern Italy on the only day of holiday she has in the whole year.

It would be wrong to think that all the Victorians were as naïve as Browning's Pippa. In fact some were so shocked by the abuses and inequalities of their society that they were forced to cling to an optimistic and theological view of the world rather than fall into despair. If they could not *be* hopeful, they would at least *believe* in hope.

So when they turned to the poet they looked for someone they could vaguely define as the poet of the age. He would give them a strong, affirmative, health-giving poetry, free from morbidity, doubt and despair. One critic asked that the poet should look at his age, 'racked and torn, haunted by ghosts', and produce a 'creative survey of modern life'; while Matthew Arnold, in a preface to his own poems, warned of 'the feeling of depression, the feeling of ennui' in modern poetry. And yet, strangely enough, it is exactly this 'feeling of depression' that turns out to be one of the dominating notes of Victorian poetry. Charles Kingsley complained, ironically, of the sadness and inaction of Arnold's early poetry – 'If he is a Whig', he remarked, 'why can't he be great upon sewerage?'

In spite of the prevailing opinion that the poet should be affirmative, the best Victorian poets sound a feeling of loss and bewilderment. And, in fact, they come much nearer to producing a 'creative survey' of their modern life when they speak of the age unofficially and unhopefully. Arnold's poem *Dover Beach* beautifully expresses a feeling of elegiac loss for a belief which has gone. A calm, glimmeringly uncertain moonlit seascape, full of the rhythmical sound of the waves, becomes the source of desolation when it is made an image for the 'ebb and flow of human misery' and the ebbing 'Sea of Faith'. The lyricism is understated – almost blanched – like the landscape itself, but it is an extraordinarily intense poem.

> The sea is calm to-night.
> The tide is full, the moon lies fair
> Upon the straits; – on the French coast the light
> Gleams and is gone; the cliffs of England stand,
> Glimmering and vast, out in the tranquil bay.
> Come to the window, sweet is the night-air!
> Only, from the long line of spray
> Where the sea meets the moon-blanch'd land,
> Listen! you hear the grating roar
> Of pebbles which the waves draw back, and fling,
> At their return, up the high strand,
> Begin, and cease, and then again begin,
> With tremulous cadence slow, and bring
> The eternal note of sadness in.
>
> Sophocles long ago
> Heard it on the Aegaean, and it brought
> Into his mind the turbid ebb and flow
> Of human misery; we
> Find also in the sound a thought,
> Hearing it by this distant northern sea.
>
> The Sea of Faith
> Was once, too, at the full, and round earth's shore
> Lay like the folds of a bright girdle furl'd.
> But now I only hear
> Its melancholy, long, withdrawing roar,
> Retreating, to the breath
> Of the night-wind, down the vast edges drear
> And naked shingles of the world.
>
> Ah, love, let us be true
> To one another! for the world, which seems
> To lie before us like a land of dreams,
> So various, so beautiful, so new,
> Hath really neither joy, nor love, nor light,
> Nor certitude, nor peace, nor help for pain;
> And we are here as on a darkling plain
> Swept with confused alarms of struggle and flight,
> Where ignorant armies clash by night.

Arnold *Dover Beach*

The poem sets up the natural ebb and flow of the sea, only to disrupt it as the Sea of Faith withdraws forever down time and history, leaving the world empty. The huge spaces in the poem, as it moves from the 'northern sea' to the Aegaean, and back from the present to Sophocles and another culture, make the lovers seem particularly isolated and threatened by flux.

Arnold found exactly the right image of flux in the sea, and echoed Victorian intellectuals, who constantly reiterated their sense of living in a state of cultural flux and instability. As the critic G. H. Lewes wrote, 'Great ideas are in the process of incarnation; great changes are taking place within the womb of society . . . but . . . we are not yet on the eve of a new birth'.

Traditional moral certainties and grounds for belief in God had been steadily eroded and many Victorian intellectuals felt stranded without a coherent religious structure to depend upon. The methods of German historical criticism had challenged the integrity of the Bible, and the discoveries of geologists and zoologists, like Lyell and Darwin, suggested that God had not made the universe in one decisive act of creation, as the book of Genesis describes; it had evolved arbitrarily over hundreds of thousands of years. The theological controversies and the varieties of religious position in the nineteenth century are a response to these undermining forces.

But many people felt that the old beliefs had completely gone, leaving nothing in their place. One world of belief was dead, Arnold wrote in *Stanzas from the Grande Chartreuse*, the other 'struggling to be born'. While Clough, the friend of Matthew Arnold, wrote a poem called *Easter Day* in which he denies the events of the Resurrection with hot, firm anger and reiterates 'Christ is not risen'. And yet there is a kind of conviction about the very uncertainty of this poem and it has a grand and resolute energy. The solidity of its rhetoric comes from the strength of Clough's irony. In stressing that Christ is not *risen*, Clough is pointing to the unimportance of the mere physical and historical facts behind the Resurrection; even if the Resurrection did not happen, we are still left with the inner meaning of the myth. The full significance of the myth is still 'struggling to be born'.

Through the great sinful streets of Naples as I past,
With fiercer heat than flamed above my head
My heart was hot within me; till at last
My brain was lightened, when my tongue had said

    Christ is not risen!

  Christ is not risen, no,
  He lies and moulders low;
    Christ is not risen.

What though the stone were rolled away, and though
    The grave found empty there! –
    If not there, then elsewhere;
If not where Joseph laid Him first, why then
    Where other men

Translaid Him after; in some humbler clay
    Long ere today.
Corruption that sad perfect work hath done,
Which here she scarcely, lightly had begun.
    The foul engendered worm
Feeds on the flesh of the life-giving form
Of our most Holy and Anointed One.

    He is not risen, no,
    He lies and moulders low;
      Christ is not risen.

    Ashes to ashes, dust to dust;
As of the unjust, also of the just –
      Christ is not risen.

What if the women, ere the dawn was grey,
Saw one or more great angels, as they say,
Angels, or Him himself? Yet neither there, nor then,
Nor afterward, nor elsewhere, nor at all,
Hath He appeared to Peter or the Ten,
Nor, save in thunderous terror, to blind Saul;
Save in an after-Gospel and late Creed
    He is not risen indeed,
      Christ is not risen.

Or what if e'en, as runs the tale, the Ten
Saw, heard, and touched, again and yet again?
What if at Emmäus' inn and by Capernaum's lake
    Came One the bread that brake,
Came One that spake as never mortal spake,
And with them ate and drank and stood and walked about?
    Ah! 'some' did well to 'doubt'!
Ah! the true Christ, while these things came to pass,
Nor heard, nor spake, nor walked, nor dreamt, alas!
    He was not risen, no,
    He lay and mouldered low,
      Christ was not risen.

121 Arthur Hugh Clough   Clough *Easter Day*, lines 1 – 47

Clough's heroic uncertainty is an exception. More typical of the prevailing mood is Tennyson's *In Memoriam*. Published in 1850, the year before the Great Exhibition, it overflows with the distress of loss. Written as an elegy for the death of his closest friend Arthur Hallam, who died in 1833, it began as a series of lyrics and grew into a long poem. But though personally inspired, it is also an elegy on the loss of belief and on the loss of energy and vitality itself. It is as if the loss of belief in God meant a loss of belief in life. The early part of this poem is full of images of darkness and emptiness, of shadows of hollow or muffled forms, as if the visible world has been emptied of meaning and significance, and human perception is untrustworthy and unreal. In writing elegiacally about the church-yard yew, the poet grasps at death just as the tree's roots grasp at the stones 'That name the under-lying dead'.

Old Yew, which graspest at the stones
    That name the under-lying dead,
    Thy fibres net the dreamless head,
Thy roots are wrapt about the bones.

The seasons bring the flower again,
    And bring the firstling to the flock;
    And in the dusk of thee, the clock
Beats out the little lives of men.

O not for thee the glow, the bloom,
    Who changest not in any gale,
    Nor branding summer suns avail
To touch thy thousand years of gloom:

And gazing on thee, sullen tree,
    Sick for thy stubborn hardihood,
    I seem to fail from out my blood
And grow incorporate into thee.

            Tennyson *In Memoriam*, II

And then, at times, *In Memoriam* becomes a cry of simple panic and desperation. The poet is as vulnerable as a child crying out in the night.

Oh yet we trust that somehow good
    Will be the final goal of ill,
    To pangs of nature, sins of will,
Defects of doubt, and taints of blood;

That nothing walks with aimless feet;
    That not one life shall be destroy'd,
    Or cast as rubbish to the void,
When God hath made the pile complete;

That not a worm is cloven in vain;
    That not a moth with vain desire
    Is shrivell'd in a fruitless fire,
Or but subserves another's gain.

Behold, we know not anything;
    I can but trust that good shall fall
    At last – far off – at last, to all,
And every winter change to spring.

So runs my dream: but what am I?
    An infant crying in the night:
    An infant crying for the light:
And with no language but a cry.

            Tennyson *In Memoriam*, LIV

Tennyson's doubt comes straight from the emotions. He was not a speculative poet and *In Memoriam* never attempts to argue out particular positions in detail. But Browning's robust, intellectual

122 Doubt and consolation go hand in hand in this delicately musing painting. A butterfly goes across a grave and green leaves grow over it. H. A. Bowler *The Doubt : 'Can these dry bones live?'*, The Tate Gallery, London

curiosity made him fascinated by religious debate. In particular, he was fascinated by the 'dangerous edge' of religious experience, by situations in which intellectual proof was untrustworthy and false feelings could deceive.

Browning expended a vast amount of imaginative and intellectual energy in arguing that religious experience defies argument. After all, nothing can test the authenticity of religious experience but the quality of the feeling itself. Browning's best poem on this theme is not, in fact, a monologue but a narrative called *Christmas Eve and Easter Day*. It describes three religious experiences – a Hell-fire sermon in a poor, dissenting chapel, a lecture by an arid German rationalist, and an extravagant Catholic service at St Peter's in Rome. Much the best part of the poem is the description of the mean Sion Chapel, on the edge of slums and alleys, surrounded by palings broken by the congregation who take short cuts across the common from unlighted streets. Browning came from a dissenting family and he describes the congregation with

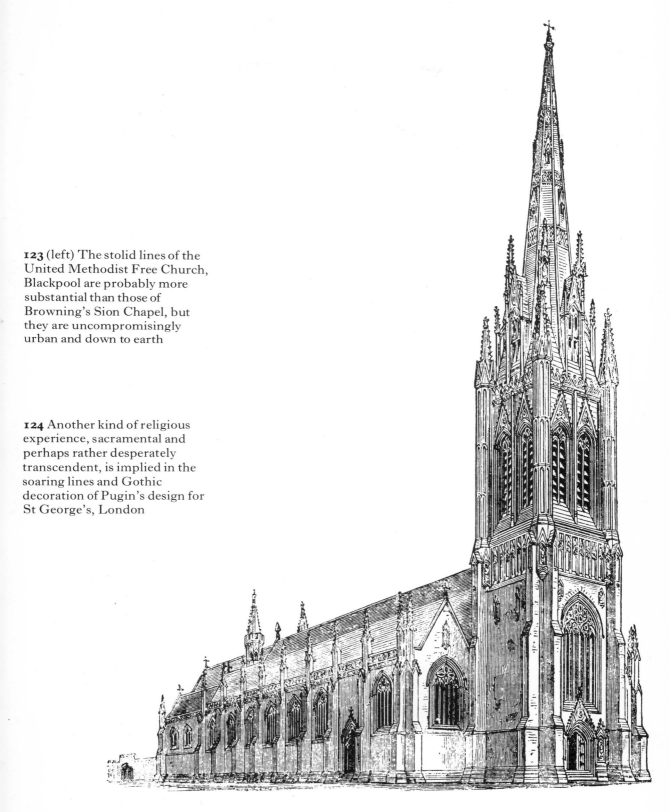

123 (left) The stolid lines of the United Methodist Free Church, Blackpool are probably more substantial than those of Browning's Sion Chapel, but they are uncompromisingly urban and down to earth

124 Another kind of religious experience, sacramental and perhaps rather desperately transcendent, is implied in the soaring lines and Gothic decoration of Pugin's design for St George's, London

comic but perceptive intimacy and a refusal to sentimentalise characters – the sickly workman, the panting, fat woman with an umbrella which is a 'wreck of whalebones' and the 'many-tattered' care-worn child – a 'Little old-faced sister-turned-mother' who clutched a baby and her wet clogs. Browning scoffs at the close suspiciousness of this group when they see him and at the crudity of the religious feeling in the chapel, and yet he has a real understanding of the needs of the congregation and returns to it at the end of the poem, granting the chapel religious authenticity and importance.

> I very soon had enough of it.
>   The hot smell and the human noises,
> And my neighbour's coat, the greasy cuff of it,
>   Were a pebble-stone that a child's hand poises,
> Compared with the pig-of-lead-like pressure
>   Of the preaching man's immense stupidity,
> As he poured his doctrine forth, full measure,
>   To meet his audience's avidity.
> You needed not the wit of the Sibyl
>   To guess the cause of it all, in a twinkling:
>   No sooner our friend had got an inkling
> Of treasure hid in the Holy Bible,
>   (Whene'er 'twas the thought first struck him,
> How death, at unawares, might duck him
> Deeper than the grave, and quench
> The gin-shop's light in hell's grim drench)
> Than he handled it so, in fine irreverence,
>   As to hug the book of books to pieces:
> And, a patchwork of chapters and texts in severance,
>   Not improved by the private dog's-ears and creases,
> Having clothed his own soul with, he'd fain see equipt yours, –
> So tossed you again your Holy Scriptures.
> And you picked them up, in a sense, no doubt:
>   Nay, had but a single face of my neighbours
>   Appeared to suspect that the preacher's labours
> Were help which the world could be saved without,
> 'Tis odds but I might have borne in quiet
> A qualm or two at my spiritual diet,
> Or (who can tell?) perchance even mustered
>   Somewhat to urge in behalf of the sermon:
> But the flock sat on, divinely flustered,
>   Sniffing, methought, its dew of Hermon
> With such content in every snuffle,
> As the devil inside us loves to ruffle.
> My old fat woman purred with pleasure,
>   And thumb round thumb went twirling faster,
> While she, to his periods keeping measure,
>   Maternally devoured the pastor.

Browning *Christmas Eve,* III

Because the discoveries of science and the new biblical criticism challenged the historical basis of Christianity, the poets fell back on

125 Butler's style admirably catches the stiffness and sanctimoniousness of family religion. Samuel Butler *Family Prayers,* St John's College, Cambridge

the private moment of vision and spiritual insight as a way of defending their beliefs. As Tennyson's *In Memoriam* simply asserts: 'I have felt'. The sceptic, though, can always refuse to accept the spiritual explanation of others' moments of insight. So Browning's Bishop Blougram says, sophisticatedly, that even the aesthetic experience of 'a chorus from Euripides' may give one the illusion of faith; and the rationalistic spirit in Clough's poem *Dipsychus* mocks a young man who is going through a crisis of faith: the moment of rapture has a crude, physical cause – it is the result of 'happier-tempered coffee'.

But though the poets spent so much energy defending the moment of vision from attack, they still had energy to spare for satirical accounts of the religious hypocrisy of their society. Clough's *The Latest Decalogue* is an ironical exposure of a morality with double standards. His readers would have been familiar with a poem written for children on the Ten Commandments by Isaac Watts, and so his sharp, blasphemous parody acquires particular bite.

Thou shalt have one God only; who
Would be at the expense of two?
No graven images may be
Worshipped, except the currency:
Swear not at all; for for thy curse
Thine enemy is none the worse:
At church on Sunday to attend
Will serve to keep the world thy friend:
Honour thy parents; that is, all
From whom advancement may befall:
Thou shalt not kill; but needst not strive
Officiously to keep alive:
Do not adultery commit;
Advantage rarely comes of it:
Thou shalt not steal; an empty feat,
When it's so lucrative to cheat:
Bear not false witness; let the lie
Have time on its own wings to fly:
Thou shalt not covet; but tradition
Approves all forms of competition.

The sum of all is, thou shalt love,
If any body, God above:
At any rate shall never labour
More than thyself to love thy neighbour.

Clough *The Latest Decalogue*

Of course, doubt was a luxury which only the middle and upper classes could afford. If you were poor in the Victorian period there were just two courses open to you: either you did not believe in anything – and the 1851 Religious Census showed that a large proportion of the working classes attended no religious services of any kind – or you could take comfort in the ghoulish rhetoric of Evangelical hymns, with their emphasis on the sacrificial blood of Christ and inevitable punishment for sin. Sometimes these hymns sounded more up to date: one describes spiritual life in terms of a railway train – God's love is the fire and his grace is the steam. But such hymns tended to encourage and console only the poorer classes.

There *were* also poets who offered consolation and comfort to the middle and upper classes. And so, if you found the poetry of doubt disturbing, you could turn to more reassuring writing. Even *In Memoriam* struggles through to a position of 'honest doubt', and Tennyson tries to convince himself that evolutionary ideas also point to the *moral* progression of man.

Perplext in faith, but pure in deeds,
　　At last he beat his music out.
　　There lives more faith in honest doubt,
Believe me, than in half the creeds.

He fought his doubts and gather'd strength,
　　He would not make his judgement blind,
　　He faced the spectres of the mind
And laid them: thus he came at length

To find a stronger faith his own;
　　And Power was with him in the night,
　　Which makes the darkness and the light,
And dwells not in the light alone,

But in the darkness and the cloud,
　　As over Sinaï's peaks of old,
　　While Israel made their gods of gold,
Altho' the trumpet blew so loud.

Tennyson *In Memoriam,* XCVI, stanzas 3 – 6

126 Alfred Tennyson

Interestingly enough, though, the comforting parts of *In Memoriam* are the least convincing, both as ideas and as poetry, and almost all Victorian consolatory verse has this weakness. Because *In Memoriam* is so full of doubt and insecurity it is surprising that John Keble's cycle of religious poems *The Christian Year* was an important influence on Tennyson. Published in 1827, *The Christian Year* became a Victorian best-seller, but it is difficult now to see why. The poems are mild, sweet and earnest, full of familiar biblical and pastoral images. They often have hints of Wordsworth, but it is a Wordsworth muted and domesticated into hymn-like Christian orthodoxy. Here, for instance, is Keble's poem *Evening,* part of which was later to be turned into the hymn *Abide with me.*

In darkness and in weariness
The traveller on his way must press,
No gleam to watch on tree or tower,
Whiling away the lonesome hour.

Sun of my soul! Thou Saviour dear,
It is not night if Thou be near:
Oh! may no earth-born cloud arise
To hide Thee from Thy servant's eyes.

When round Thy wondrous works below
My searching rapturous glance I throw,
Tracing out Wisdom, Power, and Love,
In earth or sky, in stream or grove; –

*

Abide with me from morn till eve,
For without Thee I cannot live:
Abide with me when night is nigh,
For without Thee I dare not die.

Keble *Evening,* lines 5 – 16, 29 – 32

Keble is essentially an undisturbing poet – even his few moments
of doubt are unworrying, and I think this explains his popularity.
It is also true of popular, consolatory poets such as Eliza Cook and
Martin Tupper. Tupper's *Proverbial Philosophy* – thousands of
lines of unrhymed verse in imitation of the Psalms – was another
best-seller. Here is a typical example of the self-righteous moral
cliché which dominates Tupper's work.

Yet hear, for my speech shall comfort thee: reverently, but
with boldness,
I would raise the sable curtain, that hideth the symmetry of
Providence.
Pain and sin are convicts, and toil in their fetters for good;
The weapons of evil are turned against itself, fighting under
better banners:
The leech delighteth in stinging, and the wicked loveth to do
harm,
But the wise Physician of the Universe useth that ill tendency
for health.
Verily, from others' griefs are gendered sympathy and
kindness;
Patience, humility, and faith, spring not seldom from thine own:

Tupper *Proverbial Philosophy,* 'Of Good in Things Evil', paragraph 2

But Tupper is part of the forgotten heavy mahogany of Victorian
verse: the poetry of doubt has been more lasting and compelling.
When Matthew Arnold warned against 'a feeling of depression' in
poetry, he failed to see that this could provide Victorian poetry with
its most eloquent voice. Arnold feared morbid, introspective
poetry: he called it poetry written out of 'the dialogue of the mind
with itself'. Yet the dialogue of the mind with itself gave poetry one
of its most subtle idioms: it provided a way of analysing many

kinds of feeling, including those of doubt and loss. Arnold's love poem *To Marguerite* illustrates this eloquent introspectiveness.

> Yes! in the sea of life enisled,
> With echoing straits between us thrown,
> Dotting the shoreless watery wild,
> We mortal millions live *alone*
> The islands feel the enclasping flow,
> And then their endless bounds they know.
>
> *
>
> Who order'd, that their longing's fire
> Should be, as soon as kindled, cool'd?
> Who renders vain their deep desire? –
> A God, a God their severance ruled!
> And bade betwixt their shores to be
> The unplumb'd, salt, estranging sea.
>
> Arnold *To Marguerite,* lines 1 – 6, 19 – 24

A few poets of the nineteenth century were able to write truly great religious poems, which were neither simply consolatory nor written out of the questioning dialogue of the mind with itself. Perhaps they managed to do this because they were isolated, either willingly or by accident, from the main currents of thought in the nineteenth century.

So far I have looked at the work of poets who felt that they *had* to enter into the religious controversies of their age. Either they wrote of their own sadness and insecurity in an age where God had disappeared, or they debated religious problems or satirised hypocrisy. Other poets – admittedly minor writers – felt confident of the continuing importance of religious hope and belief.

I turn now to the minority of writers who celebrated God and his universe with simple lyric strength and joy. Gerard Manley Hopkins decided in 1868, when he was in his early twenties, to become a priest and a Jesuit. For a time he even gave up writing poetry. His poems are full of passionate celebration of the variety and detail God has created in the physical world. It is as if every poem tries strenuously to concentrate the sensuous richness of this experience within itself.

> Glory be to God for dappled things –
>   For skies of couple-colour as a brinded cow;
>   For rose-moles all in stipple upon trout that swim;
> Fresh-firecoal chestnut-falls; finches' wings;
> Landscape plotted and pieced – fold, fallow, and plough;
>   And áll trádes, their gear and tackle and trim.
> All things counter, original, spare, strange;
>   Whatever is fickle, freckled (who knows how?)
>   With swift, slow; sweet, sour; adazzle, dim;
> He fathers-forth whose beauty is past change;
>   Praise him.
>
> Hopkins *Pied Beauty*

A much earlier poet, Emily Brontë, whose poems sold only two or three copies in her short lifetime, lived almost all her life in a remote part of Yorkshire. Her poems have the simple rhythms and imagery of hymns, but they transform the language of hymns into a granite firmness and uncompromising severity of statement and express unorthodox and passionate spiritual feeling.

No coward soul is mine
No trembler in the world's storm-troubled sphere
I see Heaven's glories shine
And Faith shines equal arming me from Fear.

O God within my breast
Almighty ever-present Deity
Life, that in me hast rest
As I, Undying Life, have power in Thee.

Vain are the thousand creeds
That move men's hearts, unutterably vain,
Worthless as withered weeds
Or idlest froth amid the boundless main

To waken doubt in one
Holding so fast by thy infinity
So surely anchored on
The steadfast rock of Immortality.

With wide-embracing love
Thy spirit animates eternal years
Pervades and broods above,
Changes, sustains, dissolves, creates and rears.

Though earth and moon were gone,
And suns and universes ceased to be
And thou wert left alone
Every Existence would exist in thee.

There is not room for Death
Nor atom that his might could render void
Since thou art Being and Breath
And what thou art may never be destroyed.

Emily Brontë *No Coward Soul is Mine*

THE QUESTION OF SEX

Women, love, and the Victorian poets

'Lady Jingly! Lady Jingly!
   Sitting where the pumpkins blow,
      Will you come and be my wife?'
   Said the Yonghy-Bonghy-Bò.
'I am tired of living singly, –
On this coast so wild and shingly, –
      I'm a-weary of my life:
      If you'll come and be my wife,
      Quite serene would be my life!' –
Said the Yonghy-Bonghy-Bò,
Said the Yonghy-Bonghy-Bò.

'On this Coast of Coromandel,
   Shrimps and watercresses grow,
      Prawns are plentiful and cheap,'
   Said the Yonghy-Bonghy-Bò.
'You shall have my Chairs and candle,
And my jug without a handle! –
      Gaze upon the rolling deep
      (Fish is plentiful and cheap)
      As the sea, my love is deep!'
   Said the Yonghy-Bonghy-Bò,
   Said the Yonghy-Bonghy-Bò.

Lady Jingly answered sadly,
   And her tears began to flow, –
      'Your proposal comes too late,
   Mr Yonghy-Bonghy-Bò!
I would be your wife most gladly!'
(Here she twirled her fingers madly,)
      'But in England I've a mate!
      Yes! you've asked me far too late,
      For in England I've a mate,
   Mr Yonghy-Bonghy-Bò!
   Mr Yonghy-Bonghy-Bò!'

Lear *The Courtship of the Yonghy-Bonghy-Bò*, stanzas 3 – 5

In Edward Lear's pathetic-comic narrative the poor Lady Jingly Jones is forced to reject the proposals of the Yonghy-Bonghy-

Bò and all his worldly goods, his chairs and his jug without a handle. She is respectably married to Handel Jones, Esquire, & Co. When the Yonghy-Bonghy-Bò departs, she weeps for him into the broken jug, never moving from her heap of stones. The poem probably reproduces Lear's own story. He was unable to make up his mind to marry a woman who was clearly fond of him, and eventually she married someone else. But this poem, at once absurd and sad, also points to the inflexible stiffness of the Victorian institution of marriage, its formality, its conventions, its concern with property and the economics of supporting a wife in respectable social state. Behind the poem is a longing for a franker and less repressed feeling between men and women in love. 'I can merely be your friend' says the Lady Jingly Jones, and the distant word 'friend' seems to sum up the rigidity of the codes governing sexual behaviour. Lear's poem is an absurd but truthful reflection of many of the feelings and situations in Victorian poetry about love.

Christina Rossetti's poem *Winter: My Secret* hints at a love which has to be closely concealed, and guarded from the uncongenial trappings which accompany a public declaration of love. Christina Rossetti was never married and there is evidence that she did have a secret love. She uses the idea of exposure to cold, withering weather to suggest how damaging the public possession of her love would be.

> I tell my secret? No indeed, not I:
> Perhaps some day, who knows?
> But not today; it froze, and blows, and snows,
> And you're too curious: fie!
> You want to hear it? well:
> Only, my secret's mine, and I won't tell.
>
> Or, after all, perhaps there's none:
> Suppose there is no secret after all,
> But only just my fun.
> Today's a nipping day, a biting day;
> In which one wants a shawl,
> A veil, a cloak, and other wraps:
> I cannot ope to every one who taps,
> And let the draughts come whistling through my hall;
> Come bounding and surrounding me,
> Come buffeting, astounding me,
> Nipping and clipping through my wraps and all.
> I wear my mask for warmth: who ever shows
> His nose to Russian snows
> To be pecked at by every wind that blows?
> You would not peck? I thank you for good will,
> Believe, but leave that truth untested still.
>
> Spring's an expansive time: yet I don't trust
> March with its peck of dust,
> Nor April with its rainbow-crowned brief showers,
> Nor even May, whose flowers
> One frost may wither through the sunless hours.

Perhaps some languid summer day,
When drowsy birds sing less and less,
And golden fruit is ripening to excess,
If there's not too much sun nor too much cloud,
And the warm wind is neither still nor loud,
Perhaps my secret I may say,
Or you may guess.

Christina Rossetti *Winter : My Secret*

Behind the cool, clear words of this poem there is, I think, a resolute, almost aggressive determination to preserve the privacy and independence of emotional life: 'I wear my mask for warmth' she writes. The language of the poem, though very direct, is also curiously impersonal and reserved.

A more overtly expressed frustration with the social conventions governing sexual relationships is found in Tennyson's *Maud*. This poem was published in 1855 and Tennyson had been happily married for some years; but the poem has an autobiographical basis in a youthful love affair which was broken off. *Maud* is a series of monologues spoken by a violent, unbalanced young man, who is in love with the Squire's daughter. A great social and economic rift has opened between them because the hero has been left penniless by his dead father. Though extremely melodramatic, the poem presents an extraordinarily successful study of a tense, over-excitable and unstable nature, full of violent hatreds and incipiently violent sexual feeling. The hero hates Maud's brother for keeping them apart, and the oppressive conventions which scarcely allow them to greet one another in church.

It was, of course, impossible for Tennyson to write directly of sexual feeling, and yet the love lyrics of *Maud* are full of intensely erotic feeling. In one poem, the hero, who has become secretly engaged to Maud, waits to meet her at the end of a ball from which, as a social exile still, he is excluded. The first lines of the poem – 'Come into the garden, Maud' – have become famous as a Victorian ballad; in fact, it is easy to regard them as almost a parody of the Victorian ballad. Yet the poem as a whole is anything but this. The rhythm beautifully suggests a quickening waltz and the poem increases in tension as the tempo of the waltz increases and the lover watches the dawn break. Tennyson uses the conventional love-symbols of lily, rose and passion flower, but these are set in a landscape flushed with violent, sensuous colour, and everything in it sighs for the consummation of dawn and the arrival of Maud. And so the evening star faints for love of the sun 'On a bed of daffodil sky'. The poem ends in a flush of colour and feeling: the lover's heart will 'blossom in purple and red' when his beloved arrives. There is a subtle quickening of emotion from the cool image of the slender acacia to the impassioned heat of the ending.

The slender acacia would not shake
One long milk-bloom on the tree;

The white lake-blossom fell into the lake
　　As the pimpernel dozed on the lea;
But the rose was awake all night for your sake,
　　Knowing your promise to me;
The lilies and roses were all awake,
　　They sigh'd for the dawn and thee.

Queen rose of the rosebud garden of girls,
　　Come hither, the dances are done,
In gloss of satin and glimmer of pearls,
　　Queen lily and rose in one;
Shine out, little head, sunning over with curls,
　　To the flowers, and be their sun.

There has fallen a splendid tear
　　From the passion-flower at the gate.
She is coming, my dove, my dear;
　　She is coming, my life, my fate;
The red rose cries, 'She is near, she is near';
　　And the white rose weeps, 'She is late';
The larkspur listens, 'I hear, I hear';
　　And the lily whispers, 'I wait.'

She is coming, my own, my sweet;
　　Were it ever so airy a tread,
My heart would hear her and beat,
　　Were it earth in an earthy bed;
My dust would hear her and beat,
　　Had I lain for a century dead;
Would start and tremble under her feet,
　　And blossom in purple and red.

Tennyson *Maud,* Part 1, XXII, stanzas 8 – 11

This indirect expression of passion, which convention imposed on the poets, is often very moving: forced to be discreet, they took refuge in symbol and allegory. It is not surprising to find Tennyson being influenced by Edward Fitzgerald's opulent translations of Persian poetry. The most famous of these is, of course, the translation of *The Rubà'iyàt of Omar Khayyàm* in 1859. And other poets, such as Dante Gabriel Rossetti and Swinburne, wrote poems which suggest and explore erotic feeling. Perhaps one does not immediately think of the Victorian poets as expressing sexual passion, but in fact they are surprisingly preoccupied with this theme; sufficiently at least during the eighteen sixties that the critic Robert Buchanan launched a bitter attack on what he called 'the fleshly school of poetry'.

Of course there were still poets who seemed quite content to work within the social taboos and restrictions. Coventry Patmore's *Angel in the House* charts the decorous courtship and marriage of a happy pair of lovers. This passage has a fresh, rather over-protected charm and naïveté, which is typical of the earlier scenes. The young man courts the Dean's daughter in the garden and talks about a flower show and ball.

A voice, the sweeter for the grace
    Of suddenness, while thus I dream'd,
'Good morning!' said or sang. Her face
    The mirror of the morning seem'd.
Her sisters in the garden walk'd,
    And would I come? Across the Hall
She led me; and we laugh'd and talk'd,
    And praised the Flower-show and the Ball;
And Mildred's pinks had gain'd the Prize;
    And, stepping like the light-foot fawn,
She brought me 'Wiltshire Butterflies,'
    The Prize-book; then we paced the lawn,
Close-cut, and with geranium-plots,
    A rival glow of green and red;
Then counted sixty apricots
    On one small tree; the gold-fish fed.

Patmore *Angel in the House,* Book 1, Canto 4, 'The Morning Call', Section 2

Only seven years after Patmore's poem was completed John Stuart Mill published his essay on *The Subjection of Women*, which attacks all the conventional assumptions about women. Patmore's poem, for instance, assumes without question that women will be dependent upon and subservient to men in the marital state. It is worth remembering that until 1852 a husband could quite legally compel the wife who had deserted him to return, and it was not until 1870, a year after the essay, that the law began to tackle the problem of a husband's appropriation of his wife's property. There were also neither votes nor jobs for women. So Mill spoke of

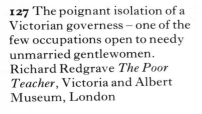

127 The poignant isolation of a Victorian governess – one of the few occupations open to needy unmarried gentlewomen. Richard Redgrave *The Poor Teacher*, Victoria and Albert Museum, London

128 Woman as comforter: the black-edged letter and envelope have brought the news of a sudden bereavement to the husband. His wife leans tenderly against him, representing a typical Victorian image of womanhood, such as we find in Patmore's *Angel in the House*. G. E. Hicks *Woman's Mission; Companion of Manhood*, The Tate Gallery, London

The pair of lovers in Hughes' *The Long Engagement* (see plate **75**, p. 145) have never even reached the married state. They are doomed to perpetual courtship because the man's income is inadequate for respectable middle-class marriage. These two pictures are very different studies in Victorian pathos.

women as an 'enslaved class' whose minds have been kept under-developed because 'Men do not want solely the obedience of women, they want their sentiments'.

> The masters of women wanted more than simple obedience and they turned the whole force of education to effect their purpose. All women are brought up from the very earliest years in the belief that their ideal of character is the very opposite to that of men; not self-will, and government by control of will, but submission, and yielding to the control of others. All the moralities tell them that it is the duty of women, and all the current sentimentalities that it is their nature, to live for others; to make complete abnegation of themselves, and to have no life but in their affections. And by their affections are meant the only ones they are allowed to have.

Mill *The Subjection of Women*, Chapter I

Mill's essay is part of a protest against the status of women, which gathered force throughout the nineteenth century: Patmore's *Angel in the House* represents the view of women's capacities which the reformers protested against. At one point the husband reads out grave news about the war and the number of dead, and the wife merely continues to think how attractive she is. The husband, who is the speaker throughout the poem, is strangely complacent about this, just as he is complacent when, a little after this incident, he says that his wife uses the submissiveness of the dove combined with the artful cunning of the snake to get her own way with him.

Luckily, some poets took part in the debate about women much more open-mindedly than this. Clough's earliest long poem, set in Scotland and called *The Bothie of Tober-Na-Vuolich,* is about a party of students who have come there to work in the vacation. One of the party is a young man with radical sympathies, who energetically condemns the conventional middle-class girl as 'a pink-paper comfit with motto romantic inside it', and claims for the working-class girl all the dignity of labour. Clough beautifully catches the high-spirited tones, the raised voices and exaggerated arguments which come of strong feeling, and the movement from strong feeling to laughter as the young man claims that a girl 'uprooting potatoes' is nobly beautiful as well as worthy.

> Home from the river or pump moving stately and calm to the
>   laundry;
> Ay, doing household work, as many sweet girls I have looked at,
> Needful household work, which some one, after all, must do,
> Needful, graceful therefore, as washing, cooking, and scouring,
> Or, if you please, with the fork in the garden uprooting potatoes. –
>   Or, – high-kilted perhaps, cried Lindsay, at last successful,
> Lindsay, this long time swelling with scorn and pent-up fury,
> Or high-kilted perhaps, as once at Dundee I saw them,
> Petticoats up to the knees, or even, it might be, above them,
> Matching their lily-white legs with the clothes that they trod in
>   the wash-tub!

Clough *The Bothie of Tober-Na-Vuolich,* ii, lines 102 – 11

Clough's hero has, quite seriously, to 'study the question of sex', as one of his friends puts it, for his views of women are over-romantic and sentimental. The poem therefore tries to explore a more reasonable view of love, women and marriage. In fact all Clough's long poems 'study the question of sex', and his investigations of the 'woman problem', as it was sometimes called, always move toward the comic and satirical.

The Princess, Tennyson's only sustained poem on the relationships between the sexes, is similar. It is part lyric poem, part burlesque, part pantomime. Princess Ida, the heroine, becomes a firm feminist and believer in female education, and sets up a women's college from which she excludes all men. The poem has a robust, farcical humour that one does not expect from Tennyson, whose bent is for lyric feeling. However, the farcical element is completely successful, as the two men in search of Ida, disguised as women, trip in their long garments and have trouble with their falsetto voices. There are deft, mock-heroic touches, as when the Prince conceals himself from his pursuers behind a statue of Judith beheading Holofernes. Male ineptitude and clumsiness is lampooned as the hero is finally brought down by one of the feminist sculptures.

> Scarce had I ceased when from a tamarisk near
> Two Proctors leapt upon us, crying, 'Names:'
> He, standing still, was clutch'd; but I began
> To thrid the musky-circled mazes, wind
> And double in and out the boles, and race
> By all the fountains: fleet I was of foot:
> Before me shower'd the rose in flakes; behind
> I heard the puff'd pursuer; at mine ear
> Bubbled the nightingale and heeded not,
> And secret laughter tickled all my soul.
> At last I hook'd my ankle in a vine,
> That claspt the feet of a Mnemosyne,
> And falling on my face was caught and known.
>
> Tennyson *The Princess*, IV, lines 239 – 51

In *The Princess* Tennyson argued seriously for men's and women's mutual regard of each other's qualities – 'For woman is not undevelopt man/But diverse . . .' It was a humane argument for 1847 when the poem was published, but it would not have satisfied Mill in the sixties, because Mill asked for a complete transformation of women's education. Elizabeth Barrett Browning's *Aurora Leigh* approaches more nearly to Mill's views, though she was no extremist. The heroine of the poem acrimoniously attacks the cramped education in femininity which she receives. The whole poem is a cry for a richer and more intelligent understanding of what it is like to be a woman.

> I learnt the royal genealogies
> Of Oviedo, the internal laws
> Of the Burmese empire, – by how many feet
> Mount Chimborazo outsoars Teneriffe,
> What navigable river joins itself
> To Lara, and what census of the year five
> Was taken at Klagenfurt, – because she liked
> A general insight into useful facts.
> I learnt much music, – such as would have been
> As quite impossible in Johnson's day
> As still it might be wished – fine sleights of hand
> And unimagined fingering, shuffling off
> The hearer's soul through hurricanes of notes
> To a noisy Tophet; and I drew . . . costumes

From French engravings, nereids neatly draped,
(With smirks of simmering godship) – I washed in
Landscapes from nature (rather say, washed out).
I danced the polka and Cellarius,
Spun glass, stuffed birds, and modelled flowers in wax,
Because she liked accomplishments in girls.
I read a score of books on womanhood
To prove, if women do not think at all,
They may teach thinking (to a maiden-aunt
Or else the author), – books that boldly assert
Their right of comprehending husband's talk
When not too deep, and even of answering
With pretty 'may it please you,' or 'so it is,' –
Their rapid insight and fine aptitude,
Particular worth and general missionariness,
As long as they keep quiet by the fire
And never say 'no' when the world says 'aye,'
For that is fatal, – their angelic reach
Of virtue, chiefly used to sit and darn,
And fatten household sinners . . .

Elizabeth Barrett Browning *Aurora Leigh,* Book 1

Aurora Leigh later introduces the theme of the fallen woman and her illegitimate child; but Elizabeth Barrett Browning deals far less confidently with this theme, and even the most open-minded of Victorian poets found it difficult to deal with socially unacceptable material such as prostitution. Meredith's poem about the break-up of a marriage, *Modern Love*, was received with more than doubt in 1862, though it seems fairly innocuous now. But it is a very subtle poem and very much aware of the complexities of feeling that can grow between estranged people. I find that Meredith sometimes fails to control his feeling of resentment at the woman, who has fallen in love with someone else; but he suggests beautifully the appalling deadness and remoteness that can come upon two people.

. . . they from head to feet
Were moveless, looking through their dead black years,
By vain regret scrawled over the blank wall.
Like sculptured effigies they might be seen
Upon their marriage-tomb, the sword between;
Each wishing for the sword that severs all.

Meredith *Modern Love* 1, lines 11 – 16

Meredith is splendid on the labyrinthine contradictions of feeling which come when the husband feels his isolation from the wife: he struggles with jealousy and the paradox that only the woman who has created it can comfort him.

I bade my Lady think what she might mean.
Know I my meaning, I? Can I love one,

And yet be jealous of another? None
Commits such folly. Terrible Love, I ween,
Has might, even dead, half sighing to upheave
The lightless seas of selfishness amain:
Seas that in a man's heart have no rain
To fall and still them. Peace can I achieve,
By turning to this fountain-source of woe,
This woman, who's to Love as fire to wood?

Meredith *Modern Love,* XL, lines 1 – 10

And then there is the awkwardness, the fencing, the guessing
that goes on under the attempted small-talk.

Madam would speak with me. So, now it comes:
The Deluge or else Fire! She's well; she thanks
My husbandship. Our chain on silence clanks.
Time leers between, above his twiddling thumbs.
Am I quite well? Most excellent in health!
The journals, too, I diligently peruse.
Vesuvius is expected to give news:
Niagara is no noisier. By stealth
Our eyes dart scrutinizing snakes. She's glad
I'm happy, says her quivering under-lip.
'And are not you?' 'How can I be?' 'Take ship!
For happiness is somewhere to be had.'
'Nowhere for me!' Her voice is barely heard.
I am not melted, and make no pretence.
With commonplace I freeze her, tongue and sense.
Niagara, or Vesuvius, is deferred.

Meredith *Modern Love,* XXXIV

So far, I've talked about the difficulties the Victorian poets experienced in writing about sexual feeling, and about the ways they
participated in the debate about the status of women. I shall end
with two poets who managed to write more uninhibitedly about
love: Clough who, as I have said, returns to the theme of women
throughout his work, and Browning, who wrote by far the most
confident poems on sexual feeling and passion. It may well be that
because the Victorians were so worried by woman and her status,
so puzzled by the relationships between men and women, that they
were unable to write *love* poetry; though Clough almost manages a
love poem when in *Amours de Voyage* his hero is fascinated by a
girl, in spite of his determination not to be affected by her.

I am in love, meantime, you think; no doubt you would think so.
I am in love, you say; with those letters, of course, you would say
    so.
I am in love, you declare. I think not so; yet I grant you
It is a pleasure indeed to converse with this girl. Oh, rare gift,
Rare felicity, this! she can talk in a rational way, can
Speak upon subjects that really are matters of mind and of
    thinking,

129 The drama of female unfaithfulness. Note the emphatically moral iconography of the house of cards and the, as yet, unfinished apple, recalling, of course, Eve

130 The just deserts of immorality. The wife, probably a prostitute, certainly destitute, cowers under one of the bridges of the Thames

Augustus Egg *Past and Present*, No's 1 and 3, The Tate Gallery, London

Yet in perfection retain her simplicity; never, one moment,
Never, however you urge it, however you tempt her, consents to
Step from ideas and fancies and loving sensations to those vain
Conscious understandings that vex the minds of man-kind.
No, though she talk, it is music; her fingers desert not the keys; 'tis
Song, though you hear in the song the articulate vocables sounded,
Syllabled singly and sweetly the words of melodious meaning.
I am in love, you say: I do not think so, exactly.

*

Hopeless it seems, – yet I cannot, though hopeless, determine to
    leave it:
She goes, – therefore I go; she moves, – I move, not to lose her.

Clough   *Amours de Voyage*, Canto II, XIII, 'Claude to Eustace'

The poet who comes closest to expressing lyrically the complexities and intensities of love is Robert Browning. His *Two in the
Campagna* begins in the middle of an experience of passionate
puzzlement. Why is feeling so elusive, so involuntary, so much
beyond control and definition? The rapid, associative thought
process which begins the poem embodies the poet's feeling about
the elusiveness of so much of his emotion.

I wonder do you feel today
    As I have felt since, hand in hand,
We sat down on the grass, to stray
    In spirit better through the land,
This morn of Rome and May?

For me, I touched a thought, I know,
    Has tantalized me many times,
(Like turns of thread the spiders throw
    Mocking across our path) for rhymes
To catch at and let go.

Help me to hold it! First it left
    The yellowing fennel, run to seed
There, branching from the brickwork's cleft,
    Some old tomb's ruin: yonder weed
Took up the floating weft,

Where one small orange cup amassed
    Five beetles, – blind and green they grope
Among the honey-meal: and last,
    Everywhere on the grassy slope
I traced it. Hold it fast!

*

No. I yearn upward, touch you close,
    Then stand away. I kiss your cheek,
Catch your soul's warmth, – I pluck the rose
    And love it more than tongue can speak –
Then the good minute goes.

Already how am I so far
 Out of that minute? Must I go
Still like the thistle-ball, no bar,
 Onward, whenever light winds blow,
Fixed by no friendly star?

Just when I seemed about to learn!
 Where is the thread now? Off again!
The old trick! Only I discern
 Infinite passion, and the pain
Of finite hearts that yearn.

    Browning *Two in the Campagna*, stanzas 1 – 4, 10 – 12

Browning is preoccupied with the limits of what seems to be infinite feeling; but despite this resonant statement about infinite passion and finite hearts he could write with a marvellously confident passion. In *Meeting at Night* he uses sexual imagery with a relaxed, happy intensity. The 'pushing prow' of the speaker's boat carries him to the sudden flare of a match and 'two hearts beating, each to each'.

The grey sea and the long black land;
And the yellow half-moon large and low;
And the startled little waves that leap
In fiery ringlets from their sleep,
As I gain the cove with pushing prow,
And quench its speed i' the slushy sand.

Then a mile of warm sea-scented beach;
Three fields to cross till a farm appears;
A tap at the pane, the quick sharp scratch
And blue spurt of a lighted match,
And a voice less loud, thro' its joys and fears,
Than the two hearts beating each to each!

   Browning *Meeting at Night*

Browning's love poetry is always bold. In this poem he writes of a free and adventurous love, in which the man and woman create and exchange each other's sexuality.

Teach me to flirt a fan
 As the Spanish ladies can,
  Or I tint your lip
With a burnt stick's tip
And you turn into such a man!
  Just the two spots that span
Half the bill of the young male swan.

   Browning *A Lovers' Quarrel*, lines 64 – 70

Browning is probably at his most haunting, though, when he writes of love as an experience of loss, as a continual, strenuous, imaginative *search* for the other person. In *Love in a Life* the lover repeatedly hunts through a house, just missing the lady and always encountering emptiness. For Browning, the experience of love *is* all-consuming search.

Room after room,
I hunt the house through
We inhabit together.
Heart, fear nothing, for, heart, thou shalt find her –
Next time, herself! – not the trouble behind her
Left in the curtain, the couch's perfume!
As she brushed it, the cornice-wreath blossomed anew:
Yon looking-glass gleamed at the wave of her feather.

Yet the day wears,
And door succeeds door;
I try the fresh fortune –
Range the wide house from the wing to the centre.
Still the same chance! she goes out as I enter.
Spend my whole day in the quest, – who cares?
But 'tis twilight, you see, – with such suites to explore,
Such closets to search, such alcoves to importune!

Browning *Love in a Life*

131 Robert Browning

THE CITY'S HEEDLESS DIN

The city in Victorian poetry

Forget six counties overhung with smoke,
Forget the snorting steam and piston stroke,
Forget the spreading of the hideous town;
Think rather of the pack-horse on the down,
And dream of London, small, and white, and clean,
The clear Thames bordered by its gardens green

*

A nameless city in a distant sea,
White as the changing walls of faërie,
Thronged with much people clad in ancient guise
I now am fain to set before your eyes;
There, leave the clear green water and the quays,
And pass betwixt its marble palaces,
Until ye come unto the chiefest square;
A bubbling conduit is set midmost there,
And round about it now the maidens throng,
With jest and laughter, and sweet broken song,
Making but light of labour new begun
While in their vessels gleams the morning sun.

Morris *The Earthly Paradise,* lines 1 – 6, 17 – 28

The Victorian poets are often blamed for their horrified retreat from the city. The extract you have just heard comes from the beginning of William Morris' poem *The Earthly Paradise,* in which Morris rejects the hideous environment of London as the material of poetry and turns instead to the white walls and marble palaces created in the world of imagination. His poem re-tells myths and legends from old Greek and Nordic sources and resembles a highly decorative piece of tapestry. In fact it is rather like the handmade textiles and wallpapers made by Morris' own craftsmen. The poem was meant to embody the beauty and freedom which, he thought, art alone can achieve. But Morris was realist enough to know, as he said later in a socialist pamphlet, that most of the population were cut off from beauty and art; they lived in towns, among 'miserable makeshifts', accepting 'coarse food', 'rotten raiment' and 'wretched houses'. For Morris, the great, new, industrial cities of Britain were

132 Factory workers are here romanticised into an urban pastoral. Eyre Crowe *The Dinner Hour, Wigan,* City of Manchester Art Galleries

an outrage on human existence. Workers produced goods for the rich, but at impossibly low wages. These low wages meant that the poor could only afford to buy cheap, mean goods. Therefore they were forced into factories to produce such inferior goods for themselves. And so people co-operated in perpetuating the wretched conditions of the cities; and the wretchedness of the Victorian city, especially London, was such that one can hardly blame Morris for urging his readers to forget it.

In 1868, the year Morris began publishing *The Earthly Paradise,* Henry James, the novelist, made his first visit to London from America and later described the 'sudden horror of the whole place' which came upon him after he had been there for a few days. He had been amazed by the 'immensity' and sinister drama of the urban landscape, 'the miles of house-tops and viaducts, the complication of junctions and signals'. He found London 'hideous, vicious, cruel'.

The low black houses were as inanimate as so many rows of coal-scuttles, save where at frequent corners, from a gin-shop, there was a flare of light more brutal still than the darkness.

Henry James *London* (1888)

Protest against the city begins in the Romantic period, but Blake's condemnation of London in his *Songs of Experience* was just as relevant to the Victorian London described by James as it was to the city of his own day. His terse, economical language expresses in four concentrated stanzas the abuses of the city. The simplest words in this poem have disturbing suggestions: there are the 'charter'd' streets and river – chartered because they have been created by the City's ancient charter, but also chartered in the sense that the land of the City was being used for commercial profiteering; there are the 'black'ning' churches, blackening in the smoke and blackening into moral decay, and the diseases of the prostitute which blight not the marriage bed but the 'marriage hearse'.

I wander thro' each charter'd street,
Near where the charter'd Thames does flow,
And mark in every face I meet
Marks of weakness, marks of woe.

In every cry of every Man,
In every Infant's cry of fear,
In every voice, in every ban,
The mind-forg'd manacles I hear.

How the chimney-sweeper's cry
Every black'ning church appals;
And the hapless soldier's sigh
Runs in blood down palace walls.

But most thro' midnight streets I hear
How the youthful harlot's curse
Blasts the new-born infant's tear,
And blights with plagues the marriage hearse.

Blake *Songs of Experience,* London

On the whole it was the novelists, rather than the poets, who co-operated with the reformers to expose the conditions of London, by mid-century the biggest city in Europe, where wealth co-existed with overcrowded, disease-ridden and polluted slums. Henry Mayhew, whose *London Labour and the London Poor* documented the conditions of London, described the abuses of overcrowding, particularly in slum lodging houses 'without ventilation, cleanliness, or decency, and with forty people's breaths perhaps mingling together in one foul choking steam of stench'. And Charles Kingsley noticed, after one of the periodic cholera outbreaks which hit the cities at least until the eighteen-sixties, that people drank

133 One of the notoriously over-crowded slum areas of London. Sheets dry on a makeshift pole poked from the window of a lodging house and a woman emerges from a cellar. Cellar dwellings were illegal at this time

from a stream into which the sewerage of their houses ran. In novels such as *Bleak House* Dickens' imagination seized upon facts like these and fused them into an account of a diseased society. The poets, on the other hand, record the moods engendered by the city environment rather than its appearance, or the social facts behind the appearance. They register the shock of a generation which had seen England become, within three decades, the first densely urbanised country in Europe. They follow the example of Romantic poets, such as Wordsworth, in rejecting the city, seeing it as the epitome of a society where people live in isolation from one another, massed together, but without communicating. So Wordsworth, in *The Prelude*, describes a blind beggar whose communication with others is reduced to a brief note pinned to him, which recounts his history. He cannot even *see* the people who read it.

> . . . 'twas my chance
> Abruptly to be smitten with the view
> Of a blind Beggar, who, with upright face,
> Stood propp'd against a Wall, upon his Chest
> Wearing a written paper, to explain
> The story of the Man, and who he was.
> My mind did at this spectacle turn round
> As with the might of waters, and it seem'd
> To me that in this Label was a type,
> Or emblem, of the utmost that we know,
> Both of ourselves and of the universe;
> And, on the shape of the unmoving man,
> His fixèd face and sightless eyes, I look'd
> As if admonish'd from another world.

Wordsworth *The Prelude*, VII, lines 609 – 622

It is interesting that Tennyson made an urban scene the setting for a moment of absolute loneliness and desolation, and that it comes from *In Memoriam*, a poem with strong pastoral elements. But it is only in such an environment that the full meaning of his friend's death comes to the poet as 'On the bald street breaks the blank day'. The heavy stresses on 'bald' and 'blank' suggest that there is no real interaction between the sun and the buildings it would normally light up: the light falls blankly upon them and the buildings are unchanged because they do not respond to the light, just as there is no response from Tennyson's dead friend when the poet arrives before the house his friend inhabited.

> Dark house, by which once more I stand
>   Here in the long unlovely street,
>   Doors, where my heart was used to beat
> So quickly, waiting for a hand,
>
> A hand that can be clasp'd no more –
>   Behold me, for I cannot sleep,
>   And like a guilty thing I creep
> At earliest morning to the door.
>
> He is not here; but far away
>   The noise of life begins again,
>   And ghastly thro' the drizzling rain
> On the bald street breaks the blank day.

Tennyson *In Memoriam*, VII

In Dante Gabriel Rossetti's poem *Jenny*, a series of meditations on a beautiful prostitute who lies asleep on the speaker's knee as he reflects about her life, the best parts are those where the man thinks of her early life in the country and then imagines her alone and rejected in the London streets, growing old. As a child, Jenny 'would lie in fields and look/Along the ground through the blown grass'. Before long, aged by prostitution, she will be by herself in the dirty

231

streets underneath the 'cold lamps'. Rossetti makes the cold lamps take on Jenny's feelings about them. Street lamps are not supposed to warm people but, in being cold, even the physical elements of the city seem to be rejecting her. The snaking, labyrinthine streets become an image for the sense of imprisonment felt by the girl.

> Jenny, you know the city now,
> A child can tell the tale there, how
> Some things which are not yet enroll'd
> In market-lists are bought and sold
> Even till the early Sunday light
> When Saturday night is market-night
> Everywhere, be it dry or wet,
> And market-night in the Haymarket.
> Our learned London children know,
> Poor Jenny, all your pride and woe;
> Have seen your lifted silken skirt
> Advertise dainties through the dirt;
> Have seen your coach-wheels splash rebuke
> On virtue; and have learned your look
> When, wealth and health slipped past, you stare
> Along the streets alone, and there,
> Round the long park, across the bridge,
> The cold lamps at the pavement's edge
> Wind on together and apart,
> A fiery serpent for your heart.

Dante Gabriel Rossetti *Jenny*, lines 135 – 54

The Victorian poets nearly always think of the city as a night scene, luridly lit by gas. Matthew Arnold's poem on Kensington Gardens is an exception. The poet lies in a quiet, protected glade, disturbed only by children and their nurses. He assures himself, and us, that his calm state of mind protects him from the 'city's hum' and the 'huge world, which roars hard by'. But the whole poem suggests how vulnerable he is, because the sound of the city is always invading him, and even his description of the teeming insect life in the grass seems just like a city crowd – 'What endless, active life is here!'

> Sometimes a child will cross the glade
> To take his nurse his broken toy;
> Sometimes a thrush flit overhead
> Deep in her unknown day's employ.
>
> Here at my feet what wonders pass,
> What endless, active life is here!
> What blowing daisies, fragrant grass!
> An air-stirr'd forest, fresh and clear.
>
> *
>
> Calm soul of all things! make it mine
> To feel, amid the city's jar,

That there abides a peace of thine,
Man did not make, and cannot mar.

Arnold *Lines, written in Kensington Gardens*, stanzas 3, 4, 10

134 James Thomson

The most masterly and sustained of all Victorian poems on the city is James Thomson's *The City of Dreadful Night*. This poem was not widely known in Thomson's lifetime and is not very widely known today. It is long and made up of twenty-one sections. Instead of the narrative structure the Victorians liked to give their long works, it is ordered like the sequences of a dream; for Thomson's city is not the real, solid, bustling city of Arnold's poem, which hums and roars in a brute physical way; it is a dead, silent place, an image for an inner, psychological world of horror and despair. It is very repetitive, because this is what dreams are like. At one point in the poem Thomson writes of the way a familiar dream continually recurs: a dream which begins to have more reality for the dreamer than his waking life because he begins to *expect* the insistent pattern of repetitions.

The City of Dreadful Night is structured, then, as a 'recurrence, with recurrent changes'; its silent darkness, its continually burning street lamps, its dead buildings and tenements, the un-named voices and figures who emerge fitfully, the inexplicable acts of violence and outrage, these are the things which recur with 'recurrent changes' discontinuously. Thomson seems to have been very interested in the strange transitions and even stranger continuities which occur in dreams. He wrote to a friend, describing a dream he had had, saying that he had been with his friend 'with two or three more who were very vague people and apt to change into other persons'. The landscape of the City of Dreadful Night is phantasmagoric in this way, but prevented from being too hazy or uncertain because of Thomson's wonderful control of the stress and movement of his verse. His ability to rhyme many-syllabled words slows the movement of the poem to a somnambulistic sureness and deliberation, like the pacing footsteps of a walker at night.

> The City is of Night; perchance of Death,
>   But certainly of Night; for never there
> Can come the lucid morning's fragrant breath
>   After the dewy dawning's cold grey air;
> The moon and stars may shine with scorn or pity;
> The sun has never visited that city
>   For it dissolveth in the daylight fair.
>
> Dissolveth like a dream of night away;
>   Though present in distempered gloom of thought
> And deadly weariness of heart all day.
>   But when a dream night after night is brought
> Throughout a week, and such weeks few or many
> Recur each year for several years, can any
>   Discern that dream from real life in aught?

*

The street-lamps burn amidst the baleful glooms,
  Amidst the soundless solitudes immense
Of rangèd mansions dark and still as tombs.
  The silence which benumbs or strains the sense
Fulfils with awe the soul's despair unweeping:
Myriads of habitants are ever sleeping,
  Or dead, or fled from nameless pestilence!

Yet as in some necropolis you find
  Perchance one mourner to a thousand dead,
So there; worn faces that look deaf and blind
  Like tragic masks of stone. With weary tread,
Each wrapt in his own doom, they wander, wander,
Or sit foredone and desolately ponder
  Through sleepless hours with heavy drooping head.

Mature men chiefly, few in age or youth,
  A woman rarely, now and then a child:
A child! If here the heart turns sick with ruth
  To see a little one from birth defiled,
Or lame or blind, as preordained to languish
Through youthless life, think how it bleeds with anguish
  To meet one erring in that homeless wild.

Thomson *The City of Dreadful Night,* I, lines 1 – 14, 43 – 63

The City of Dreadful Night has both the precision and the appalling vagueness of a dream: 'I wandered in a suburb of the North . . . I took the left-hand lane' the poet writes; but this precision collapses when he sees a crawling 'something', a man who violently accuses him of discovering his 'secret'. Again, Thomson describes the weary, insecure penetration by the eye of endless shadows within shadows.

Although lamps burn along the silent streets,
  Even when moonlight silvers empty squares
The dark holds countless lanes and close retreats;
  But when the night its sphereless mantle wears
The open spaces yawn with gloom abysmal,
The sombre mansions loom immense and dismal,
  The lanes are black as subterranean lairs.

And soon the eye a strange new vision learns:
  The night remains for it as dark and dense,
Yet clearly in this darkness it discerns
  As in the daylight with its natural sense;
Perceives a shade in shadow not obscurely,
Pursues a stir of black in blackness surely,
  Sees spectres also in the gloom intense.

Thomson *The City of Dreadful Night,* III, lines 1 – 14

Perhaps it is easy to exaggerate the tragedy of Thomson's life; but in between his bouts of insomnia and cycles of depressive illness, during which he drank heavily, he seems to have been a buoyant and energetic man. He was valued by his friends, even though on one occasion he was found dead drunk next to a whelk stall when invited to dinner and, eventually, died of alcoholism. Towards the end of his life he became more isolated, living in cheap rooms in Pimlico and Bloomsbury, thoroughly familiar with the poor man's tramp for cheap lodging: 'Dusty, musty, fusty, rusty, and *dear*' he described them after one hunt.

But though Thomson must have been only too familiar with the social needs of the poor in London, *The City of Dreadful Night* is not a directly social poem. There are references to the poor and half-starved, but Thomson is more interested in suggesting a state of mind where all energy and hope have been annihilated. He had read Dante and Shelley and had assimilated from them ways of idealising and symbolising moral states and feelings. He never explicitly defines the state he is portraying, but allows the city and its voices to define it. Here, for example, two 'bodiless voices' talk enigmatically of their futile attempts to escape from the city.

> I sat forlornly by the river-side,
>   And watched the bridge-lamps glow like golden stars
> Above the blackness of the swelling tide,
>   Down which they struck rough gold in ruddier bars;
> And heard the heave and plashing of the flow
> Against the wall a dozen feet below.
>
> Large elm-trees stood along that river-walk;
>   And under one, a few steps from my seat,
> I heard strange voices join in stranger talk,
>   Although I had not heard approaching feet:
> These bodiless voices in my waking dream
> Flowed dark words blending with the sombre stream: –
>
> And you have after all come back; come back.
> I was about to follow on your track.
> And you have failed: our spark of hope is black.
>
> That I have failed is proved by my return:
> The spark is quenched, nor ever more will burn,
>
> Thomson   *The City of Dreadful Night,* VI, lines 1 – 18

It is rare to find a poet celebrating the city, responding to its busyness and vitality as well as to its miseries; after reading Thomson it is easy to see why. Just a few poets did achieve this, however, and without false optimism or sentimentality. Clough, who lived in Liverpool, managed largely because he knew the environment of the poor intimately. In this passage from *The Bothie of Tober-Na-Vuolich* he shows he knew that the city, with its raw 'unfinished houses, lots for sale, and railway outworks', is a 'great wicked artificial civilised fabric' but, all the same, he has a dogged desire to accept and transform the ordinary and the mean. The coming of dawn, in this passage, is a revelation as beautiful in the city as in the country.

135 Few poets think of the town with this artist's zest. The brilliantly poster-plastered wall advertises performing fleas and, significantly but with gay irony, the last days of Pompeii; a pickpocket steals a handkerchief. John Orlando Parry *A London Street Scene*. 1835

But as the light of day enters some populous city,
Shaming away, ere it come, by the chilly day-streak signal,
High and low, the misusers of night, shaming out the gas lamps –
All the great empty streets are flooded with broadening clearness,
Which, withal, by inscrutable simultaneous access
Permeates far and pierces to the very cellars lying in
Narrow high back-lane, and court, and alley of alleys: –
He that goes forth to his walks, while speeding to the suburb,
Sees sights only peaceful and pure; as labourers settling
Slowly to work, in their limbs the lingering sweetness of slumber;
Humble market-carts, coming-in, bringing-in, not only
Flower, fruit, farm-store, but sounds and sights of the country
Dwelling yet on the sense of the dreamy drivers; soon after
Half-awake servant-maids unfastening drowsy shutters
Up at the windows, or down, letting-in the air by the doorway;
School-boys, school-girls soon, with slate, portfolio, satchel,
Hampered as they haste, those running, these others maidenly
      tripping;
Early clerk anon turning out to stroll, or it may be
Meet his sweetheart – waiting behind the garden gate there;
Merchant on his grass-plat haply, bare-headed; and now by this
      time
Little child bringing breakfast to 'father' that sits on the timber
There by the scaffolding; see, she waits for the can beside him;
Meantime above purer air untarnished of new-lit fires:
So that the whole great wicked artificial civilised fabric –
All its unfinished houses, lots for sale, and railway outworks –
Seems reaccepted, resumed to Primal Nature and Beauty: –

Clough *The Bothie of Tober-Na-Vuolich*, IX, lines 82 – 107

    When Clough's poem was published, in 1848, Liverpool was still crammed with back-to-back houses, which had almost no light or ventilation. One might well ask how one could sustain even the moderate optimism of *The Bothie* in these conditions. I find, even so, that Clough's poem has a soberness about it, a sense of the difficulties of living in the nineteenth century: and it is not just a facile gesture; he arrived at his belief in improvement after a great deal of thought.

    A very much more buoyant poet is Browning. He lived in Italy for much of his poetic life, and when he writes of towns they are the exotic, untidy, but essentially humane towns of Italy, places for people to live in, with their markets and squares, places in which to be, as well as to work. This account of an Italian market, which comes at the beginning of *The Ring and the Book,* exuberantly describes the junk and jumble of a stall, its old picture frames and prints and chest knobs. Browning's description of these objects vividly suggests the chance elements which have brought together this diverse collection of bric-a-brac.

'Mongst odds and ends of ravage, picture frames
White through the worn gilt, mirror-sconces chipped,
Bronze angel-heads once knobs attached to chests,
(Handled when ancient dames chose forth brocade)
Modern chalk drawings, studies from the nude,
Samples of stone, jet, breccia, porphyry
Polished and rough, sundry amazing busts
In baked earth, (broken, Providence be praised!)
A wreck of tapestry, proudly-purposed web
When reds and blues were indeed red and blue,
Now offered as a mat to save bare feet . . .

Browning *The Ring and the Book,* Book I, lines 53–63

As the century progressed, the poets seem to have become less worried about the abuses of the town and more conscious of the enjoyments to be had from it. The poets of the eighties and nineties are rather self-consciously wicked in their enjoyment of music halls, pubs, arty life. This poem by Arthur Symons, *In Bohemia*, is written with a rather pleased frisson of concern when the dawn shows up the haggard faces of the hard-drinking ladies.

Drawn blinds and flaring gas within,
And wine, and women, and cigars;
Without, the city's heedless din;
Above, the white unheeding stars.

And we, alike from each remote,
The world that works, the heaven that waits,
Con our brief pleasures o'er by rote,
The favourite pastime of the Fates.

We smoke, to fancy that we dream,
And drink, a moment's joy to prove,
And fain would love, and only seem
To live because we cannot love.

Draw back the blinds, put out the light!
'Tis morning, let the daylight come.
God! how the women's cheeks are white,
And how the sunlight strikes us dumb!

Symons *In Bohemia*

In spite of this acceptance of the urban scene later in the century, there were still poets who felt the threat of the great anonymous cities and their capacity for reducing human beings to nothing. In *Midnight on the Great Western* Thomas Hardy describes a boy on a railway train. The 'journeying boy' is alone, with his ticket tucked for safety into his hat. The isolation of the boy and his detachment from a world which will most certainly make demands on him fills Hardy with awe. There is a curious resilient, almost stoic, quality about the boy, in spite of his defencelessness and pathos; and Hardy manages to suggest all these in a bare simplicity of statement.

In the third-class seat sat the journeying boy,
    And the roof-lamp's oily flame
Played down on his listless form and face,
Bewrapt past knowing to what he was going,
    Or whence he came.

In the band of his hat the journeying boy
    Had a ticket stuck; and a string
Around his neck bore the key of his box,
That twinkled gleams of the lamp's sad beams
    Like a living thing.

What past can be yours, O journeying boy
    Towards a world unknown,
Who calmly, as if incurious quite
On all at stake, can undertake
    This plunge alone?

Knows your soul a sphere, O journeying boy,
    Our rude realms far above,
Whence with spacious vision you mark and mete
This region of sin that you find you in,
    But are not of?

Hardy *Midnight on the Great Western*

So far I have looked at the way in which the Victorian poets saw the city as a symbol of gloom and oppression, and at the few poets who enjoyed its busy streets and crowds. But, if the poets did not entirely retreat from the city, the city certainly made them more intensely interested in the natural world than at almost any other period. In every poet one can find wonderfully accurate lyric descriptions of landscape, trees or sky. Here, to end, is a brief extract by A. E. Housman on trees and one by George Meredith on the sky.

The chestnut casts his flambeaux, and the flowers
    Stream from the hawthorn on the wind away,
The doors clap to, the pane is blind with showers.

Housman *Last Poems* IX, lines 1 – 3

Sharp is the night, but stars with frost alive
Leap off the rim of earth across the dome.

Meredith *Winter Heavens,* lines 1 – 2

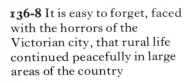

136-8 It is easy to forget, faced with the horrors of the Victorian city, that rural life continued peacefully in large areas of the country

SO BLACK A RIDDLE

The poet and the problems of the age

There were many problems that troubled the Victorian poets, and in previous programmes I have talked about some of them: doubt, scientific discovery, feminism and the threat of the city. Today I want to talk about the issue which puzzled them most: the problem of the poet's function. The Victorians found this problem deeply disturbing. Their society valued thrusting, practical energy and many of the poets, having no practical involvement with this society, felt very guilty. Either they were deeply out of sympathy with the values of their contemporaries, or they did not see how they could write directly of contemporary affairs. There was a notion about that the poet should 'reflect' the age in some way, but it was difficult to know exactly *how* he should 'reflect the age'. Perhaps it meant writing directly topical poetry, or perhaps it meant that he should only look at the good side of his age. Another view of the poet suggested that he had, in some sense, the function of a prophet; again it was difficult to know what this really meant. Perhaps he should write about great public issues, maybe he should exhort and attack society, or maybe hold out a golden vision of the future.

The most uncomfortable and apologetic of the poets was Tennyson. In *The Princess*, his first poem on a directly contemporary issue, he explored the problem of the status of women through a fairy tale, and called it, deprecatingly, a 'medley'. The topical and the fairy story elements are all, as he puts it, 'jumbled together'. So though he meant to represent the solid worth of the landowning gentry in the eighteen forties, even the 'great broad-shoulder'd genial Englishman' described at the end of the poem has unequal qualities which are jumbled together. He is a 'Lord of fat prize-oxen' and 'A quarter-sessions chairman, abler none', a 'patron of thirty charities' and a 'raiser of huge melons'. But in *Locksley Hall*, in spite of his doubts about festering social disorder and a 'hungry people' ready to spring like a lion, Tennyson holds out a grandiose, utopian vision of the future. To express his confidence he uses the symbols of progress beloved of the Victorians – commerce and the railway train. 'Let the great world spin for ever down the ringing grooves of change', he wrote; Tennyson, because he was short-sighted, thought that trains ran in grooves and not on rails.

139 Turner's painting suggests the excitement rather than the social horrors of railway age. *Rain, Steam and Speed,* The National Gallery, London

For I dipt into the future, far as human eye could see,
Saw the Vision of the world, and all the wonder that would be;

Saw the heavens fill with commerce, argosies of magic sails,
Pilots of the purple twilight, dropping down with costly bales;

Heard the heavens fill with shouting, and there rain'd a ghastly
    dew
From the nations' airy navies grappling in the central blue;

Far along the world-wide whisper of the south-wind rushing
    warm,
With the standards of the peoples plunging thro' the thunder-
    storm;

Till the war-drum throbb'd no longer, and the battle flags were
    furl'd
In the Parliament of man, the Federation of the world.

*

Not in vain the distance beacons. Forward, forward let us range,
Let the great world spin for ever down the ringing grooves of
    change.

Thro' the shadow of the globe we sweep into the younger day:
Better fifty years of Europe than a cycle of Cathay.

Tennyson *Locksley Hall,* lines 119 – 28, 181 – 84

Tennyson's ignorance of the detail of railway lines perhaps reflected a similar ignorance when it came to talking of larger things.
The agitations of the Chartists were making it clear just how
wretched the condition of the poor was. They were not just meta-

140 The city forced the poor to outrageous scavenging

phorically, but literally, hungry. *Locksley Hall* was published two or three years after Carlyle's polemical essay on Chartism, but deals only superficially with social problems. Only two or three years later Frederick Engels, in *The Condition of the Working Class in England*, describes the kind of food which a workman could afford: 'The potatoes are usually poor ... the vegetables wilted, the cheese old and of poor quality, the bacon rancid, the meat lean, tough; taken from old, often diseased, cattle'. In such conditions there is something obtuse about the belief in progress Tennyson shows in *Locksley Hall*; a preference for 'fifty years of Europe' against 'a cycle of Cathay' seems almost perverse. But despite such poems, Tennyson could sometimes write impressively on contemporary events. His poem on the disastrous charge of the Light Brigade, ordered in the Crimean War, has a simple, direct drama, worthy of the tragedy. There is a telling force in its laconic message: 'Some one had blunder'd'.

> Half a league, half a league,
>   Half a league onward,
> All in the valley of Death
>   Rode the six hundred.
> 'Forward, the Light Brigade!
> Charge for the guns!' he said:
> Into the valley of Death
>   Rode the six hundred.
>
> 'Forward, the Light Brigade!'
> Was there a man dismay'd?
> Not tho' the soldier knew
>   Some one had blunder'd:
> Their's not to make reply,
> Their's not to reason why,
> Their's but to do and die:
> Into the valley of Death
>   Rode the six hundred.

Tennyson *The Charge of the Light Brigade,* lines, 1 – 17

The public poems, written while Tennyson was Laureate, were, on the whole, better than those of another Victorian Laureate, Alfred Austin. When Austin, in his poem *Why England is Conservative,* praises the traditions of England – 'Mother of happy homes and Empire vast' – one feels that he simply does not know enough about the realities. It was not so with Kipling, perhaps the only poet who, towards the end of the century, managed to write convincingly of Britain's public, imperialistic rôle.

Kipling was born in India and returned there to become a journalist when he was still a young man. Here is a poem about a soldier sent to an overworked post in a killing climate. Behind the ironically cheerful, marching rhythms, the popular ballad style and colloquial language, is an insider's knowledge of a region, its pattern of life, its slang and the ruthless impersonality of its administrators

– the bungling which ignores the human cost of decisions. Ironically suggesting that the soldier's wife is as heartless as the administrators, Kipling says she 'mourned' only five months. But she died, of course, having no money.

'Now there were two men in one city ; the one rich and the other poor'

Jack Barrett went to Quetta
    Because they told him to.
He left his wife at Simla
    On three-fourths his monthly screw.
Jack Barrett died at Quetta
    Ere the next month's pay he drew.

Jack Barrett went to Quetta.
    He didn't understand
The reason of his transfer
    From the pleasant mountain-land.
The season was September,
    And it killed him out of hand.

Jack Barrett went to Quetta
    And there gave up the ghost,
Attempting two men's duty
    In that very healthy post;
And Mrs. Barrett mourned for him
    Five lively months at most.

Jack Barrett's bones at Quetta
    Enjoy profound repose;
But I shouldn't be astonished
    If *now* his spirit knows
The reason of his transfer
    From the Himalayan snows.

And, when the Last Great Bugle Call
    Adown the Hurnai throbs,
And the last grim joke is entered
    In the big black Book of Jobs,
And Quetta graveyards give again
    Their victims to the air,
I shouldn't like to be the man
    Who sent Jack Barrett there.

Kipling   *The Story of Uriah*

In spite of the poets' worries about their social function, there was a considerable amount of poetry of social protest in England throughout the century, though little of it by major poets. Interestingly, the major poets either could not, or would not, write polemical verse. In 1843 Thomas Hood published in *Punch* his *Song of the Shirt* to make people aware of the long hours and starvation wages of the seamstress – a widow with two children earned only seven shillings a week for hours of punishing labour. Hood drives his point home by a bold and obvious rhetoric; the heavy repetition is meant to suggest the wearily repeated task, and the emphatic paradoxes – the shirt which is a shroud; the bread which is so dear, the life which is so cheap – drive home the message.

> O! Men! with Sisters dear!
>   O! Men! with Mothers and Wives!
> It is not linen you're wearing out,
>   But human creatures' lives!
>   Stitch – stitch – stitch,
>   In poverty, hunger, and dirt,
> Sewing at once, with a double thread,
>   A Shroud as well as a Shirt.
>
> 'But why do I talk of Death?
>   That Phantom of grisly bone,
> I hardly fear his terrible shape,
>   It seems so like my own –
>   It seems so like my own,
>   Because of the fasts I keep,
> Oh! God! that bread should be so dear,
>   And flesh and blood so cheap!
>
> 'Work – work – work!
>   My labour never flags;
> And what are its wages? A bed of straw,
>   A crust of bread – and rags.
> That shatter'd roof – and this naked floor –
>   A table – a broken chair –
> And a wall so blank, my shadow I thank
>   For sometimes falling there!

Hood *The Song of the Shirt*, lines 25 – 48

Another emphatic protest is Thomas Noel's *The Pauper's Drive*. This poem relies for its effect upon crude, aggressive irony and a rousingly satirical refrain. The only time the friendless pauper reaches the gentility of a coach ride is when he is in his coffin. The poet exhorts the driver to get the job over quickly with the refrain 'Rattle his bones . . .'

> There's a grim one-horse hearse in a jolly round trot,
> To the churchyard a pauper is going, I wot;
> The road it is rough and the hearse has no springs;
> And hark to the dirge which the sad driver sings:
>   *Rattle his bones over the stones!*
>   *He's only a pauper, whom nobody owns!*
>
> O, where are the mourners? Alas! there are none –
> He has left not a gap in the world now he's gone –
> Not a tear in the eye of child, woman, or man;
> To the grave with his carcass as fast as you can:
>   *Rattle his bones over the stones!*
>   *He's only a pauper, whom nobody owns!*

What a jolting, and creaking, and splashing and din!
The whip how it cracks, and the wheels how they spin!
How the dirt, right and left, o'er the hedges is hurled!
The pauper at length makes a noise in the world!
  Rattle his bones over the stones!
  He's only a pauper, whom nobody owns!

Poor pauper defunct! he has made some approach
To gentility, now that he's stretched in a coach!
He's taking a drive in his carriage at last;
But it will not be long, if he goes on so fast!
  Rattle his bones over the stones!
  He's only a pauper, whom nobody owns!

Noel *The Pauper's Drive*, lines 1 – 24

Elizabeth Barrett Browning's poem *The Cry of the Children* was another product of the stress of the forties. She had read the reports of the Children's Employment Commissioners on the use of children in factories and mines, and the poem is full of her shocked response to it, of her realisation that brutalising conditions create people who understand neither love nor religion. The poem is best where the children speak of their utter physical weariness: they have no energy for joy.

'For oh,' say the children, 'we are weary,
    And we cannot run or leap;
If we cared for any meadows, it were merely
    To drop down in them and sleep.
Our knees tremble sorely in the stooping,
    We fall upon our faces, trying to go;
And, underneath our heavy eyelids drooping,
    The reddest flower would look as pale as snow;
For, all day, we drag our burden tiring
    Through the coal-dark, underground –
Or, all day, we drive the wheels of iron
    In the factories, round and round.

'For, all day, the wheels are droning, turning, –
    Their wind comes in our faces, –
Till our hearts turn, – our head, with pulses burning,
    And the walls turn in their places:
Turns the sky in the high window blank and reeling,
    Turns the long light that drops adown the wall,
Turn the black flies that crawl along the ceiling,
    All are turning, all the day, and we with all.
And all day, the iron wheels are droning,
    And sometimes we could pray,
"O ye wheels" (breaking out in a mad moaning),
    "Stop! be silent for to-day!"'

Elizabeth Barrett Browning *The Cry of the Children*, lines 65 – 88

Poverty is the perpetual theme of the social criticism in nine-teenth-century poetry. In the latter part of the century John

141 The remorseless activity of a poorly ventilated factory

142 The compensations of the rural poor – air and sun

Davidson, a poet who was perpetually hard up and who once, like the speaker of this poem, worked as a clerk, tried to express a cheerful, cockney resilience to hardship in the style of a music-hall ballad. He rather overdoes the slang, with his 'bloomings' and 'ballys' and sentimentalises the enforced stoicism of the poor; but some vigorous jokes save the poem. Perhaps we are all in hell 'And lost and damn'd and served up hot to God'.

> But I don't allow it's luck and all a toss;
>> There's no such thing as being starred and crossed;
> It's just the power of some to be a boss,
>> And the bally power of others to be bossed:
> I face the music, sir; you bet I ain't a cur;
>> Strike me lucky if I don't believe I'm lost!
>
> For like a mole I journey in the dark,
>> A-travelling along the underground
> From my Pillar'd Halls and broad Suburbean Park,
>> To come the daily dull official round;
> And home again at night with my pipe all alight,
>> A-scheming how to count ten bob a pound.
>
> Davidson *Thirty Bob a Week,* stanzas 2 – 3

Many of the directly topical poems of social criticism come nearer to being journalistic polemic than poetry; for some reason it is hard to make good poetry out of social criticism, the reformer's shock or anger too often takes over. But there is a superb moment in Tennyson's *Maud* when the speaker attacks the exploitation of the poor and, particularly, the evil of adulterated food. Flour was frequently adulterated with chalk or poisonous alum to make it cheaper to produce, and so, wrote Tennyson, 'the spirit of murder works in the very means of life'. The intensity of his attack comes from the accumulation of meanings concentrated into the word 'works': living yeast 'works' in dough; poison 'works' to destroy the body. For all his optimism, Tennyson handles language with true virtuosity.

> Peace sitting under her olive, and slurring the days gone by,
> When the poor are hovell'd and hustled together, each sex, like
>> swine,
> When only the ledger lives, and when only not all men lie;
> Peace in her vineyard – yes! – but a company forges the wine.
>
> And the vitriol madness flushes up in the ruffian's head,
> Till the filthy by-lane rings to the yell of the trampled wife,
> And chalk and alum and plaster are sold to the poor for bread,
> And the spirit of murder works in the very means of life,
>
> Tennyson *Maud,* Part 1, 1, stanzas 9 – 10

Another poet who wrote with a quiet, careful, understated observation, without writing merely documentary poetry, is a much lesser known poet, William Ernest Henley, whose series of poems *In Hospital* records with delicacy and literalness the events and people in the life of a hospital. He describes the 'tragic meanness' of 'corridors and stairs of stone and iron', and the staff nurses, cleaners and probationers whom he saw from his bed. This poem is about a suicide case.

Staring corpselike at the ceiling,
    See his harsh, unrazored features,
    Ghastly brown against the pillow,
    And his throat – so strangely bandaged!

Lack of work and lack of victuals,
    A debauch of smuggled whisky,
    And his children in the workhouse
    Made the world so black a riddle

That he plunged for a solution;
    And, although his knife was edgeless,
    He was sinking fast towards one,
    When they came, and found, and saved him.

Stupid now with shame and sorrow,
    In the night I hear him sobbing.
    But sometimes he talks a little.
    He has told me all his troubles.

In his broad face, tanned and bloodless,
    White and wild his eyeballs glisten;
    And his smile, occult and tragic,
    Yet so slavish, makes you shudder!

Henley *In Hospital* Suicide

143 A queue of needy poor,
painted with a compassionate
emotion which the circumstances
justify. Sir Luke Fildes
*Applicants for Admission to a
Casualty Ward,* Royal Holloway
College, University of London,
Egham

Swinburne was perhaps one of the few Victorian poets to write of contemporary events without losing his characteristic poetic voice. In *The Halt Before Rome*, a poem about the liberation of Italy, he transforms elemental, biblical imagery of sword, flame and dust into his own familiar, surging rhythms.

> The blind, and the people in prison,
>   Souls without hope, without home,
> How glad were they all that heard!
> When the winged white flame of the word
> Passed over men's dust, and stirred
> Death; for Italia was risen,
>   And risen her light upon Rome.
>
> The light of her sword in the gateway
>   Shone, an unquenchable flame,
> Bloodless, a sword to release,
> A light from the eyes of peace,
> To bid grief utterly cease,
> And the wrong of the old world straightway
>   Pass from the face of her fame.

Swinburne   The Halt Before Rome, stanzas 14 – 15

In 1853 Matthew Arnold wrote a preface to his poems in which he criticised the demands of his contemporaries for a poetry which dealt with 'matters of present import'. He condemned poetry which explored 'the problems of modern life, moral, intellectual, social'. He condemned poets with a 'mission', who talked of 'interpreting their age' and who were too preoccupied with 'the great ideas of industrial development and social amelioration'. Instead, he proposed a poetry which returned to the pure, essential realities of life, the permanent emotions and situations embodied in the 'great' subjects of classical or ancient legend. Arnold's notion of the 'great' subject in poetry is extremely limiting, but behind it, I think, is a feeling that poetry with direct social purpose is ugly and superficial, that a 'mission' somehow deflects the poet from the more profound work of imaginative exploration which ought to be involving him. Arnold's friend, Arthur Hugh Clough, criticised him for perpetually 'twisting and turning' in an effort to see life as an ancient Greek might have done. Clough urged a poetry of everyday life, a poetry which would irradiate the world we *have* to live with, the literal world of 'positive matters of fact'. Accordingly he wrote verse novels and contemporary satire. This poem is a fierce attack on a laissez-faire money-making attitude, which is thoroughly philistine and self-indulgent.

> As I sat at the café, I said to myself,
> They may talk as they please about what they call pelf,
> They may sneer as they like about eating and drinking,
> But help it I cannot, I cannot help thinking
>   How pleasant it is to have money, heigh ho!
>   How pleasant it is to have money.

I sit at my table *en grand seigneur,*
And when I have done, throw a crust to the poor;
Not only the pleasure, one's self, of good living,
But also the pleasure of now and then giving.
    So pleasant it is to have money, heigh ho!
    So pleasant it is to have money.

I drive through the streets, and I care not a d–mn;
The people they stare, and they ask who I am;
And if I should chance to run over a cad,
I can pay for the damage if ever so bad.
    So pleasant it is to have money, heigh ho!
    So pleasant it is to have money.

    Clough *Dipsychus,* Scene IV, lines 130–41, 148–53

Clough's poem would not be so successful if it were not part of a much larger poem. It is spoken by a figure ambiguously called 'Spirit', who mocks with his practical, rational wisdom a young man, Dipsychus, who is going through a crisis of conscience about his religion and about his society. Clough's presentation of the Spirit is much more than a satire on current social attitudes; he presents us with a character whose views are morally thin, imaginatively impoverished and essentially arid and mechanistic. 'Our age', wrote Carlyle in a very early article called *Signs of the Times,* 'is above all others, the Mechanical Age. It is the Age of Machinery, in every outward and inward sense of that word; the age which, with its whole undivided might, forwards, teaches and practises the great art of adapting means to ends'. Clough's poem is the more searching because it probes to the inner meaning of a mechanistic belief as well as recording its outward form.

The best Victorian social poetry is that which one feels is responding to, and struggling with, a mechanistic culture. Paradoxically it need not even be directly topical in form to do this. Tennyson's *The Lotos-Eaters* is based on an episode in the Odyssey, where the sailors are drugged and enchanted into forgetfulness by magic fruit: they give in to the experience with a mesmerised, dreamy nihilism. Yet this is not a poem which escapes from life, it is rather a poem *about* escaping from life, about the temptation to retreat from a deeply unsympathetic environment.

In the afternoon they came unto a land
In which it seemèd always afternoon.
All round the coast the languid air did swoon,
Breathing like one that hath a weary dream.
Full-faced above the valley stood the moon;
And like a downward smoke, the slender stream
Along the cliff to fall and pause and fall did seem.
A land of streams! some, like a downward smoke,
Slow-dropping veils of thinnest lawn, did go;
And some thro' wavering lights and shadows broke,
Rolling a slumbrous sheet of foam below.
    Tennyson *The Lotos-Eaters,* lines 3–13

Browning, like Tennyson, doesn't always write of the present. He chooses a Renaissance painter for instance, Fra Lippo Lippi, in order to describe a man fighting desperately to assert the values of imaginative energy and the transforming power of creative life. Again one feels he is dramatising a contemporary fight against a deadening, mechanistic thought.

> . . . you've seen the world
> – The beauty and the wonder and the power,
> The shapes of things, their colours, lights and shades,
> Changes, surprises, – and God made it all!
> – For what? Do you feel thankful, ay or no,
> For this fair town's face, yonder river's line,
> The mountain round it and the sky above,
> Much more the figures of man, woman, child,
> These are the frame to? What's it all about?
> To be passed over, despised? or dwelt upon,
> Wondered at? oh, this last of course!

Browning *Fra Lippo Lippi*, lines 282 – 92

So far I've talked of the difficulties the Victorians experienced in writing poetry about topical issues, the kind of writing one might call 'public' poetry. Some writers, often by using popular songs and ballads as models, did write successful 'public' poems, but they are minor poets – and often minor poems. On the other hand, like *The Lotos-Eaters* and *Fra Lippo Lippi*, a lot of Victorian poetry is not directly about contemporary themes at all. But such poems are about far more than their surface material suggests: for one thing they celebrate the profound importance of myth, as does Arnold's *Sohrab and Rustum*. This poem takes the tragic pattern of son fighting against father from Persian legend. It celebrates incantation, like Swinburne's choruses from *Atalanta in Calydon*, which are full of reverberating phrases: 'Before the beginning of years . . . Time with a gift of tears . . . Grief with a glass that ran'. It celebrates magical sound, like Rossetti's inexplicable but resonant-sounding numbers in *The Blessed Damozel* : 'She had three lilies in her hand/And the stars in her hair were seven'. Tennyson puts the dilemma of the Victorian poet beautifully in his legendary poem *The Lady of Shalott*. The enchanted lady is compelled to weave a web whose design is taken from the reflections of the outside world in her mirror. But this, perhaps the artist's life, is life at second hand, however beautiful: 'I am half sick of shadows said/The Lady of Shalott'. However, when real life breaks in, the mirror cracks and the lady dies. The dream has to be *about* something, about life; but life might destroy the dream. Holman Hunt's picture of the scene, plate **64**, appears on page 134.

Lastly, I will mention one source of social criticism in poetry which leads neither to direct and defiant polemic, nor to indirect legend and myth. The Victorian poets were particularly successful when they satirised middle-class values, the values which, more than anything, created the philistine, mechanical Victorian world. My last two examples are of poems which describe and criticise middle-class life. Clough's hero, Claude, in *Amours de Voyage* is almost choked by his middle-class snobbishness as he tries to assess, with minute attention to accent and taste, the exact status of the family of the girl he is trying not to fall in love with. Notice the fussy superciliousness – and self-disgust – in these lines.

Is – shall I call it fine? – herself she would tell you refined, and
Greatly, I fear me, looks down on my bookish and maladroit
    manners;
Somewhat affecteth the blue; would talk to me often of poets;
Quotes, which I hate, Childe Harold; but also appreciates
    Wordsworth;
Sometimes adventures on Schiller; and then to religion diverges;
Questions me much about Oxford; and yet, in her loftiest flights
    still
Grates the fastidious ear with the slightly mercantile accent.
Is it contemptible, Eustace – I'm perfectly ready to think so, –
Is it, – the horrible pleasure of pleasing inferior people?

Clough *Amours de Voyage,* Canto I, XI, lines 206 – 14

In the next poem, Browning's *The Inn Album*, there is satirised buoyantly, with great energy, the standardised bourgeois vulgarity of a private house turned tourist inn, with its Landseer stag and inevitable reproduction of Holman Hunt's *Light of the World* (see plate **62**, page 132).

Two personages occupy this room
Shabby-genteel, that's parlour to the inn
Perched on a view-commanding eminence;
– Inn which may be a veritable house
Where somebody once lived and pleased good taste
Till tourists found his coign of vantage out,
And fingered blunt the individual mark
And vulgarized things comfortably smooth.
On a sprig-pattern-papered wall there brays
Complaint to sky Sir Edwin's dripping stag:
His couchant coast-guard creature corresponds;
They face the Huguenot and Light o' the World.
Grim o'er the mirror on the mantelpiece,
Varnished and coffined, *Salmo ferox* glares
– Possibly at the List of Wines which, framed
And glazed, hangs somewhat prominent on peg.

Browning *The Inn Album,* I, lines 26 – 41

*Acknowledgment is due to the following for permission
to reproduce illustrations :*

CHRISTIES (photo A. C. Cooper) plate 74; THE COLMAN & RYE LIBRAR-
IES OF LOCAL HISTORY, NORWICH CENTRAL LIBRARY plate 142;
THOS. COOK & SON plates 29, 31 and 32; ALFRED DUNHILL LTD plate 135;
DEPT. OF THE ENVIRONMENT plate 54; from FABER & FABER *The Love
Letters of Walter Bagehot & Eliza Wilson* edited by their sister MRS
RUSSELL BARRINGTON, 1933; THE FAWCETT LIBRARY plates 33, 34 and
36; PHOTOGRAPHIE GIRAUDON plate 105; W. E. R. HALLGARTH plate
116; HEANOR & DISTRICT LOCAL HISTORICAL SOCIETY plate 14; by
permission of THE WARDEN & FELLOWS OF KEBLE COLLEGE, OXFORD
plate 62; LIBRAIRIE HACHETTE, PARIS plate 22; THE MANSELL COLLEC-
TION plates 39, 40 and 41; MARY EVANS PICTURE LIBRARY plate 19;
NATIONAL LIBRARY OF WALES plate 1; RADIO TIMES HULTON PICTURE
LIBRARY plates 3, 5, 9, 10, 12, 13, 15, 16, 17, 18, 21, 23, 24, 27/8, 37, 38,
47, 117, 118, 120, 121, 123, 126, 131, 133, 134, 136, 137, 138 and 140;
THE MASTER AND FELLOWS OF ST JOHN'S COLLEGE, CAMBRIDGE plate
125; SALVATION ARMY plate 35; TRADES UNION CONGRESS plate 20;
WHITBY LITERARY & PHILOSOPHICAL SOCIETY plate 11.

*Acknowledgment is also due to the following for permission
to reproduce poems :*

MRS GEORGE BAMBRIDGE and EYRE METHUEN LTD for Kipling's 'The
Story of Uriah' from *Departmental Ditties;* CURTIS BROWN LTD for
Hardy's 'Before Life and After' and 'Midnight on the Great Western';
MARTIN SECKER AND WARBURG publishers of Symons' 'In Bohemia'
from *Arthur Symons' Collected Poems;* THE SOCIETY OF AUTHORS for
the ESTATE OF A. E. HOUSMAN and JONATHAN CAPE publishers of
A. E. Housman's Collected Poems for Housman's 'A Shropshire Lad'.